Roy F. Melugin
The Formation of Isaiah 40—55

Roy F. Melugin

# The Formation of Isaiah 40-55

W
DE
G

Walter de Gruyter · Berlin · New York
1976

**CBPac**

Beiheft zur Zeitschrift für die alttestamentliche Wissenschaft

Herausgegeben von Georg Fohrer

141

*Library of Congress Cataloging in Publication Data*

Melugin, Roy F
   The formation of Isaiah 40—55.
   (Beihefte zur Zeitschrift für die alttestamentliche Wissenschaft ; 141)
   Bibliography: p.
   1. Bible. O.T. Isaiah XL-LV--Criticism, interpretation, etc. I. Title.
II. Series: Zeitschrift für die alttestamentliche Wissenschaft.
   Beihefte ; 141.
   BS401.Z5 vol. 141 [BS1520] 224'. 1'06 76-13519
   ISBN 3-11-005820-0

*CIP-Kurztitelaufnahme der Deutschen Bibliothek*

**Melugin , Roy F.**
The formation of Isaiah 40—55 [forty to fiftyfive]. — 1. Aufl. —
Berlin, New York : de Gruyter, 1976.
   (Zeitschrift für die alttestamentliche Wissenschaft : Beih. ; 141)
   ISBN 3-11-005820-0

© 

1976

by Walter de Gruyter & Co., vormals G. J. Göschen'sche Verlagshandlung —
J. Guttentag, Verlagsbuchhandlung — Georg Reimer — Karl J. Trübner —
Veit & Comp., Berlin 30

Printed in Germany

Satz und Druck: Saladruck, Berlin 36
Bindearbeiten: Lüderitz & Bauer, Berlin 61

To Sylvia
and
our daughters, Annella and Cynthia

# Preface

This work grew out of a suggestion several years ago by Brevard Childs that the nature of the literature contained in Isaiah 40—55 needed re-examination. I am indebted to him for his insight and guidance which led to a dissertation presented to the faculty of Yale University. Since the dissertation was completed in 1968 my approach to the problem has changed significantly, so that this work differs markedly from its predecessor. I am indebted also to W. Eugene March and Prescott Williams of the Austin Presbyterian Theological Seminary and to my colleague, Peter Lucchesi of the Department of English at Austin College, for a lively dialogue which led to major changes in my thinking on the subject. I am grateful also to John Van Seters of the University of Toronto for his insights at various points along the way, and to J. William Whedbee of Pomona College, who contributed to my thinking at the outset of my work on this topic and who read the danuscript before it was submitted for publication.

I wish to thank Professor D. Dr. Georg Fohrer, who accepted the monograph for the *Beihefte* series, for his encouragement and patience. I am grateful also to Sue Glenn and Margaret Grigg for preparation of the manuscript. For financial support I would express my gratitude to Austin College and to the Sid W. Richardson Foundation.

Finally, I am deeply indebted to my wife, who helped proofread the manuscript and gave much-needed moral support, and to my parents, who taught me the importance of studying the scriptures.

# Contents

# Abbreviations

| | |
|---|---|
| ANET | Ancient Near Eastern Texts Relating to the Old Testament, ed. J. B. Pritchard, 1955. 1959. |
| BZAW | Beihefte zur Zeitschrift für die alttestamentliche Wissenschaft |
| CBQ | Catholic Biblical Quarterly |
| ET | English translation |
| EvTh | Evangelische Theologie |
| ExpT | The Expository Times |
| JBL | Journal of Biblical Literature |
| JNES | Journal of Near Eastern Studies |
| JR | Journal of Religion |
| LXX | Septuagint |
| RGG | Die Religion in Geschichte und Gegenwart |
| SEA | Svensk Exegetisk Arsbok |
| SJTh | Scottish Journal of Theology |
| VT | Vetus Testamentum |
| ZAW | Zeitschrift für die alttestamentliche Wissenschaft |
| ZThK | Zeitschrift für Theologie und Kirche |
| 1QIsaᵃ | The Isaiah Scroll of St. Mark's Monastery |

# Chapter One: Introduction

In recent decades form criticism has made a major impact on research in prophetic literature. Names such as Gunkel, Mowinckel, Wolff, Zimmerli, and Westermann loom large in scholarly circles. Even among those who are not primarily form critics one finds a tendency to use form criticism.[1] Although *Formgeschichte* is not without its critics, the widespread assumption that most pre-exilic prophets uttered relatively short pronouncements distinguishable by form is not yet showing signs of being abandoned by the majority of scholars.[2]

This consensus prevails because the isolation of the originally separate speeches is often relatively easy. Sometimes a change in the historical period shows us that we have more than one unit.[3] In other cases we can separate two speeches from the same historical period by showing that the two utterances were spoken in quite different circumstances, such as the difference between the situation producing argumentative speech and a setting in which an oracle was spoken.[4] Or we may find a shift in the person(s) to whom the prophet speaks the ground for postulating a new unit.[5] Still another means of isolating originally separate utterances is the analysis of form. A speech whose structure is remarkably stereotyped may be identified as a particular genre (*Gattung*), a type of utterance whose form has been shaped by repeated use in a certain institution or set of circumstances — the *setting* or *Sitz im Leben* of the genre. Generally it has been assumed that a change in genre is a probable sign of a new self-contained unit.[6]

---

[1] E. g., H. Huffmon, The Covenant Lawsuit in the Prophets, JBL 78 (1959), 285—295; R. B. Y. Scott, The Literary Structure of Isaiah's Oracles, Studies in Old Testament Prophecy, 1950, 175—186.

[2] A recently emerging interest in "structural" and "rhetorical" analysis may result in a breakdown of this consensus.

[3] For example, Isa 14, 24—27 must be separated from the preceding context because Assyria, rather than Babylon, is the subject of the poem.

[4] Isa 28, 23—29 is the *prophet's* attempt to dispute the contention that his word is not from God; 29, 1 ff. is an *oracle*.

[5] Am 4, 1—3 is directed to wealthy women in Samaria; v. 4—5 are intended for a masculine plural audience.

[6] For instance, Am 3, 1—2 is an *oracle*, to be distinguished in genre, purpose, and setting from the disputation in v. 3—8.

Those widely held views regarding the pre-exilic prophets do not extend to Deutero-Isaiah. Scholars disagree whether Second Isaiah is a collection of originally separate utterances which can be distinguished because each betrays a form stereotyped by long usage in oral tradition. Perhaps, on the contrary, the structure of these chapters is primarily the artistic creation of a poet, a literary genius unfettered by traditional ways of speaking. Variations of both views have been espoused in the last several decades, but the problem remains unresolved.

The recent debate over the literary product in Deutero-Isaiah is the result of various attempts to employ form critical methodology. The story begins in 1914 with H. Gressmann.[7] Gressmann viewed the Deutero-Isaianic corpus as a collection of originally separate speeches.[8] Sometimes they could be isolated by means of opening and closing formulae. Using these formulae and other indicators of form, Gressmann attempted to lift speeches from their context by demonstrating that they exhibit traditional genres: promises *(Verheissungen)*, threats *(Drohungen)*, exhortations *(Mahnworte)*, along with certain non-prophetic forms of speech, notably the hymn. Deutero-Isaiah did not employ the customary forms unchanged, however; Gressmann believed that the prophet lived in a period in which the traditional genres were loosed from their settings and in a state of flux.[9] Thus Deutero-Isaiah was able to transform them significantly. The hymn he fused with alien genres, such as the prophetic formula, "Thus says Yahweh." Moreover, he abandoned the traditional prophetic association of invective with threat and exhortation with promise.

In 1923 L. Köhler continued the form critical approach initiated by Gressmann.[10] He too viewed Deutero-Isaiah as a collection of self-contained units which were literary imitations of oral forms of speech. Indeed, the traditional genres were so greatly modified that they served only as the primitive material upon which the prophet exercised his poetic craft. To this extent Köhler's conclusions largely parallel those drawn by Gressmann. The genres which Köhler postulated were quite different, however, from those described by Gressmann.[11]

Gressmann and Köhler were content to argue that Deutero-Isaiah is composed of originally separate speeches; they showed no interest in the arrangement of the collection. In 1931 S. Mowinckel, who believed also that the Deutero-Isaianic corpus is a collection of independent utter-

---

[7] Die literarische Analyse Deuterojesajas, ZAW 34 (1914), 254—297.
[8] Ibid. 264.
[9] Ibid. 295—296.
[10] Deuterojesaja stilkritisch untersucht, 1923, 102 ff.
[11] Köhler's primary *Gattungen* are the *Prädikation*, the messenger speech *(Botenspruch)*, and the disputation *(Streitgespräch)*.

ances, studied the arrangement of the collection.[12] Speeches were arranged, he argued, by means of thematic similarity and catchword connection. Each speech was placed in its context on the basis of its association with the preceding speech.[13] This mechanical means of association has no significance for understanding the prophet's message, for there is no progression of thought in the juxtaposition of units.

The hypothesis of Mowinckel sparked a lively response from K. Elliger.[14] Although he agreed that Deutero-Isaiah is a collection of originally separate utterances, he believed that the arrangement of units is significant theologically. Deutero-Isaiah's disciple Trito-Isaiah arranged his master's speeches in such a way that the collection manifests continuity in thought.[15] In some instances it was necessary for Trito-Isaiah to rework the speeches of his predecessor or even to insert words of his own.[16] As Elliger saw it, this process resulted in groups of *message* units, most of which included more than one *formal* unit.[17]

Gressmann, Köhler, Mowinckel, and Elliger advanced the study of the Hebrew scriptures by introducing form criticism into Deutero-Isaianic research. Nevertheless, their work was but a beginning. Gressmann's analysis was limited by his failure to undertake a detailed examination of the forms of Deutero-Isaiah's speeches. For the most part, he simply adopted the genres which had already been discovered in form critical research and assumed that the prophet simply modified these forms.[18] A similar lack of careful attention to structure is characteristic of Köhler, Mowinckel, and Elliger.[19] It was left to J. Begrich to

---

[12] Die Komposition des deuterojesajanischen Buches, ZAW 49 (1931), 87—112, 242—260.

[13] Ibid. 242.

[14] Deuterojesaja in seinem Verhältnis zu Tritojesaja, 1933, 219—272.

[15] In the discussion of the arrangement of the units we find terms such as *Gedankenfortschritt* and *Gedankengang* (p. 232), *Gedanken des Sammlers* (235), and *sachlicher Zusammenhang* (239).

[16] The bulk of Elliger's book (1—218) presents the argument that Trito-Isaiah's work can be detected in chapters 40—55.

[17] Beginning on 225 Elliger undertakes a systematic examination of the relationship of each unit to its context.

[18] For example, Gressmann employs several of the *Gattungen* discussed by Gunkel, such as *Drohungen* and *Scheltworte*. Cf. RGG[1] IV, 1866—1886; RGG[2] IV, 1538—1554.

[19] Illustrations: Mowinckel's arguments for the original unity of Isa 40, 12—31 are not based on a careful study of the structure and setting of the passage (Komposition 90, footnote 2), and this kind of form critical analysis is characteristic of his work. A typical illustration from Elliger is his study of chapter 41 (229 ff.). There one looks in vain for precise information concerning formal structures and their

perform the first thorough form critical study on Deutero-Isaiah.[20]
Aware of the disagreements among his predecessors, Begrich undertook a
fresh analysis — this time a minute examination of the structure and
setting of each genre. This resulted in conclusions markedly different
from those who preceded him. For example, Begrich was not content
with the general category *Verheißung* as a description of Deutero-
Isaiah's assurances concerning the future; careful analysis led him to
view Deutero-Isaiah's promises as imitations of a salvation oracle form
used by priests in answer to the lament psalm.[21] In similar fashion,
detailed inquiry prompted him to distinguish trial speeches from disputation speeches,[22] the former of which he identified as forms of speech
customarily employed in the legal proceedings of the town gate.[23]

Like Gressmann and Köhler, Begrich believed that Deutero-Isaiah's
speeches are literary imitations of oral genres.[24] The circumstances of
the exile, Begrich believed, made oral preaching impossible. Moreover,
Deutero-Isaiah's use of speech-forms customarily employed in non-
prophetic circles Begrich regarded as a sign of an imitative process of
composition. Begrich's concurrence with Gressmann and Köhler that
Deutero-Isaiah's speech-forms are imitations must not be construed to
imply, however, that Begrich agreed with Gressmann that the forms of
the traditional genres had almost completely broken down.[25] On the
contrary, Begrich's delineation of the genres makes Deutero-Isaiah's
imitation of them often appear surprisingly exact. The difficulty with
the form critics before Begrich, one might argue from the perspective of
Begrich's analysis, is that they had not identified the genres correctly.

---

setting. Instead, criteria such as content, poetic meter, and strophe are used to
separate units. In the case of Köhler, numerous utterances are included under the
genre of the messenger speech, but the author does not present a thorough analysis
of the way in which Deutero-Isaiah used and modified the structure of this genre.
He contents himself with presenting a list of messenger speeches, distinguishing only
the presence or absence of introductory or closing formulae (cf. 102—109). A
discussion of the internal structure of the genre is conspicuously missing. His
analysis of the disputation genre is equally sketchy (cf. 110—120). His lack of
attention to the structure of the theophany form makes us wonder whether a genre
with an identifiable form has actually been discovered (cf. 124—127).

[20] Das priesterliche Heilsorakel, ZAW 52 (1934), 81—92, and Studien zu Deuterojesaja,
1938, 1963. Page numbers are from the 1963 edition.

[21] Begrich, Heilsorakel, 91—92, and Studien, 17 ff.

[22] Studien 48.

[23] Ibid. 26—48.

[24] Ibid. 97.

[25] In fact, Begrich denies that traditional prophetic genres are prominent in Deutero-
Isaiah. Cf. Studien 67.

Begrich's work has been widely accepted. Most form critical analyses since that time have on the whole adopted Begrich's categories.[26] To be sure, H. E. von Waldow staked out new territory.[27] He disagreed with Begrich's contention that Deutero-Isaiah's speeches are literary imitations of oral speech-forms. Deutero-Isaiah was in his opinion a cultic prophet, and the *Heilsorakel* is a genuine prophetic genre.[28] The trial speeches, too, originate in the cult; thus they are not imitations of forms of speech used in the town gate.[29] Despite these differences, von Waldow depends heavily upon Begrich; his form critical analysis is but a modification of the work of Begrich. Indeed, Begrich's conclusions have so dominated all subsequent form critical studies that his analysis can be called the classical treatment of the subject.

A number of years elapsed without substantial criticism of the form critical work on Deutero-Isaiah. S. Smith viewed the disagreements among the form critics as a sign that the method is unsatisfactory for Deutero-Isaiah, but his critique was brief and his constructive alternative programmatic.[30] J. Muilenburg's commentary represents the best critique and alternative approach.[31] He granted that the pre-exilic prophets spoke in short utterances, but in the seventh century, he argued, a literary revolution took place in Israel — perhaps in the entire Near East — in which the ancient oral patterns disintegrated and gave way to a new process of composition. Writers, no longer bound to traditional genres, were free to employ and modify conventional forms of speech in almost any way they chose. This literary revolution is visible, according to Muilenburg, in Deuteronomy, Jeremiah, Ezekiel, and Deutero-Isaiah. Deutero-Isaiah, to be sure, made use of traditional oral forms of speech, but they were not binding on the form of his literary product. The prophet combined certain genres with other genres and elements of genres, molding them and transforming them in whatever ways suited his purpose.[32] Although remnants of traditional forms of speech are now and then observable, they cannot be the basis for isolating units. The prophet instead constructed his poems by means of stanzas or strophes, which are in turn subdivisions of larger units.[33] Strophes can be isolated

---

[26] Cf., e. g., H. E. von Waldow, Anlaß und Hintergrund der Verkündigung des Deuterojesaja, 1953; R. Rendtorff, Die theologische Stellung des Schöpfungsglaubens bei Deuterojesaja, ZThK 51 (1954), 3—13; W. Zimmerli, Erkenntnis Gottes nach dem Buche Ezechiel, 1954, 30 ff.

[27] Anlaß und Hintergrund.

[28] Ibid. 26, 124—133.

[29] Ibid. 37—47.

[30] Isaiah Chapters XL—LV: Literary Criticism and History, 1940, 1944, 6 ff.

[31] The Interpreter's Bible, V 1956, 381 ff.

[32] Ibid. 385, 389—390.

[33] Ibid. 385.

by analysis of style. A strophe often begins, for example, with an emphatic personal pronoun; or exclamations like "behold" or a call to hear in imperative style may signify the beginning of a strophe. The strophes are frequently linked by similar introductions, conclusions, or the repetition of key words.[34]

Muilenburg also sees a kind of progression in the prophet's thought. Admittedly it is not the kind of continuity habitually expected in Western literature, for in Deutero-Isaiah verses and strophes break in without any apparent relation to the context. Nevertheless, a rough progression is observable. Chapters 40—55 open with the announcement in the heavenly council that God is about to appear, coming as a conqueror of Israel's enemies to usher in his kingdom, and as a shepherd to comfort and heal. Then follows a poem on Yahweh as Creator. After that, the nations are confronted by means of a trial in which Yahweh speaks comfort to Israel his servant. The servant, though summoned for a high destiny, is blind and deaf; but Yahweh is gracious and promises redemption. Cyrus is then named as the conqueror of Babylon, and the city is defeated. At that time, the servant enters, calling on the nations to hear, and the promise of redemption continues. The climax occurs with the coming of the King and the cry, "Yahweh has become king!" Next comes the announcement of the exaltation of the servant, after which appears the nations' confession and Yahweh's vindication of the servant. Chapters 40—55 close with a final cry of joy.[35]

The work of Muilenburg provided the impetus for C. Westermann to enter the discussion.[36] Westermann concurs with Muilenburg that Deutero-Isaiah is for the most part made up of units longer than the form critics had believed. Furthermore, these longer units do not manifest any one genre. But he disagrees with Muilenburg's view that traditional forms of speech played a quite limited role in the formation of units; on the contrary, Westermann argues that genres long used in oral tradition were quite decisive. The long poetic units composed by the prophet are not totally free compositions as Muilenburg would have it; they are instead a complex interweaving of various genres with the

---

[34] Ibid. 391—393.
[35] Ibid. 385—386.
[36] Westermann has made three important contributions to the study of Deutero-Isaiah: Das Heilswort bei Deuterojesaja, EvTh 24 (1964), 355—373; Sprache und Struktur der Prophetie Deuterojesajas, in: Forschung am alten Testament, 1964, 92—170; Das Buch Jesaja: Kapitel 40—66, 1966 (ET, Isaiah 40—66, 1969). Westermann was influenced to a large extent regarding the overall structure of Deutero-Isaiah by Eva Hessler, Gott der Schöpfer: Ein Beitrag zur Komposition und Theologie Deuterojesajas, 1961. Nevertheless, Westermann's chief point of departure is a dialogue with Muilenburg (Sprache und Struktur 106—110).

structure of one genre serving as the formal model for the organization of the poem. In Isaiah 49, 14—26, for example, elements of disputation speech and the announcement of salvation *(Heilsankündigung)* are arranged in accordance with the structure of the lament psalm. This long unit of meaning is an original poem which cannot be described as any *one* genre; at the same time, its structure cannot be understood apart form critical analysis.[37]

One cannot possibly fail to see the differences among the scholars discussed above. The disagreements perhaps would not matter if they differed merely on details. But their differences are fundamental; they disagree about the very nature of the process of composition. Did the prophet speak in short utterances which betray the structures of traditional oral speech? Or did he as artist create his own forms? Have we to do with a collector? Or have we a long poem? What methods of analysis should be used? Is form criticism appropriate? Or should we, like Muilenburg, look for strophic structure? Recent scholarship has led us to these questions, all of which may be reduced to one: what is the nature of the poetry and the literary arrangement of the Deutero-Isaianic corpus? That question is the subject of this book.

## II. THE QUESTION OF METHOD

The question about the nature of the poetry and the literary arrangement of Deutero-Isaiah is first of all a problem of method. Our survey has produced two opposite methods of approach: form criticism and the approach employed by Muilenburg. Westermann's method may be viewed in part as a synthesis between the two, thus deserving a place as a third major alternative. Which should we employ? We obviously should not decide on the basis of preference. We must instead try to discover which method corresponds best to the process of composition employed by Deutero-Isaiah.

We begin our analysis of method with Muilenburg, for it is he who has most effectively challenged the dominance of the form critical approach to Deutero-Isaiah. His attack is doubly forceful because he affirms on the one hand the impact of oral forms of speech on the prophet's style while maintaining on the other that form criticism must be supplemented by a study of the writer's literary creativity.[38] In particular, Muilenburg's method depends upon the assumption that the poet's

---

[37] Westermann, Heilswort, 366—368; Sprache und Struktur 121; Das Buch Jesaja 175—180.

[38] See in particular the methodological considerations discussed by Muilenburg, Form Criticism and Beyond, JBL 88 (1969), 1—18.

individual creativity so dominated the process of composition that
strophe analysis is far more important than study of genre units.

Analysis of strophes is not a new undertaking in the study of the
Hebrew scriptures.[39] But it suffers from lack of agreement on the criteria
for detecting strophes. On occasion they are clearly marked off by
refrains, but this is a rare phenomenon.[40] Sometimes one may discover
strophes in acrostic poems, but most poems are not acrostics.[41] Occasionally we find strophes on the basis of regularity in the number of lines
as in Psalm 104, but this is the exception rather than the rule.[42] If one
wishes to analyze strophes, he must recognize, as does Muilenburg, that
they are not normally regular in length or in meter. Indeed, says
Muilenburg, strophes may be detected, not on the basis of meter or
number of lines, but rather by means of a study of various rhetorical
devices, such as similarity at the beginning or end of the strophes, or
repetition of key words.[43]

How successful are Muilenburg's criteria? Are there any controls
on his method, or is his approach, as C. R. North suggests, almost
entirely arbitrary?[44] We can hardly answer these questions in the
abstract; it is instead necessary to observe Muilenburg at work. For this
purpose we shall examine his analysis of Isaiah 41, 1—42, 4.[45]

Muilenburg considers Isaiah 41, 1—42, 4 to be a long poem por-
traying dramatically a trial between the nations with their gods and
Yahweh. Yahweh first speaks to the nations, challenging them to claim
credit for Cyrus' victories in terms of their own religion (v. 1—7). When
they cannot answer, Yahweh demonstrates that he alone is the power

---

[39] Cf., e. g., K. Budde, Poetry (Hebrew), in: James Hastings, A Dictionary of the
Bible, IV 1902, 2—13; W. H. Cobb, A Criticism of Systems of Hebrew Metre,
1905; A. Condamin, Le livre d'Isaïe, 1905; K. Fullerton, The Feeling for Form in
Psalm 104, JBL 40 (1921), 43—56; The Original Form of the Refrains in Isaiah
2, 6—21, JBL 38 (1919), 64—76; The Rhythmic Analysis of Isaiah 1, 10—20, JBL
38 (1919), 53—63; and The Strophe in Hebrew Poetry and Psalm 29, JBL 48
(1929), 274—290; G. B. Gray, The Forms of Hebrew Poetry, 1915; C. F. Kraft,
The Strophic Structure of Hebrew Poetry, 1938; R. Lowth, Lectures on the
Sacred Poetry of the Hebrews, 1847; T. J. Meek, The Structure of Hebrew Poetry,
JR 9 (1929), 523—550; H. Möller, Strophenbau der Psalmen, ZAW 50 (1932),
240—256; D. H. Müller, Die Propheten in ihrer ursprünglichen Form, 1896, and
Strophenbau und Responsion, 1898.
[40] Kraft, Strophic Structure, 7—8.
[41] Ibid. 9.
[42] Fullerton, The Feeling for Form in Psalm 104, 43—56. Note that Fullerton finds it
necessary to make emendations to secure his strophic pattern.
[43] Muilenburg, Interpreter's Bible, V 391—393.
[44] The Second Isaiah, 1964, 10.
[45] Muilenburg, Interpreter's Bible, V 447 ff.

behind Cyrus. As the trial continues, Yahweh turns to Israel, speaking words of comfort and hope (v. 8—16). Following a lyrical interlude (v. 17—20), Yahweh resumes the trial by demanding that the gods prove that they are indeed worthy of that title (v. 21—29). They cannot, and the case is closed (v. 29). Then comes the finale: the destiny of the nations is disclosed as the object of Israel's role as servant (42, 1—4).

Muilenburg argues for the unity of the poem on literary grounds:

The literary character of the poem is determined throughout by its setting in the court of law, its formal construction, and its prevailing dramatic style. The want of transitions, the exclamations (*behold*, etc.), the imperatives (41, 1.21—23), the carefully wrought repetitions (e. g., *strengthen*, 41, 6.7.12; *fear not*, 41, 10.13c.14, cf. v. 5; *I will help you*, 41, 10c.13d.14c, cf. v. 6a; *behold*, 41, 24.29.; 42, 1), the directness of address to Israel (41, 8 ff.) and the nations (41, 1 ff.21 ff.), the pronouncement of the verdict (41, 11.24.29), and the climactic emphases, similar to those encountered in the preceding poem, all betray a dramatic style that binds the work into a literary unity.[46]

Muilenburg believes that the poem is composed of nine strophes grouped in triads (v. 2—4.5—7.8—10; 11—13.14—16.17—20; 21—24. 25—29.42, 1—4). The third member of each triad marks a point of climax. Particles of transition show that the strophes are part of a larger literary unity: e. g., "but thou Israel" (41, 8), "behold" in 42, 1 following the twofold judgment of the nations also introduced by this particle (41, 24.29). As Muilenburg argued in the passage quoted above, literary unity is apparent in yet another way; the entire passage hangs together as a trial. The word *mišpaṭ* introduces the poem (41, 1), and it dominates the final strophe (42, 1—4). And one can hardly fail to see the trial imagery in 41, 1 ff.21 ff.

Without doubt these arguments are impressive. At the same time, certain questions arise. One wonders whether the *entire* passage actually reflects the language of a trial. Few would object that 41, 1—4(7) and 41, 21—29 mirror legal proceedings. But on what grounds does Muilenburg argue that 41, 8—16 belong to the trial? It has been argued by Begrich, von Waldow, Westermann, and others that v. 8—13 and v. 14—16 exhibit the structure of an oracle originally employed in the cult rather than the language of legal speech.[47] Muilenburg is of course not unaware of this,[48] but he makes nothing of the repeated occurrences in Deutero-Isaiah and elsewhere in which we find poetry which manifests this same structure.[49] Even a superficial study of these texts reveals

---

[46] Ibid. 447.

[47] Begrich, Heilsorakel; von Waldow, Anlaß und Hintergrund, 11—27; Westermann, Heilswort.

[48] Muilenburg, Interpreter's Bible, V 389, 458.

[49] Cf. Isa 41, 8—13.14—16; 43, 1—7; 44, 1—5 Jer 30, 10.11 = 46, 27.28.

that their form is higly stereotyped, both within Deutero-Isaiah and
without: (1) "Fear not," (2) direct address, (3) substantiating clause
indicating the nearness of Yahweh's help, usually in the form of a
nominal sentence, (4) assurance that Yahweh has heard and has turned
to help, verbalized in the perfect tense, and (5) announcement of the
future, usually in the imperfect. The regularity in structure has all the
earmarks of a traditional form of speech. Even Muilenburg admits that
it reflects the language of a priestly genre.[50] How then can he assume
that Deutero-Isaiah considers 41, 8—16 as part of the trial? The same
questions might be asked about 41, 17—20 and 42, 1—4, since there is
no evidence that they are forms of legal speech.

Muilenburg would probably answer by arguing that we do not have
before us true oral genres but rather imitations of them in a long poem
composed of several strophes. Indeed, I suspect that he would consider
his strophe analysis the strongest evidence of an originally unified poem
organized on the basis of trial language. But his analysis of the strophes
of 41, 1—42, 4, though ingenious, is problematical. His strophes do not
rest upon objective criteria such as regularity in meter or number of
lines. This in itself does not disprove his theory, although it indicates
how subjective it is. But when his strophic analysis comes into conflict
with what appear to be sound form critical observations, his conclusions
are thrown into jeopardy. And this is precisely what happens; the
climax (41, 8—10) of one of his triads of strophes (v. 2—4.5—7.8—10)
breaks the *Heilsorakel* genre in two (v. 8—13).[51]

This critique has by no means demolished Muilenburg's position.
His contribution is far too great to be so easily shattered. Yet the
analysis above indicates that he has passed over form criticism too
lightly. Perhaps we shall ultimately agree with him that the creativity
of the prophet is so dominant that form critical analysis is of marginal
value, but such a conclusion would be justified only on the basis of a
more detailed form critical study than we find in Muilenburg. Thus a
sound methodological study should first analyze the form critical
approach in relation to Deutero-Isaiah — both to explore its possibilities
and to determine its limits.

We shall begin, then, with a careful analysis of form. But we
should not stop there; we should inquire about the arrangement of the
Deutero-Isaianic corpus as a whole. Is the present arrangement of the
text significant kerygmatically or artistically? Or have we an arrangement which is only mechanical? The plan of this book reflects both the
questions of form and arrangement — Part One: The Analysis of
Genres, and Part Two: The Arrangement of the Text.

---

[50]  Muilenburg, Interpreter's Bible, V 389—390.
[51]  See the discussions of the form by Begrich, von Waldow, and Westermann in the
      works cited in footnote 47.

Part One: The Analysis of Genres

# Chapter Two: Salvation Speeches

No one denies that Deutero-Isaiah announced salvation. But there is considerable difference of opinion concerning the literary character of this type of speech. Can we discern a traditional oral genre (or genres) which can be isolated from the context by form and whose setting can be identified? And, if we can, is the genre used in its original setting, or have we a prophetic imitation of a form of speech at home in another realm of life? In addition, we must ask whether these forms can be isolated from their context as originally separate units of tradition or whether they are parts of longer poetic compositions. Finally, we must remain open to the possibility that no oral genre can be found, or at least that Deutero-Isaiah employs only snippets of a traditional form of salvation speech with the result that form criticism would be virtually useless in analyzing these texts.

## I. THE "PRIESTLY SALVATION ORACLE"

Begrich began the dialogue about the form of Deutero-Isaiah's salvation speeches. In 1934 he produced an epoch-making article in which he attempted to demonstrate that several texts in Deutero-Isaiah, as well as two passages in Jeremiah, are prophetic imitations of the oracle-form spoken in the cult by priests in response to the lament psalm of the individual.[1] A priest uttered this oracle, in Begrich's judgment, following the complaint and petition sections of the lament psalm, preceding the certainty of hearing.[2]

Always a word of Yahweh to an individual, the form is as follows: (1) "Fear not,"[3] (2) direct address,[4] (3) substantiating clause indicating the nearness of Yahweh's help, usually in the form of a nominal sentence,[5] (4) expression that Yahweh has heard, presented in the perfect tense with Yahweh as grammatical subject,[6] and (5) announcement of

---

[1] Begrich, Das priesterliche Heilsorakel, ZAW 52 (1934), 81—92. The texts are: Isa 41, 8—13.14—16; 43, 1—3a.5; (44, 2—5); 48, 17—19; 49, 7.14—15; 51, 7—8; 54, 4—8 Jer 30, 10 = 46, 27; 30, 11 = 46, 28.

[2] Ibid. 82.

[3] Isa 41, 10.13.14; 43, 1.5; 44, 2; 51, 7; 54, 4    Jer 30, 10 = 46, 27; 46, 28.

[4] Isa 41, 8.14; 44, 2; Jer 30, 10 = 46, 27; 46, 28.

[5] Cf. e. g., Isa 41, 10; 43, 5.

[6] Isa 41, 10.14; 43,1.

the future, usually in the imperfect. Yahweh is often the grammatical subject,[7] but other subjects sometimes occur.[8]

The structure of this salvation oracle corresponds to various parts of the individual lament psalm. The relationship of "Fear not" to the lament psalm can be seen in Lamentations 3, 57. The substantiating clause corresponds to the expression of confidence. The expression that Yahweh has heard corresponds to the certainty of hearing in the lament psalm. The announcement of the future reflects the language of the petition.[9] Deutero-Isaiah's speeches are imitations of the genre instead of actual cultic texts, for Deutero-Isaiah uses them to address the whole people rather than a single individual.[10]

A later study by Begrich,[11] which builds on the 1934 article, adds a series of texts not included in the original study,[12] five of which Begrich regards as imitations of the answer to the communal lament psalm.[13] In these additional texts the structure differs from the one outlined in the 1934 article: (1) "Fear not" is missing; (2) the direct address is often lacking; (3) the substantiating clause in nominal sentence form is usually missing.[14]

In spite of these formal differences, Begrich believed that both the texts discussed in the 1934 article and those added in *Studien zu Deuterojesaja* reflect the same genre. In his view the structure of the texts discussed in *Studien zu Deuterojesaja* is similar to that of the texts analyzed in 1934. He posits the following form for all texts: (a) announcement of Yahweh's intervention, often expressed in the perfect tense,[15] (b) the consequences of Yahweh's intervention, expressed in the imperfect,[16] and (c) the purpose of Yahweh's intervention.[17]

---

[7] Cf. e. g., 43, 5b.6; 44, 3.

[8] Cf. e. g., 41, 11—12; 43, 2.

[9] For additional details about the correspondence between the salvation oracle and the lament psalm, see Begrich, Heilsorakel, 82—85, 87 ff.

[10] Ibid. 81, 82.

[11] Begrich, Studien zu Deuterojesaja, 1938. 1963, 14—26. Page numbers are from the 1963 edition.

[12] Isa 41, 17—20; 42, 14—17; 43, 16—21; 45, 1—7.14—17; 46, 3—4.12—13; 49, 8—12 (13).22—23.24—26; 51, 12—16; 54, 11—12+13b.14a+13a—17; 55, 8—13. Cf. Begrich, Studien, 14.

[13] Isa 14, 17—20; 42, 14—17; 43, 16—21; 51, 6—8; 55, 8—13. Cf. Begrich, Studien, 14.

[14] Begrich, Studien, 15.

[15] 44, 21—22; 45, 4; 46, 13; 49, 6c.8.16; 51, 22; 54, 8.9.16; 55, 4.11. Cf. Begrich, Studien, 16. Sometimes, however, Yahweh's intervention is expressed in the imperfect (41, 17—20; 43, 16—21; 49, 22—23.24—26). Begrich's member *a* in his Studien zu Deuterojesaja corresponds to the expression that Yahweh has heard as Begrich discussed it in the 1934 journal article. See my discussion above.

[16] This corresponds to the announcement of the future in the 1934 article.

[17] For Begrich's delineation of this structure see his Studien 16.

That these speeches are imitations can be seen in the modification of the form by a direct reference to (or quotation of) the complaint.[18] This alteration reflects the prophet's strongly felt need to answer the specific complaints uttered in the circumstances of the exile. Another indication that Deutero-Isaiah is imitating comes in 43, 16—21, where "Fear not" becomes "Do not remember the former things..." (43, 18). This modification arises out of the prophet's experience of controversy with his hearers.[19] In 55, 8—13 imitation can be seen, according to Begrich, in the transformation of the pure oracle form by the style of disputation.[20]

Von Waldow continues the tradition begun by Begrich, but he differs from Begrich in that he sees Deutero-Isaiah's salvation oracles, not as imitations of a priestly genre, but rather as speeches actually spoken by the prophet Deutero-Isaiah in the cult. Indeed, for von Waldow, the salvation oracle is a prophetic genre.[21] The priest uses only technical means for obtaining revelation, while the prophet is grasped by Yahweh's spirit.[22] The messenger formula, which often introduces the salvation oracle, indicates that the oracle was spoken by the prophet.[23] Moreover, von Waldow points to the concreteness of detail in the promises. Begrich had seen this detail as prophetic imitative expansion of the more general priestly statements such as, "I am with you." But von Waldow views it as evidence that the genre is native to the prophetic institution. Most important of all, von Waldow argues that Deutero-Isaiah's salvation oracles have a regularity in structure which can be explained only if they are viewed as speeches which were uttered in their original setting. If they had been imitations, the structure would have become blurred.[24]

The structure, according to von Waldow, is as follows:[25]

Introduction, including an introductory formula — either messenger formula[26] or call to attention[27] followed by "Fear not"[28] and direct address;

---

[18] 54, 7.8; 42, 14; 41, 17. Cf. Studien 17.

[19] Studien 21.

[20] Ibid. 22. See 21 ff. for other modifications which suggest to Begrich that Deutero-Isaiah's speeches are imitations.

[21] H. E. von Waldow, Anlaß und Hintergrund der Verkündigung des Deuterojesaja, 1953, 83 ff. II Chr 20 is a good example of a lament psalm answered by a salvation oracle, and the speaker of the oracle shows the traditions of the prophetic institution.

[22] Cf. II Chr 20, 14.     [23] Cf. II Chr 20, 15.

[24] Von Waldow, Anlaß und Hintergrund, 26.

[25] Ibid. 12 ff.     [26] 43, 1.16 f.; 44, 2 etc.

[27] Cf. e. g., 44, 1; 46, 3.

[28] 41, 10.14; 43, 1.5a; 44, 2; 51, 7; 54, 4. More often than not this element is missing. Cf. von Waldow, Anlaß und Hintergrund, 12.

A: statement of Yahweh's intervention, beginning with a clause with general content,[29] usually with Yahweh as subject,[30] followed by the elaboration of Yahweh's intervention with the deity as grammatical subject in either the perfect or imperfect[31] and the substantiation of the intervention (often not present);[32]

B: statement of the consequences of Yahweh's intervention, a statement in which Yahweh is no longer the subject; the statement is always in the imperfect;[33]

C: the purpose of Yahweh's intervention.[34]

Von Waldow recognizes that modification in structure sometimes occurs. For example, member A sometimes takes the form of a direct comment or disputation on the complaint uttered in the lament psalm.[35] Isaiah 51, 17—23, 55, 1—5, 54, 11—17, and 51, 9—15 are additional examples of modification of the genre.[36] Nevertheless, in von Waldow's judgment, the structure is not blurred, so that there is no reason to believe that Deutero-Isaiah did not employ the genre in its original setting.[37]

Begrich and von Waldow agree that Deutero-Isaiah's salvation speeches are derived from the cultic salvation oracles whose structure is: (a) Yahweh's intervention, (b) consequences of Yahweh's intervention, and (c) purpose of Yahweh's intervention. The differences in formal structure are to be seen in von Waldow's attempt to postulate a more complex original form than the one suggested by Begrich — chiefly by means of his distinction between the elaboration of Yahweh's intervention (in member A) and the consequences of Yahweh's intervention (member B).

The precision of von Waldow's analysis turns out to be its problem. For example, the distinction between the elaboration of Yahweh's inter-

---

[29] This element appears mostly in the perfect tense (e. g., "I have redeemed you"), but it also occurs in the imperfect (41, 17b; 42, 14) and in nominal sentences (43, 19a).

[30] Exceptions are 49, 24—26; 51, 7—8; 54, 4—6.

[31] Cf. 41, 17 (intervention) / v. 18 f. (elaboration); 43, 19a (intervention) / v. 19b (elaboration); 44, 3a (intervention) / v. 3b (elaboration); 46, 13a (intervention) / v. 13b (elaboration). 51, 22—23 is an exception. Cf. von Waldow, Anlaß und Hintergrund, 183 footnote 17.

[32] Cf. e. g., 54, 10; 43, 4a.

[33] Examples of the transition from A to B: 41, 8—13 (10/11); 41, 14—16 (15a/15b); 42, 14—17 (16/17); 43, 16—21 (19/20); 44, 1—5 (3/4); 49, 8—10 (9a/9b); 49, 11—13 (11/12); 49, 14—21 (19a/17); 49, 22—23 (22a/22b); 55, 3b—5 (4/5).

[34] 41, 16b.20; 43, 7b.21; 49, 23c.26b; 55, 5b.

[35] 49, 14—21.24—26; 54, 4—6; 42, 14—17. In 51, 7—8 member A is also modified to deal directly with the complaint. Cf. von Waldow, Anlaß und Hintergrund, 16—18.

[36] Cf. von Waldow's discussion, Anlaß und Hintergrund, 21 ff.

[37] Ibid. 26—27.

vention expressed in the first person with Yahweh as grammatical subject and the consequences of Yahweh's intervention, in which Yahweh is never the subject, cannot be sustained as a formal principle. Admittedly, the shift in subject often occurs in those clauses which elaborate in detail upon the general expression of Yahweh's intervention, but the style is too fluid to make the change in subject a formal category. In Isaiah 41, 8—13, for instance, Yahweh appears as the grammatical subject, but only in the clauses with general content reflecting the intervention proper (v. 10). The clauses with more concrete detail do not have Yahweh as grammatical subject at all (v. 11—12). 41, 14—16 and 44, 1—5, on the other hand, betray the shift in subject. But in 41, 17—20, Yahweh is the grammatical subject throughout. Several other texts do not reflect von Waldow's distinction between elaboration of Yahweh's intervention and consequences of that intervention.[38]

Moreover, von Waldow's rigid structure necessitates unworkable distinctions between Yahweh's intervention and the elaboration of that intervention.[39] Can Isaiah 44, 3a really be distinguished as intervention over against v. 3b as elaboration? And is not the distinction just as arbitrary between 46, 13a and v. 13b?

Thus von Waldow has been unsuccessful in demonstrating the existence of *one* basic structure to which all of Deutero-Isaiah's salvation speeches conform. The fact that some speeches contain "Fear not" and some do not, that some are highly disputational and some are not, and that other diversities occur, suggests that we are not dealing with one speech-form still employed in its original setting. Indeed, the tendency of certain salvation speeches to become arguments counteracting the complaint instead of simply promising deliverance gives weight to Begrich's view that these particular speeches, if not all of Deutero-Isaiah's salvation speeches, were not uttered in the cult. There is no evidence at all that the cultic answer to the lament psalm was uttered in disputational style. It is more likely that Deutero-Isaiah, speaking to the special situation of doubt in the exile, combined disputation style with the language of salvation speeches.

The variety in Deutero-Isaiah's speeches of salvation causes us not only to reject von Waldow's position, but also with Westermann to question Begrich's derivation of all of Deutero-Isaiah's salvation speeches from one basic form.[40] Westermann begins with the differences between

---

[38] 46, 3—4.12—13; 49, 24—26; 54, 4—6.

[39] See footnote 31.

[40] Or perhaps two: the salvation oracle directed to the individual supplicant and the oracle which answers the communal lament.

Begrich's 1934 article and his *Studien zu Deuterojesaja*.[41] Westermann agrees with Begrich that six of the texts which appeared in the 1934 essay reflect the oracle-form used in the cult to declare salvation to an individual.[42] The structure is essentially the one seen by Begrich: It opens with direct address and the *assurance* of salvation *(Heilszuspruch)*, expressed by "Fear not." The direct address and assurance of salvation are substantiated by two kinds of clauses. The first of these signifies by means of nominal sentences that Yahweh has turned his attention to the supplicant.[43] The second, in the form of verbal sentences in the perfect tense, contains statements that Yahweh has now turned to intervene on the supplicant's behalf. Yahweh is always the subject of these verbs. The action expressed by the verbs is not very specific; it is dominated by generalities like, "I have redeemed you."[44] Following the direct address and the substantiated assurance of salvation, the tense changes to the imperfect, and the consequences *(Folge)* of Yahweh's intervention are described in considerable detail.[45] This section Westermann calls the *announcement of salvation (Heilsankündigung)*. Finally, the purpose of Yahweh's intervention sometimes appears.[46]

Only the texts discussed by Begrich in 1934 belong to the priestly salvation oracle; the texts added in *Studien zu Deuterojesaja* are in Westermann's opinion too varied to be derived from the form just discussed. They lack "Fear not" and sometimes the direct address. Often they are in the plural rather than the singular. They also lack the expression of Yahweh's intervention in the perfect tense; instead, Yahweh's turning to help and his intervention appear in the imperfect. In view of these differences Westermann postulates another genre — the *announcement of salvation*. The structure is as follows: (1) reference to the complaint, (2) announcement of salvation, including Yahweh's turning to help and direct statements of his intervention and its consequences, and (3) the purpose of Yahweh's intervention.[47]

---

[41] Westermann, Das Heilswort bei Deuterojesaja, EvTh 24 (1964), 355—373, and Sprache und Struktur der Prophetie Deuterojesajas, in Forschung am alten Testament, 1964, 117—124. Two other important form critical works are: P. B. Harner, The Salvation Oracle in Second Isaiah, JBL 88 (1969), 418—434; A. Schoors, I Am God Your Saviour: A Form Critical Study of the Main Genres in Isaiah XL—LV, 1973, 32—175.

[42] 41, 8—13.14—16; 43, 1—4.5—7; 44, 1—5; (54, 4—6).

[43] E. g., "I am with you" (41, 10; 43, 5); "I am your God" (41, 10; 43, 3).

[44] 41, 10b.14b; 43, 1b.

[45] 41, 11—12.15—16 etc.

[46] 41, 16b; 43, 7; 44, 5.

[47] 41, 17—20; 42, 14—17; 43, 16—21; 45, 14—17; 49, 7—12. Cf. Westermann, Heilswort, 365—366.

The oracles containing "Fear not" are imitations of the answer to the individual lament psalm. The lack of concreteness in the *assurance of salvation* and its substantiation suggests that it was derived by the technical means of the priesthood rather than in prophetic circles where the *announcement of salvation* was habitually produced.[48] When Deutero-Isaiah imitated the priestly assurance of salvation, argues Westermann, he added at the end of it the more specific announcement of salvation.[49] The prophet modified the assurance of salvation in still another way; he spoke to the people Israel by means of a genre normally used to address individuals.

In addition to his imitation of the priestly assurance of salvation by supplementing it with the announcement of salvation,[50] the prophet sometimes employed the announcement of salvation by itself — a pure salvation-announcement oracle.[51] Although Deutero-Isaiah's pure announcements of salvation are related to the communal lament psalm, their rather free structure suggests to Westermann that this genre is at home in prophetic circles rather than among the priests.

Thus far our discussion of the assurance-of-salvation oracle and the salvation-announcement oracle has been in terms of self-contained units of speech. But in addition to these forms of speech, argues Westermann, the prophet also employed the basic structure of the announcement of salvation in combination with elements from other genres to create larger poetic units. Isaiah 49, 14—26 is a good example of Westermann's view:[52] reference to the complaint appears in v. 14. Then follows the announcement of salvation in v. 15 ff. The announcement of salvation is, however, thoroughly intertwined with disputational elements, which are designed to overcome the complaint reflected in v. 14. This structure repeats itself in v. 21—23 and v. 24—26. The three parts of this long poem (v. 14—26) are tied together, not only by content, but also by their adherence to the structure of the lament psalm. Each part is a disputational announcement of salvation modeled on a different part of the lament psalm — v. 14 ff. on the complaint against Yahweh, v. 21 ff. on the complaint about what is happening to the supplicant, and v. 24 ff. on the complaint against the enemy.

Westermann's research on the speeches of salvation is a decisive step forward. The Deutero-Isaianic speeches in the second person singular which contain *'ăl tîra'* should be separated form critically from the rest of the prophet's salvation speeches. The original setting for these

---

[48] Westermann, Heilswort, 372.
[49] I refer here to the portion dominated by the imperfect tense.
[50] The *announcement* originated in prophetic circles.
[51] 41, 17—20; 42, 14—17; 43, 16—21; 45, 14—17; 49, 7—12.
[52] Westermann, Heilswort, 366—368.

speeches is the answer to the individual lament psalm.[53] The correspon-
dences to the lament psalm have already been shown by Begrich.[54] In
addition, we have evidence from Mesopotamia showing this genre in its
true setting as answer to the lament psalm:

> Kniend sitzt auf seinen Unterschenkeln Assurbanipal, wendet sich immer
>   wieder an seinen Herrn Nabu:
> "Ich habe dich lieb gewonnen, Nabu; verlaß mich doch nicht!
> Mein Leben ist vor dir aufgeschrieben, meine Seele dem Schoß der Ninlil
>   übergeben;
> Ich habe dich lieb gewonnen, überlegen-starker Nabu, verlaß mich doch nicht
>   inmitten meiner Neider!"
> Es antwortet ein 'Windhauch' von seinem Herrn Nabu her:
> "Fürchte dich nicht, Assurbanipal; ich werde dir ein langes Leben schenken!
> Gute *Winde* werde ich *für* dein Leben *einsetzen;*
> Jener mein Mund, der gut *wurde,* segnet dich immer wieder in der
>   Versammlung der großen Götter!"[55]

From Israel as well comes an example of this genre clearly set in the
context of the individual lament. In Genesis 21, 17—18 such an oracle is
an answer to Hagar's weeping.[56] *Wättebk* (v. 16) should be understood
as a reference to the utterance of a lament.[57] God hears and as an
answer sends his messenger who says, "Fear not!" This assurance is substantiated by the verb *šmʿ* in the perfect tense. Finally, the assurance of
salvation is followed by a more detailed promise expressed in the
imperfect (v. 18).

It now seems clear that the assurance of salvation is an oracle form
not to be confused with other types of salvation speech. We have yet to
determine whether its occurrence in Deutero-Isaiah imitates a non-
prophetic genre or whether it is a genuine prophetic form of speech
(von Waldow). We must admit at the outset that we cannot resolve
here the complex problem of the relationship between the role of priest
and prophet in the cult. But certain important observations can be made
as the problem borders on our form critical study. First of all, the view
of Begrich and Westermann that this genre was derived from a technical,

---

[53] Westermann is correct that this form is to be distinguished from those speeches in
which "Fear not" is used in a theophany (Gen 15, 1; 26, 24; 46, 3  Judg 6, 23  Dan
10, 8 ff.  Mk 14, 28). This distinction is overlooked by H. Dion, The "Oracle of
Salvation," CBQ 29 (1967), 198—206.

[54] Begrich, Heilsorakel, 82 ff.

[55] A. Falkenstein and W. von Soden, Sumerische und akkadische Hymnen und Gebete,
1953, 293.

[56] Westermann, Heilswort, 360.

[57] In Judg 21, 2 the phrase, "They lifted up their voices and wept," clearly refers to
the lament which follows (v. 3).

and thus priestly, means of revelation is open to question. Particularly unlikely is Westermann's view that the unspecified nature of the assurance of salvation proper indicates the technical means of the priest while the announcement of salvation is a Deutero-Isaianic addition of a prophetic *Gattung* to a priestly form of speech. Every example of the salvation-assurance oracle outside Deutero-Isaiah contains a section which elaborates on the general statements of Yahweh's intervention.[58] It is almost certain, therefore, that the detailed announcement of the future belongs to the genre in its original form. Whether the genre was uttered by a priest or prophet remains, however, unknown.

The view of Begrich and Westermann that the salvation-assurance oracle in Deutero-Isaiah is an imitation because it employs a form of speech originally used for an individual as an address to Israel is also open to question. It seems almost certain that some of the "individual laments" reflect the need of an entire people.[59] Moreover, outside Deutero-Isaiah this genre is sometimes addressed to Jacob-Israel (Jer 30, 10 = 46, 27). There is no evidence of literary dependence between the two prophets; thus it is unlikely that Deutero-Isaiah addresses a group different from the one to whom the genre could normally be directed.

It is difficult to determine whether Deutero-Isaiah's salvation-assurance oracles are imitations. Since almost all our examples of this genre in the Hebrew scriptures are found in prophetic texts rather than in cultic literature, it is not easy to decide whether Deutero-Isaiah has modified the original form in order to use it for different purposes in a different setting. Because some of the appositions to the direct address are apparently unique to Deutero-Isaiah's style,[60] one might be tempted to argue that Deutero-Isaiah has *imitated* the cultic genre. Yet other expansions of the direct address may well be native to the original genre.[61] Moreover, we cannot exclude the possibility that even in cultic usage the cultic official (priest or prophet?) felt free to include appositions in his own style without significantly modifying the basic structure of the genre, much as a modern supplicant may add attributive clauses

[58] Jer 46, 27(27b).28(28b) = Jer 30, 10—11 (a conflation of two oracles) Gen 21, 17—18(18b). The oracle to Ashurbanipal also has concrete promises.

[59] Cf. e. g., Ps 7 (v. 8.9); 54 (v. 5); 56 (v. 8); 59 (v. 6.9); 102 (v. 13—18).

[60] I refer to phrases such as "whom I choose" (41, 8.9; 44, 1.2) and "your creator." Appeal to Yahweh as creator of Israel is notably absent from the lament psalms. Moreover, the fact that Deutero-Isaiah employs language about Yahweh as creator in such appositions in other genres reinforces the supposition that this is Deutero-Isaiah's own style. Cf. 44, 24—28 and 45, 1—7.

[61] The appearance of 'æbæd in the non-Deutero-Isaianic Jer 46, 27—28 suggests that this particular apposition may be native to the genre in its cultic setting.

to the direct address in a prayer without doing violence to the genre
or wrenching it from its normal setting.

A closer look at the speeches in Deutero-Isaiah, however, suggests
that the appositions concerning Yahweh as creator stand outside the
framework of the original genre. In each case they occur as expansions
of the messenger formula (43, 1; 44, 2); in 41, 8—13.14—16, both of
which lack the messenger formula, the appositions naming Yahweh as
creator do not appear. The same is true of Jeremiah 30, 10—11 = 46,
27—28. Add to this the observation that the direct address appears twice
in Isaiah 44, 1—5 — in the introduction (v. 1—2a) and in the assurance
of salvation proper. One suspects, then, that the introduction did not
originally belong to the salvation-assurance oracle and is thus a sign of
the prophet's own work. If the introduction is not original to the genre,
we might guess that the appositions, always in the introduction, are
creations of Deutero-Isaiah. It would of course be foolhardy to draw
sweeping conclusions from so little evidence. Nevertheless, a tentative
conclusion is warranted: Deutero-Isaiah imitated a cultic genre, wrested
it from its original setting in worship, and modified it with his own
style and with the messenger formula for prophetic purposes. This conclusion grows in credibility when one considers that the prophet was
free to employ types of salvation speech other than the salvation-
assurance oracle.[62] If he had uttered his oracles in the original cultic
setting, surely he would not have had the option of using so many forms
of salvation speech.

Whether or not Deutero-Isaiah's salvation-assurance oracles are
imitations is admittedly not completely certain, but it is clear that they
exhibit a genre which can be isolated from its context by form. Now we
turn to the rest of the salvation speeches of Deutero-Isaiah. Do they
manifest one *Gattung*? Or have we several types? Are all of them self-
contained units? Or are some, as Westermann suggests, parts of longer
poetic compositions?

## II. OTHER FORMS OF SALVATION SPEECH

Deutero-Isaiah contains more than one form of salvation speech.
This Westermann has effectively shown. Whether he is right that some
of the utterances which did not contain the assurance "Fear not" are
independent utterances while others are parts of longer poems remains
to be seen. Before we can deal with the issue of shorter versus longer
poems, however, we must challenge Westermann's assumption that all
of Deutero-Isaiah's salvation speeches, other than the salvation-assurance oracles, reflect one basic genre called *Heilsankündigung*. To be
sure, all of Deutero-Isaiah's speeches of salvation include the "announce-

ment of salvation" — i. e., some kind of announcement of the future; but the structures in which this occurs are quite varied.[63] It shall be our task to determine whether we have one genre with one primary *Sitz im Leben*, whether we have different genres, each with a different setting, or whether the variety in structure is the result of a poetic creativity fundamentally unfettered by traditional genres. A form critical analysis of several texts should help answer the question.

1. *Isaiah 41, 17—20 and 42, 14—17*. The form of these texts is as follows: (1) reference to the complaint (41, 17a; 42, 14a), (2) announcement of Yahweh's intervention, expressed in the imperfect with Yahweh as subject (41, 17b; 42, 14b), and (3) the elaboration of the announcement of Yahweh's intervention (41, 18—19; 42, 15—16). In 42, 14—17 the oracle concludes with a summary statement, "These are the things I will do to them . . ."[64] 41, 17—20 ends with the purpose of Yahweh's saving activity (v. 20). Israel is spoken of in third person throughout. These two texts appear to reflect a cultic genre used to answer communal laments, as Psalm 12 shows. The oracle in that psalm speaks of Israel in third person plural rather than by direct address. Moreover, a similar structure appears: reference to the complaint (v. 6aα) and announcement of Yahweh's intervention in the imperfect (v. 6aβ). V. 6b resembles to some extent the elaboration of the intervention expressed in Isaiah 41, 17—18 and 42, 15—16, although Psalm 12, 6b is much more general and abbreviated. One might even argue that Psalm 12, 6b is part of the generalized announcement of intervention and that the oracle contains no elaboration. In any case, the formal relationships between Psalm 12, 6 and Isaiah 41, 17—20 and 42, 14—17 indicate that Deutero-Isaiah has made use of a genre originally at home in the cult.

2. *Isaiah 46, 1—4*. These verses are a fusion of two genres. V. 1—2, on the one hand, imitate a song of victory, a genre exhibited elsewhere by Jeremiah 50, 2b.[65] The defeat of the foe is depicted by verbs in the perfect. These verbs connote defeat and shame. If the text in 46, 1—2 is correct,[66] these verses are addressed *formally*[67] to the Babylonians, as *nᵉśuʾotêkæm* shows. V. 3—4, on the other hand, take on the form of

---

[62] See the discussion below in part II of this chapter.

[63] Compare, for example, 41, 17—20 with 45, 14—17 or 43, 16—21.

[64] This seems to be Deutero-Isaiah's imitation of the "summary appraisal." Cf. B. S. Childs, Isaiah and the Assyrian Crisis, 1967, 128—136; J. W. Whedbee, Isaiah and Wisdom, 1971, 75—79. Normally the "summary appraisal" is not a word of Yahweh (cf. e. g., Isa 14, 26; 17, 14). Deutero-Isaiah transforms it into a divine word at the end of an oracle.

[65] Cf. Begrich, Studien, 61.62.

[66] The versions have third person suffix.

[67] It is unlikely that the prophet is actually addressing the Babylonians.

salvation speech. The imperative *šimʿû* in Deutero-Isaiah often introduces a salvation speech.[68] The addressee, in contrast with v. 1—2, is
Israel — most often the case in salvation speeches. Finally, the announcement of the future in v. 4b is typical of salvation speeches.

Nevertheless, v. 1—4 cannot be separated into two parts. V. 3—4
differ from most of Deutero-Isaiah's salvation speeches in that the
announcement of the future is depicted only in general terms, and this
general assertion is the climax of the speech instead of merely the
substantiation as in the salvation-assurance oracles. The uniqueness in
structure is because of the contrast between v. 3—4 and v. 1—2. In
response to Israel's doubt concerning Yahweh's power in relation to the
Babylonian gods, the prophet utters a polemical speech of salvation. The
Babylonian gods, who must be carried, differ radically from Yahweh,
who has always carried Israel. Unable to deny the validity of the contrast, Israel may believe that Yahweh who has always "done" this in
the past[69] will in the future carry and deliver.

The fusion of genres in Isaiah 46, 1—4 hardly has a long history
in oral tradition prior to the exile. The structure is rather the creation
of Deutero-Isaiah; he has combined and transformed traditional genres
in a way hitherto unknown in order to convey his message to the exiles.
Whether 46, 1—4 was originally uttered apart from its present context
will occupy us later; for the moment we must content ourselves with the
recognition that v. 1—4 are independent by form. These verses are to
be distinguished form critically from the disputation speech which
follows (v. 5—11).[70] Both by form and content 46, 1—4 can also be
isolated from the exhortation and oracle of salvation in 45, 22—25,
which is itself held together by a common theme and set of images.

3. *Isaiah 51, 17—23.* Begrich is probably correct that v. 17—20 are
derived from speech used to comfort mourners.[71] The use of the root
*qwm* in II Samuel 12, 20 suggests that the verb might be employed in
imperative form, along with other appropriate imperatives, as a speech
to comfort mourners. The appearance of *yanûd* in v. 19 gives added
weight to the notion that this is a speech-form used to comfort mourners.[72] The verb root *nḥm* in v. 19, whether read as first person or
emended to third,[73] is added confirmation.[74] The language of
v. 17—20 is derived from the complaint sections of the lament psalm.

---

[68] Cf. e. g., 44, 1; 46, 3.12; 51, 1.7.
[69] *ʾᵃnî ʿaśîtî.*
[70] Cf. Chapter Three, II, 2.
[71] Begrich, Studien, 62.
[72] Cf. Nah 3, 7.
[73] See the commentaries.
[74] Cf. Gen 37, 35  II Sam 10, 3  Nah 3, 7  Job 2, 11 etc.

The word of comfort is transformed into a speech of salvation in v. 21—23. It begins with the introductory call to hear (v. 21) and messenger formula (v. 22a), followed by the statement that Yahweh has already intervened to take away the cup (v. 22b) and an announcement of the consequences of that act both for Jerusalem and for her enemies (v. 22c—23).

The fusion of the style of the speech of comfort and the language of salvation speech is clearly the creation of Deutero-Isaiah. Both kinds of utterance have been molded by him into one speech-unit — a speech of salvation. This speech of salvation is unified by form and content as an announcement of salvation to the mourning Jerusalem. This genre unit can be separated from the preceding salvation speech (v. 12—16) both by form and content.[75] Its relationship to 52, 1—2 is not immediately clear. 52, 1—2, as we shall see, is an imitation of a word of comfort.[76] Whether 51, 17—23 and 52, 1—2 were originally separate must await analysis in Part Two. But the two are complete units form critically. 51, 17—23 is an announcement of salvation to the one who has been forced to drink the cup; 51, 1—2, though similar in form, uses the images of ritually clean and unclean garments. Each can stand without the other as an announcement of salvation.

4. *Isaiah 55, 1—5.* Begrich views these verses as imitation of a Wisdom genre — the invitation to a meal.[77] The summons to life,[78] to eat and drink,[79] has roots in Wisdom. The form, too, has parallels in Wisdom; the invitation, marked by the imperatives in v. 1b and 3, is found in Wisdom literature (Prov 9, 5 Sir 24, 19). The content, however, is not typical of Wisdom; a modified expression of the traditions associated with the Davidic covenant is substituted for the content normally appearing in Wisdom circles. The form of v. 3b—5, moreover, is that of a salvation speech. Von Waldow differs from Begrich to the extent that he views these verses as an imitation of the speech of a street merchant who calls for people to come and buy.[80]

Von Waldow is probably correct that the form is the speech of a merchant. In apparent contrast with Proverbs 9, 4 ff. and Sirach 24, 19 ff., Isaiah 55, 1—5 clearly contains an invitation to buy. Nevertheless, the language of Wisdom is evident. Not only does the summons to receive life seem to be drawn from Wisdom, but also the imperative

---

[75] V. 12—16 will be discussed in detail in Part Two: Chapter Nine, I, D.
[76] Cf. Chapter Nine, I, D.
[77] Begrich, Studien, 59—61.
[78] Prov 3, 13—18; 4, 22; 8, 35; 9, 6 ff. Sir 4, 12.
[79] Prov 9, 2.5 Sir 1, 17; 15, 3; 24, 19.21.
[80] Von Waldow, Anlaß und Hintergrund, 22.

*hắṭṭû 'ăzn*ᵉ*kæm* is a formula at home in Wisdom.[81] Did Wisdom have a
genre imitating the cry of a street merchant from which Deutero-Isaiah
drew? Or did the prophet fuse the language of the merchant with that
of Wisdom? We cannot know, but we can be certain that the welding
of the speech of the street merchant with the language of promise in
v. 3b—5 is Deutero-Isaiah's own work.

Again, a full discussion of the relationship of Isaiah 55, 1—5 to its
context must be delayed until Part Two. It is evident, however, that
these verses distinguish themselves from their context as a promise to
Israel, a promise which employs the typical call of a merchant as a
vehicle for inviting Israel to life.


### III. CONCLUSION

Our investigation of a few of Deutero-Isaiah's speeches of salvation
has attempted to show that these poems are amenable to form critical
analysis. In some instances the prophet imitated genres traditionally
used in the cult. In others he modified the basic structure of the "announcement of salvation" by fusion with elements of other genres. In
the case of the latter, the structure of the utterance is as much the result
of the creativity of Deutero-Isaiah as it is the influence of typical forms
of salvation speech. Deutero-Isaiah's freedom in structuring his poetry
raises of course the question whether the "speeches of salvation" are
truly independent utterances (Begrich, von Waldow) or whether they
are elements of longer poems (Muilenburg, Westermann). Each genre
unit will be analyzed in Part Two; here I limit myself to two general
observations: (1) All the speeches examined thus far stand out from their
context by *form*. The salvation-assurance oracles (41, 8—13.14—16;
43, 1—7; 44, 1—5) and the two oracles which imitate the answer to the
communal lament (41, 17—20; 42, 14—17) are distinguishable by form
and traditional setting in life. The others, although given structure by
Deutero-Isaiah, are capable of standing alone both by form and content.
(2) At the same time we find in Deutero-Isaiah a number of rather
lengthy sections which reflect the same theme and similar style. Isaiah
51, 9—52, 12 is one of these. I shall argue in Part Two that the
passage can be broken down into several genre units (51, 9—11.12—16.
17—23; 52, 1—2.3—6.7—10.11—12). Yet the repetition of the doubled
imperatives of the verb *'ûr* (51, 9.17; 52, 1), the appearance of the
doubled *'anokî* (51, 12), the repetition of *libšî 'oz/'uzzek* (51, 9; 52, 1),
the juxtaposition of oracles directed to mourners (51, 17—23; 52, 1—2),
the repetition of the image of Yahweh's arm (51, 9; 52, 10), and the

---

[81] Cf. Prov 4, 20; 5, 1; 22, 17  Ps 78, 1.

repetition of *ṭame'* (52, 1.11) suggest that the arrangement of material is not accidental. 49, 14—26 is an example of another of these lengthy sections which exhibit strong connections among the various parts.[82]

If one wishes to determine whether Deutero-Isaiah is composed of originally separate units distinguishable by form or of long poems, he must take both of these factors into account. Are the long passages which reflect a similar theme and style the work of a collector? Or are they originally unified compositions with several "units" within? The relation between form and context is the subject of Part Two. But first other genres must be examined.

---

[82] Westermann, Heilswort, 366—368.

# Chapter Three: Disputation Speeches

The fundamental problem in our study of Deutero-Isaiah is whether form criticism illuminates the structure of the text. We have examined the speeches of salvation. Now we turn to the disputation speeches. The most important question is: can we find in Deutero-Isaiah's disputations forms of speech sufficiently stereotyped that form criticism may be considered a useful method of exegesis?

If we should be successful in isolating stereotyped structures, several questions arise: Are Deutero-Isaiah's disputations traditional forms of speech employed in their normal setting? Or are they imitations of speech-forms whose place in life is different from the one in which our prophet employs them? Or has Deutero-Isaiah created his own forms of speech which can be called an oral genre because the prophet has created a new stereotyped oral pattern? Finally, we must concern ourselves with the relationship of the disputation speeches to their context. Are they independent units of speech with no essential connection with the context? Or does the prophet employ them as small segments of larger poetic compositions?

## I. THE PROBLEM IN HISTORICAL PERSPECTIVE

Begrich viewed Deutero-Isaiah's disputations as independent units composed as imitations of speech-forms used in everyday situations of dispute.[1] One reason for this position was his belief that the circumstances of the exile made oral preaching impossible.[2] If Deutero-Isaiah did not dispute with opponents face-to-face, his disputation speeches would necessarily be literary imitations of speech-forms occurring in real life. But Begrich saw these speeches as imitations for another important reason. For him the forms of disputation speech have their original setting in the everyday world, and the prophets consciously imitated these non-prophetic disputation speech-forms,[3] much as they sometimes imitated priestly *tôrā*.[4] From the variety of possibilities in

---

[1] Begrich, Studien zu Deuterojesaja, 1938. 1963, 49. Page numbers are from the 1963 edition.
[2] Ibid. 97.
[3] Ibid. 49.
[4] Cf. Begrich, Die priesterliche Tora, BZAW 66 (1936), 63—88.

everyday life to develop the forms of disputation speech, one can see how the prophets' imitation would reflect that variety.

Begrich did not attempt to prove his assumption that Deutero-Isaiah's disputation speeches are imitations, but it is not difficult to see how it could be done on the basis of his approach. The variety in the structure of Deutero-Isaiah's disputation speeches could not be accounted for if they had their setting in one institution; therefore, they must be imitations of speeches used in various settings in the everyday world. Moreover, the adaptation of cultic hymn-forms to the circumstances of disputation could not be explained as a phenomenon native to prophetic circles in general, but rather must be understood as an arbitrary fusion of two genres which have different settings in life.

Von Waldow, too, recognized the various ways in which Deutero-Isaiah's disputation speeches are structured.[5] Moreover, he agreed that the lack of a common formal structure in any group of speeches of a particular type would signify the presence of an imitation no longer moored to the original setting in life.[6] But von Waldow denied the lack of such a common form in Deutero-Isaiah's disputation speeches. In spite of the admitted variety in structure, one common formal pattern can be found. The need to convince opponents of the truth of the speaker's claim provides the framework for the form. It consists of A: *disputation basis*, which provides a point of departure upon which both speaker and opponent can agree, and B: *conclusion*, which is the logical result of the argument based on the point of common agreement.[7] This formal framework, which always appears, demonstrates, in von Waldow's judgment, that the prophet employed a form of speech whose primary *Sitz im Leben* was the situation in which the prophet used it — to defend the oracles which he had uttered in the cult.[8] Both von Waldow and Begrich saw Deutero-Isaiah's disputation speeches as originally separate utterances.

Still another position is that of Westermann.[9] Contrary to von Waldow, he saw too much variety to yield one form.[10] Moreover, the setting of Deutero-Isaiah's disputation speeches is quite different from that of earlier prophets. In the beginning, prophets were aware that

---

[5] Von Waldow, Anlaß und Hintergrund der Verkündigung des Deuterojesaja, 1953, 35.

[6] Ibid. 26.

[7] Ibid. 28 ff.

[8] Ibid. 135 ff.

[9] Westermann, Sprache und Struktur der Prophetie Deuterojesajas, in: Forschung am alten Testament, 1964, 124—134.

[10] Ibid. 125.

disputation speech was not genuinely prophetic and used it rarely;[11] by Deutero-Isaiah's time, however, it had assumed an important role in the prophet's message.[12] Indeed, it sometimes appears as an inseparable part of the *announcement of salvation*.[13] Such a development means that originally non-prophetic forms have been removed from their original setting and have become prophetic speech.

Westermann's most distinctive contribution is his contention that Deutero-Isaiah's disputations are not oral speech; they are employed in lengthy poetic compositions rather than existing as separate utterances. Although disputation speech-forms are imitated, we have to do with conscious compositions which elaborate upon and transform the original genre. A good example of one of these compositions is Isaiah 40, 12—31.[14] It is composed of one complete disputation speech (v. 27—31), which is preceded by three speech fragments (v. 12—17.18—24.25—26). These parts are all related to one another as a unified attempt to deal with one subject under dispute,[15] Israel's complaint that Yahweh has forsaken her. V. 28—31 dispute the contention that Yahweh *will* not help, while the three fragments in v. 12—26 counter the assertion that Yahweh *can* not help. This long poetic composition which imitates disputation speech draws its content from the style of the cultic hymn. It is from the hymn that the structure "God can help / God will help" is derived.[16] Thus we have a poem which imitates both disputation style and hymn style in a complex way, which to Westermann is indicative of a planned composition.

Where does the work of these three scholars leave us? In my judgment Begrich and Westermann are right that more than one basic kind of speech is involved. Von Waldow's *disputation basis-conclusion* schema does not succeed in presenting us with *one* speech-form. A glance at 45, 9—13, for example, shows us that this simple schema does not fit. If v. 9—10 should be viewed as the common basis for disputation, v. 11 would be the conclusion, demonstrating that Israel cannot rightfully question Yahweh's plan. But what is to be done with v. 12—13? The *basis* (v. 12) and *conclusion* (v. 13) seem to appear again, this time in hymn style. Thus the schema is not as simple as it appears in von

---

[11] And, we may add, often without modification in form. The rhetorical-question disputation form found in Am 3, 3—8 displays without essential change the form and content of the kind of Wisdom disputation seen in Job 6, 5—6: 8, 11 ff.

[12] Westermann, Sprache und Struktur, 125—126.

[13] Ibid. 126.

[14] Ibid. 127—132.

[15] Westermann views the questions in v. 12—26 as rhetorical rather than real issues under dispute.

[16] Cf. Westermann, Das Loben Gottes in den Psalmen, 1963, 91 ff.

Waldow's discussion. Indeed, *disputation basis-conclusion* is not adequate as a description of the structure of a genre. Any disputation, regardless of structure, would probably have a common base from which to argue and a conclusion (expressed or implied). But the multiformity in structure which we find in Deutero-Isaiah's disputations betrays more than slight variations of one basic structure. As our analysis below will indicate, one of Deutero-Isaiah's disputations derives its form and content from its usage in Wisdom. But not all of Deutero-Isaiah's disputations are Wisdom genres.

The inadequacy of von Waldow's attempt to postulate a common formal framework suggests that we should not speak of one genre with one setting. Several forms of disputation speech apparently occur. But even more significant is the tendency to fuse disputation speech with other genres. Formal elements from the cult are often incorporated into the disputation; in one case both oracular formulae and the self-praise style of the hymn are fused with disputation speech (45, 9—13).

What is the significance of the variety in structure and the tendency to combine other genres with disputation speech? Should we assume that Deutero-Isaiah has quite consciously imitated forms of speech alien to the prophetic institution? Or does the messenger formula in 45,9-13 indicate that disputation speech had by Deutero-Isaiah's time become a genuine prophetic genre? Or is the structure the result of Deutero-Isaiah's creativity, as Westermann suggests? Obviously a fresh form critical analysis is needed.

## II. FORM CRITICAL ANALYSIS

1. *Isaiah 40, 12—17*.[17] A careful scrutiny of these verses reveals a particular structure and content unknown elsewhere in Deutero-Isaiah but readily available to us in Wisdom literature. The structure is as follows: (1) a series of rhetorical questions introduced by *mî*:

> Who measured the waters in the hollow of his hand and marked
>     off the heavens with a span,
> Enclosed the dust of the earth in a measure, weighed the mountains
>     with a balance, and the hills with scales?
> Who measured the spirit of Yahweh, what man taught him his counsel?
> With whom did he consult for his enlightenment,[18] who taught him the path
>     of justice,
> Taught him knowledge, and made him know the way of understanding?

---

[17] R. F. Melugin, Deutero-Isaiah and Form Criticism, VT 21 (1971), 330—333. Cf. also A. Schoors, I Am God Your Saviour: A Form Critical Study of the Main Genres in Isaiah XL—LV, 1973, 245 ff.

[18] Literally, "with the result that he enlightened him".

(2) The disputation concludes with an assertion introduced by *hen*:

> Behold, the nations are like a drop from a bucket, reckoned as dust
>   in the scales.
> Behold, the coastlands are taken up[19] like fine dust.
> Lebanon is not sufficient for burning,
>   its beasts for a burnt offering.
> All the nations are like nothing compared to him, reckoned as nothing
>   and emptiness in relation to him.

Disputations with questions introduced by *mî*, along with other forms of rhetorical questions, are typical of Wisdom.[20] Of particular interest is Job 40, 25 ff. There we find precisely the structure which we have in Isaiah 40, 12—17: rhetorical questions designed to show man's impotence against Leviathan (Job 40, 25—32), followed by a conclusion introduced by *hen* (41, 1):

> Behold, his hope[21] is false, he is cast down even at the sight of him.[22]
> He is not fierce that he can arouse him.[23]
>   Who is he then that can stand before me?[24]
> Who can stand before me that I must repay?
>   Anything under all the heavens is mine.
> Did I not silence his boasting[25] and the mighty word and _____?[26]

It might be objected that this type of disputation is not unique to Wisdom. To be sure, disputations with questions introduced by *mî* must have been used in numerous situations.[27] But it is my contention that this widely-used type of disputation speech was adopted by the wise men, specialized, and made into a Wisdom genre. In both Job 38 ff. and Proverbs 30, 4 the rhetorical questions function in a particular way; they show that mortal man is nothing compared with Yahweh the Creator. Thus the questions acquire a particular content and vocabulary to show the contrast between God and man.[28]

---

[19] Or, perhaps, the verb has to do with weighing.
[20] Cf. Job. chs. 38 ff.   Prov 30, 4.
[21] The hope of any would-be assailant.
[22] Even if the consonants '*l* were to be vocalized as '*el*, as suggested by the Peshitta and Symmachus, instead of '*æl* (MT), the contrast between a man und Leviathan would still be maintained. For a discussion of the text see M. H. Pope, Job, 1965, 282.
[23] Or, "Is he not fierce when one arouses him?"
[24] LXX has first person suffix, but see Pope, Job, 282.
[25] With Pope, Job, 283.
[26] No satisfactory solution has been offered for *ḥin 'ærkô*.
[27] Cf. e. g., Ex 4, 11   II Kings 18, 35 = Isa 36, 20.
[28] '*Eṣā* — Job 38, 2; 42, 3; *bîn/bînā* (both verb and noun) — Job 38, 4.18.36; *yādă'* — (Qal) Job 38, 4.5.21.33   Prov 30, 4 (Hiph.) Job 38, 3; *dă'ăt* — Job 38, 2; 42, 3.

Isaiah 40, 12—17 reflects both the form and content of this Wisdom genre. Who but Yahweh could measure the waters in the hollow of his hand? Who has enough wisdom to be his teacher? The similarities with Job 38 ff. and Proverbs 30, 4 are evident; thus we may conclude that Isaiah 40, 12—17 is a genre at home in Wisdom circles.[29]

2. *Isaiah 40, 18—24.25—26; 46, 5—11.*[30] These texts betray a stereotyped structure. The form is as follows: (1) the question "To whom will you compare God/me?" (Isa 40, 18.25; 46, 5). (2) Sometimes a sarcastic description of the manufacture of idols follows (40, 19—20; 46, 6—7). (3) Next the prophet's hearers are asked to remember what they have long known through the cult, sometimes by means of rhe-. torical questions,[31] sometimes through imperatives.[32] (4) What they are to remember is expressed in the participial style of the hymn.[33]

The structure has within it a certain latitude for variation. Yahweh can be the speaker (40, 25—26; 46, 5—11), but it may be the prophet (40, 18—24). Member 2 of the speech-form can be omitted (40, 25—26). Another variable is the use of the hymn. In 40, 18—24.25—26 the prophet uses the usual third person style of Israel's hymns to convey the body of tradition common to both speaker and opponents. In 46, 5—11 he begins with the self-predication, "I am God and *there is no other.*" The self-predication of Yahweh occurs in Deutero-Isaiah primarily in salvation oracles on the one hand,[34] and trial speeches[35] and disputation speeches[36] on the other. In salvation oracles it serves as the basis for announcement of salvation.[37] Hymnic expansions of the self-predication

---

[29] Von Waldow, Der traditionsgeschichtliche Hintergrund der prophetischen Gerichts-reden, 1963, 48 ff. G. von Rad also supports our notion that we are dealing with a Wisdom *Gattung.* He points to a parallel in Egyptian Wisdom literature in which the scribe Hori disputes with a colleague in rhetorical question style. Cf. von Rad, Job xxxviii and Egyptian Wisdom, in The Problem of the Hexateuch and Other Essays, 1965, 287 ff. The text to which von Rad refers can be found in ANET, 1955, 475 ff. This footnote is repeated from the article by Melugin, Deutero-Isaiah and Form Criticism, 333.

[30] Melugin, Deutero-Isaiah and Form Criticism, 333—334.

[31] *Hᵃlô' tedᵉ'û,* etc. (40, 21).

[32] 40, 26; 46, 8.9.; 46, 8 asks the hearers to reflect on the statement concerning idol making. V. 9, by contrast, exhorts reflection on Israel's tradition. Westermann's elimination of v. 5—8 on the basis of the difference in meaning of *zikrû* does not hold, however, when one compares the formal similarity of 40, 18—24; 40, 25—26, and 46, 5—11. Cf. Westermann, Sprache und Struktur, 151—152.

[33] 40, 22—24.26 (third person style); 46, 10—11 (self-praise style).

[34] Cf. e. g., 41, 13; 43, 3.15.

[35] Cf. e. g., 41, 4; 43, 10.11.12; 45, 18.19.21.

[36] Cf. e. g., 46, 9. Cf. W. Zimmerli, Ich bin Jahwe, in: Gottes Offenbarung, 1963, 31.

[37] It is sometimes introduced by *kî* (41, 13; 43, 3), or it may be asyndeton (43, 15).

style in this genre express Yahweh's saving relationship to Israel.[38] But
in trial and disputation speeches the self-predication distinguishes Yahweh from other gods in polemic fashion. Often it is continued by an
assertion that there is no other God but Yahweh.[39] The polemic use of
self-praise hymn style is not unique to Deutero-Isaiah. For instance, we
possess a Sumerian hymn in which Inanna utters self-praise:

> Mein Vater hat mir den Himmel gegeben, hat mir die Erde gegeben;
>   Die Himmelsherrin bin ich,
> Mißt sich einer, ein Gott, mit mir?[40]

Another is an Akkadian hymn of Ishtar's self-praise, preserved fragmen-
tarily:

> . . .
> Ich lasse regnen auf die Feindin(nen) einen Kampf wie einen Feuerstrahl,
> . . .
> Ich durchschreite immer wieder den Himmel . . .,
>   stürze die Erde um;
> Dann vernichte ich den Rest der Ortschaften, . . .
>   die Feindinnen des Schamasch.
> Ich bin die kriegerischste der Götter, etc.[41]

Self-praise of the deity has firm hymnic roots in the Near East,[42]
both in Mesopotamia and Egypt. Insofar as we are able to tell,[43] however, these two hymns are not fullfledged disputations like Isaiah 46,
5—11; they are simply hymns with a polemic edge. As far as I know,
self-praise of the deity did not have a traditional place in the speech-
forms of disputation. Therefore, we must conclude that Deutero-Isaiah
arbitrarily adapted a hymn style well known to him and incorporated
it within the framework of a disputation speech. He may have borrowed
a form learned in Babylon, or he may be using a self-praise form from
Israelite life not preserved to us; we cannot be sure. But we may be
certain that the speech-form is no longer employed in its original setting.

---

[38] "I am Yahweh *your* God, who strengthens *your* right hand . . ." (41, 13); "For I am
Yahweh *your* God, the Holy One of *Israel, your* savior" (43, 3); "I am Yahweh
*your* Holy One, the creator of *Israel, your* king" (43, 15).

[39] 43, 11.12—13; 45, 18.21; 46, 9.

[40] A. Falkenstein and W. von Soden, Sumerische und akkadische Hymnen und Gebete,
1953, 67—68.

[41] Ibid. 239—240.

[42] Cf. E. Norden, Agnostos Theos: Untersuchung zur Formgeschichte religiöser Rede,
1913, 207 ff. A recent treatment of the idea of the incomparability of the deity,
which includes self-praise texts, is C. J. Labuschagne, The Incomparability of
Yahweh in the Old Testament, 1966.

[43] The fragmentary character of Ishtar's hymn makes certainty impossible.

In fact, we can see traces of Deutero-Isaiah's transformation of the self-praise hymn style as he incorporated it into the framework of the disputation. He first employs hymnic participial style as a point of agreement between him and his opponents (v. 10),[44] proceeding then to a now-undeniable assertion of the disputed matter by means of a parallel clause in the same style (v. 11).[45]

Neither 40, 18—24 nor 40, 25—26 nor 46, 5—11 can claim antiquity in oral tradition, as far as form is concerned. Indeed, the structure is apparently a Deutero-Isaianic creation; the framework is from the style of disputation, while the content is from cultic style. Nevertheless, the three texts are stereotyped to the degree usually manifest in an oral *Gattung*. In this sense each is independent from its context. Whether each was actually an independent utterance has, however, not yet been determined; that must wait for Part Two. At this point it will suffice to recognize that Deutero-Isaiah created a structure which looks very much like a new genre, a genre composed of disputation and hymn elements.

3. *Isaiah 40, 27—31*.[46] These verses are a disputation calculated to overcome the complaint quoted in v. 27. The complaint is in the style well known from the individual lament psalm, and the disputation is structured in liturgical style as an argument against the cultic complaint. In order to persuade his opponents that their complaint is not justified, the prophet appeals to what they have always known from the cult: "Have you not known, have you not heard?" The disputation then proceeds in the style of the "expression of confidence" found in the individual lament psalms:[47]

> Yahweh is an everlasting God, creator of the ends of the earth.
> He does not faint or grow weary, his understanding is unsearchable.
> He gives power to the faint, to the strengthless he adds might.
> Youths may faint and be weary, young men may stumble;
> Those who wait upon Yahweh shall renew their power; they shall ascend with wings like eagles;
> They shall run and not be weary; they shall walk and faint not.

The "expression of confidence," used in the lament psalm to express the faith that Yahweh will deliver, is taken from its original setting by Deutero-Isaiah and made the content of the prophet's *argument* against the complaint. This is an example of Deutero-Isaiah's freedom to transform traditional forms of speech; the structure of this disputation is not

---

[44] 45, 12 also uses hymn style for such disputational purposes.

[45] Cf. also 45, 13.

[46] Melugin, Deutero-Isaiah and Form Criticism, 334—335.

[47] Cf. Ps 25, 8; 102, 13.

found in tradition prior to Deutero-Isaiah. Thus we cannot assert that it was an originally independent saying on the basis of a form long known in oral tradition. Yet v. 27—31 stands out from the context as a disputation on the complaint in v. 27. Whether it was originally part of the context must await discussion in Part Two; form critically it stands alone as a well-integrated disputation.

4. *Isaiah 45, 9—13.* This passage makes use of a widely known form of speech—rhetorical questions which reflect incredibility that one who handles an object should be thought inferior to the object. Our passage opens with this "handler-handled" disputation form:

> Woe is upon the one who contends with his maker, the potsherd with the potter.[48]
> Does the clay say to its maker, "What are you making?" or,
> "Your work has no handles?"
> Woe is upon the one who says to a father, "What are you begetting?"
> or to a woman, "With what are you in travail?"

This speech-form may appear with[49] or without[50] the woe sentence. The genre draws on the background of the contest fable.[51] This form of speech takes the disputational character of the contest fable into its own particular speech-pattern by means of rhetorical questions about the relationship of the handler to that which is handled. It has its place in everyday life and may be used in various ways. It may be used as a disputation proper (Isa 10, 15; 45, 9—10  Rom 9, 20 ff.). Or it may be used in situations which only approximate disputation — to lend weight to a woe sentence used as a prophetic indictment (Isa 29, 15—16) or to emphasize the truth of a didactic saying (the Sayings of Ahikar).[52] The variety in its use is accomplished by variation in the way the speaker can move from these rhetorical questions, which provide a basis of agreement with opponents, to resolve the disputed matter. In Isaiah 10, 15 the opponent is left to draw the conclusion for himself,[53] whereas

---

[48] MT now reads, "a potsherd among earthen pots." Parallelism, however, would suggest reading ḥaraś instead of ḥărśê. For a discussion of the text, cf. C. C. Torrey, The Second Isaiah, 1928, 359.

[49] Isa 29, 15; 45, 9.

[50] Isa 10, 15  Rom 9, 20 ff.

[51] Cf. H. Gressmann, Israels Spruchweisheit, 1925, 28—29; R. J. Williams, The Fable in the Ancient Near East, in: A Stubborn Faith, edited by E. C. Hobbs, 1956, 7.

[52] "Why should wood strive with the fire, meat with the knife, a man with the king?" This follows a didactic saying concerning obedience to the king. Cf. A. Cowley, Aramaic Papyri of the Fifth Century B. C., 1923, 216, 223.

[53] We need not decide here whether v. 16 ff. are original or secondary. Even if they are original, these verses are not the disputed matter but rather the announcement that can be made once the dispute is settled. The dispute has to do with the

in Romans 9, 20 ff., the application to the concrete situation of dispute appears in the form of questions concerning the disputed matter (v. 22 ff.). Isaiah 45, 9—13 resolves the dispute in the following manner:

Thus says Yahweh the Holy One of Israel and his Maker,
"Will you question me about my sons,[54] will you command me concerning
the work of my hands?"

The answer to these questions is, "No." Then Yahweh appeals to what is known about him in tradition (v. 12) in order to command assent to his claim about Cyrus (v. 13):

I made the earth, and I created mankind upon it;
My hand stretched out the heavens, and I commanded all their hosts.
I aroused him in righteousness, and I will make straight all his ways;
He will build my city and release my exiles,
Not for a price or bribe, says Yahweh Sabaoth.

Deutero-Isaiah's way of resolving the dispute based on "handler-handled" questions departs from the normal procedure. Usually the speech-form appears in human rather than divine speech. In Isaiah 29, 15—16 Yahweh is spoken of in the third person, which indicates that the speaker was understood to be human; as far as the time of Paul it was natural to use this genre as human speech. Even in Isaiah 10, 15, where Yahweh appears to be the speaker, we have an imitation of a normal dispute between two people, in which one of the parties happens to be Yahweh. Only in Isaiah 45, 9—13, where a dispute between prophet and people seems real enough, do we find Yahweh as a partner in the dispute through his prophetic *messenger*.[55] Deutero-Isaiah transforms the human "handler-handled" disputation form into a prophetic messenger speech. Moreover, apart from the introductory and closing formulae of the messenger speech, Yahweh does not speak in normal oracular form. He first speaks in disputational form, applying the language of v. 9—10 to the relationship of Yahweh and people (v. 11b). Then he carries on the disputation in self-praise hymn style (v. 12—13). Thus 45, 9—13 is an imitation and transformation of a non-prophetic genre. Deutero-Isaiah's fusion of "handler-handled" style with messenger speech and self-praise of the deity — each of which has a different setting in life — can be attributed to nothing other than his own creativity. Nevertheless, every element of this speech is employed for the

---

legitimacy of Assyria's boasts. V. 15 uses the "handler-handled" disputation form as a basis of common agreement. The opponent is left to draw the proper conclusion for himself concerning the legitimacy of Assyria's boasts.

[54] Read *hăʾattæm tišalûnî*.
[55] Note the prophetic formulae *kōʾamăr yhwh* and *ʾamăr yhwy ṣᵉbaʾôt*.

purposes of disputation. The messenger-speech style gives the prophet's words the authority of Yahweh, and the style of the cultic hymn provides part of the content of the argument in its appeal to widely-accepted Israelite tradition.

5. *Isaiah 44, 24—28.* This passage has provoked disagreement concerning its genre. Gressmann viewed it as hymnic, Köhler as a messenger speech which has incorporated the style of self-predication, and Begrich, von Waldow, and Schoors as a disputation speech.[56] All of them agree, however, that the speech is a self-contained unit. Recently a new approach has been suggested by Westermann. Although he, like Gressmann, views these verses as a hymn, he does not believe that they constitute an independent unit. Instead, 44, 24—28 is a hymnic introduction to the poetic composition 44, 24—45, 7. The participial clauses in v. 24—28 are merely appositions to the self-predication in v. 24; the main body of the text — an oracle to a king — begins in 45, 1 ff., following the expanded introductory self-predication (44, 24—28).[57]

Westermann's suggestion that 44, 24—28 is not to be separated from 45, 1—7 has merit, particularly in view of the similarity in subject matter. Thus the question must be reopened. Is it true that 44, 24—28 is only a hymnic introduction to something that follows? Or does it stand alone as a self-contained unit, possibly as a disputation or a hymn?

It seems obvious that v. 24—28 employ the style of the hymn. We have observed already that the self-praise of the deity has a firm place in the hymn.[58] The string of participial attributions is also traceable to that genre.[59] But we must determine whether the prophet has here incorporated a true hymn or whether he has imitated one. The fact that v. 24—28 begin with a messenger formula suggests that these verses are not a genuine hymn. Historically the prophets used the messenger formula to introduce oracles.[60] One suspects that Deutero-Isaiah's use of the messenger formula here is an indication that the following clauses in hymn style are employed for purposes other than praise. Indeed, Begrich is correct that these verses serve as a disputation.[61] In the situation of doubt occasioned by the exile the prophet has Yahweh argue from what Israel already knows about him in order to allay their

---

[56] Gressmann, Die literarische Analyse Deuterojesajas, ZAW 34 (1964), 285, 289; Köhler, Deuterojesaja stilkritisch untersucht, 1923, 105; Begrich, Studien, 49, 51; von Waldow, Anlaß und Hintergrund, 36; Schoors, I Am God Your Saviour, 267—273.

[57] Westermann, Sprache und Struktur, 144—151.

[58] See my discussion of 46, 5—11.

[59] Cf. e. g., Ps 103, 3 ff.   104, 2 ff.

[60] Cf. e. g., Am 5, 3.16; 7, 17   Isa 28, 16.

[61] Begrich, Studien, 50—53.

uncertainty regarding the future. In the style of the hymn Yahweh appeals to generally-accepted knowledge of his activity (v. 24—26a). With v. 26b Yahweh turns to things yet unfulfilled — the rebuilding of Jerusalem and the victory of Cyrus. Normally the hymn uses participial style for past events or for attributive statements which are essentially timeless.[62] Thus the participial clauses in v. 26b—28 are a departure from the usual practice. Moreover, they are marked by a stylistic change seen in the definite article before the participle. Thus v. 26b—28 are the conclusion of the disputation; Yahweh has argued from the known in order to convince doubters of that which is not yet generally agreed upon.

It would seem, then, that 44, 24—28 is a self-contained disputation rather than an introduction to a longer poetic unit. But Westermann's argument that v. 24—28 are incomplete grammatically remains to be considered. Unfortunately we do not possess texts which are exactly parallel to the grammatical structure of 44, 24—28. But Psalm 103 is sufficiently analogous to illumine the problem. Psalm 103, like Isaiah 44, 24—28, contains a series of participial clauses which are attached to the introduction (v. 3—7). To be sure, the participial clauses in v. 3—7 are continued by other stylistic elements (v. 8 ff.). But these participial clauses are not subordinate grammatically to what follows; they stand on their own as independent affirmations. In all likelihood this is true also of the participial clauses in Isaiah 44, 24—28. The fact that Israel is no longer the addressee in 45, 1—7 is additional evidence that 45, 1 begins a new grammatical unit. Thus Isaiah 44, 24—28 stands out from its context as a disputation in hymn style.

6. *Isaiah 48, 1—11.* The literary problems presented by this passage are vexing. Most perplexing is the curious mixture of second person singular and plural. Attempts to solve the problem along source-critical lines have proved unsatisfactory, however. The attempts of Duhm and Westermann to make separations on the basis of content are unconvincing, in part because they do not proceed along the lines of the singular-plural dichotomy.[63] But even Begrich's attempt to delineate the fusion of two originally separate texts — one in the singular (v. 4.5.6b. 7.8.9.10) and one in the plural (v. 3.6aβ.11) runs into the problem that neither text can stand alone well.[64] Therefore, we must agree with

---

[62] Ps 136 is an example of participial clauses used to praise Yahweh's past deeds. Ps 103, 3 ff. is an illustration of the participial clause used to describe Yahweh's deeds and attributes which are characteristic of him in all times.

[63] Duhm, Das Buch Jesaia übersetzt und erklärt, 1922, 360 ff.; Westermann, Sprache und Struktur, 154.

[64] Begrich, Studien, 169—170.

von Waldow that the present state of the text must be accepted.[65] Whatever the history of the text may have been, we can interpret it now only in its present form.

Although we cannot agree with von Waldow's assumption that this text displays the *one* disputation speech-form which he supposes is existent throughout Deutero-Isaiah, he is correct in classifying it as a disputation speech. V. 6a is an appeal to the prophet's opponents to declare their agreement to what is already known (v. 3—5) as a basis upon which to proceed with the rest of the disputation (v. 6b ff.). But it is a complex speech. It begins with an introduction in the style of the prophetic invective. "Hear this!" or, "Hear this word!", followed by invective in participial or relative clause style, occurs in several places in prophetic literature.[66] V. 3 ff., however, departs from the structure of the prophetic invective, and the disputation begins. Thus we have a complex disputation made up of several elements delicately balanced. It differs from most of Deutero-Isaiah's disputations, in which appeal to the long-known reliability of Yahweh's prophetic word with regard to the "former things" is the sole basis for commanding assent to the "new things" now being prophesied. In 48, 1—11 the usual simplicity of most of Deutero-Isaiah's disputation speeches is replaced with an inseparable combination of the theme of Yahweh's word *then* and *now* with the theme of Yahweh who saves rebellious Israel only for the sake of his name. These elements intertwined among one another seem at first glance to blur the sharpness of the speech. To what concrete situation of disputation is this speech addressed?

V. 3—6a provide an initial point of entry in reconstructing the situation of dispute. Yahweh presupposes agreement between him and his opponents that he prophesied the "former things" before they occurred, so that sinful Israel would not attribute them to another god. The view of the opponents which Yahweh disputes, as von Waldow correctly observes,[67] is the following: Yahweh has not told Israel long beforehand of the events now taking place. Therefore, they must not be Yahweh's deeds. But Yahweh, taking issue with this view, invites Israel to consider why he prophesied the "former things" (v. 3—6a). He did so in order that his deeds would not be attributed to another god, as the prophet's hearers can agree (v. 6a). Now Israel is told why Yahweh waits until now to declare the "new things." If he does not perform the "new things," he will forfeit his glory to another deity (v. 9.11); therefore, he determines to refine Israel rather than to destroy her (v. 10).

---

[65] Von Waldow, Anlaß und Hintergrund, 32.

[66] Cf. e. g., Am 4, 1; 8, 4. Cf. also Isa 28, 14, where the introduction is, "Hear the word of Yahweh."

[67] Von Waldow, Anlaß und Hintergrund, 33—34.

In the case of both the "former things" and "new things" Yahweh uses his prophetic word to prevent his honor from being attributed to another god. But in the case of the "new things" Yahweh must proceed in a new way. If he should announce the salvation long beforehand, Israel would know (v. 7b) and deal faithlessly (v. 8b), thereby spoiling the refinement planned by Yahweh. Thus only now when the events are appearing on the scene does he prophesy them.

As has been the case with most of Deutero-Isaiah's disputation speeches, there is no life setting for this speech-form in Israel's oral tradition. Instead, it is a free creation of Deutero-Isaiah. The style of prophetic invective (v. 1—2) is combined with disputation (v. 3—11). But even v. 3—11 have elements from other genres. Indeed, the elements of disputation are combined with the style of an aetiological narrative placed in the mouth of Yahweh as an explanation of his purposes with regard to the "former things" and the "new things." A similar aetiological narrative appears in Genesis 3, 21 ff., there appearing in third person with Yahweh's words quoted:

> Yahweh Elohim said, "Behold, the man has become like one of us, knowing good and evil. And now, *lest* he stretch out his hand and take also from the tree of life and eat and live forever . . .[68]

Deutero-Isaiah puts this kind of narrative in Yahweh's mouth for the purposes of disputation, a function not original to that narrative type.

In spite of Deutero-Isaiah's fusion of several genres in this speech, 48, 1—11 stands out from its context as a unit of reflection on the particular issue under dispute. The entire speech, although complex, deals with that particular question, and the larger context does not appear to reflect upon that issue at all.

*7. Isaiah 42, 18—25.* Up to the present time there has been no satisfactory form critical analysis of this text. Gressmann calls it a *Scheltwort,*[69] but his analysis is sketchy. Köhler calls it a *Streitgespräch,*[70] but presents no detailed arguments for his view. Begrich and von Waldow omit a discussion of the text. For my part, I see no prospect for a fully adequate form critical description of the passage. At the same time, I am convinced that Westermann's view of it as something like a disputation speech is a fruitful approach.[71]

---

[68] Cf. Ex 13, 17 for another example of such an aetiological narrative.

[69] Gressmann, Analyse, 270.

[70] Köhler, Deuterojesaja stilkritisch untersucht, 111.

[71] Westermann, Das Buch Jesaja: Kapitel 40—66, 1966, 89—94. This speech is not a trial speech as Westermann suggests in Sprache und Struktur, 143 (cf. also Schoors, I Am God Your Saviour, 202). V. 18 is not a summons to trial like 41, 1.21; 43, 8. 42,18 is an introduction to a disputation. See footnote 74.

In Westermann's view a lament psalm lies behind this text. This lament psalm contains the complaint that Yahweh is blind and deaf to Israel's need with the result that Israel has fallen prey to plunderers. In v. 18—25 Yahweh disputes the claim that he is blind. Instead, it is Israel who is blind, and they are plundered because of their lack of obedience to their role as servant. Westermann points to the questions introduced by *mî* to suggest the similarity of these verses with disputation speech. These significant insights, however, are unfortunately not developed.[72]

In spite of the apparent impossibility of a fully-satisfying form critical analysis of this text, the arguments for its function as a disputation speech can be amplified. Westermann is undoubtedly correct that v. 22 reflects the cultic complaint, "We are a people plundered and spoiled; all of us are trapped in holes . . ." He is probably also correct that Yahweh is answering a complaint that he is blind and deaf to his people's plight.[73] There are additional signs that v. 18—25 are a disputation on such a lament. By means of imperatives to "hear" and "look," the "blind and deaf" are summoned to gain a new perspective.[74] It is for their future profit that they should do so (v. 23). Even clearer than the imperatives is the transition from v. 24a to v. 24b. After summoning the hearers for the sake of the future, the prophet has Yahweh ask this question (introduced by *mî*): "Who gave Jacob to plunder and Israel to spoilers?" The answer to this question is in the form of a rhetorical question (v. 24b). V. 24b—25 constitute the conclusion to this disputation, whose argument has been presented in the preceding verses.[75]

The course of the argument is as follows: the disputation against the complaint that Yahweh has been deaf and sightless to the plundering of his people begins with a summons for the blind and deaf to "hear" and "look" in order to see (v. 18). Then the prophet has Yahweh dispute the complaint that Yahweh is blind and deaf with the question, "Who is blind but my servant . . .?" The question is rhetorical, implying that no one is blind and deaf but Yahweh's servant Israel — a nation which has seen and heard Yahweh's will and yet persisted in disobedience.

---

[72] Moreover, Westermann's work is hampered by arbitrary emendations of the text.

[73] This occurs in the complaint section of lament psalms (cf. Hab 1, 13) and also in the petition (e. g., Ps 28, 1; 35, 22; 39, 13; 83, 2; 109, 1).

[74] The imperatives in v. 18 are indications that this is a disputation speech. Such imperatives occur elsewhere in speeches designed to present an argument against an opposing view. For example, in II Sam 20, 16 ff., a wise woman employs an imperative to introduce a speech designed to convince Joab that he should not destroy the city of Abel. In Job 33, 1.31.33 Elihu tries to convince Job of the validity of his position over against what Job has said.

[75] Note the stylistic similarity of the conclusion to the argument in 45, 21c.

Then the typical style of the hymn of thanksgiving influences the language of the argument (v. 21). We have examples of similar phraseology from Israel's hymns, in which Yahweh is praised for "magnifying"[76] his saving power[77] on behalf of Israel (or Israel's anointed). It was precisely for delivery out of difficult circumstances, often political,[78] that the psalmist customarily gave thanks. Deutero-Isaiah employs this kind of hymnic phrase as a point of agreement between him and his hearers. Every Israelite should be able to give assent to such a statement about Yahweh. Having reached this point of agreement, the prophet has Yahweh point out that Israel is not saved but plundered.[79] What does this desperate state of affairs signify? That Yahweh is blind and deaf? That Yahweh has allowed Israel to be plundered for no good reason? No! It is instead Israel's sin, so v. 24b—25 argue, that accounts for their present plight. Deutero-Isaiah has used the contrast between what is known by Israelites of Yahweh's saving power (v. 21) and the miserable plight of Israel (v. 22) to undermine Israel's complaint concerning Yahweh's inactivity. If Yahweh is known to be a God who saves his people, yet his people are plundered with no one to deliver, then it must be that Israel has sinned, not that Yahweh has been sightless and unhearing. Israel must see and hear this in order to profit for the future.

It is clear that this disputation is not a real disputation between Yahweh and people. Although Yahweh is cast as the speaker, we can see that the role of Yahweh as speaker of the disputation is not firm; for Yahweh is sometimes spoken of in the third person (v. 21.24b$\beta\gamma$), and the speaker once identifies himself with the people (v. 24b$\alpha$). That this speech is an imitation of a real disputation is shown also by the fact that there was no setting in Israel for Yahweh to answer a lament psalm with a disputation.

Isaiah 42, 18—25 is a result of Deutero-Isaiah's creativity; the form is not rooted in centuries of oral tradition. Nevertheless, v. 18—25 can be distinguished from the preceding oracle of salvation (42, 14—17) and the assurance of salvation which follows (43, 1 ff.). The precise relationship of Isaiah 42, 18—25 to its context will be discussed in Part Two. Here we limit ourselves to the recognition that it is independent by form and content.

---

[76] Hiph'il of *gdl*.
[77] That is to say, his *y*e *šû ʿā* and his *ḥæsæd* (Ps 18, 51). Cf. also Ps. 138, 2, although the text appears to be in disarray.
[78] Cf. e. g., Ps 18.
[79] Note the contrast implied by the conjunction at the beginning of v. 22.

## III. CONCLUSION

The results of our study indicate that, for the most part, the structure of Deutero-Isaiah's disputation speeches is his own creation. On occasion, admittedly, he appears to have used traditional genres without significant modification (Isa 40, 12—17). But in most instances we can see that he was free to create his own poetry. In so doing, however, he was not oblivious to or totally independent from customary conventions of speech. As we have seen, the impact of various traditional genres is observable. Thus the most significant result of our study is that the prophet did not abandon speaking in stereotyped forms. Even when the prophet has created a new structure, it sometimes becomes a pattern which can occur in several contexts (40, 18—24.25—26; 46, 5—11). Indeed, it appears that Deutero-Isaiah has taken genre elements from the cult and has on occasion created a new stereotyped genre. At the same time, the prophet has not bound himself to any one structure; in several of his disputations we see considerable poetic creativity. But even here the utterances are disputations throughout and in this sense can be distinguished from their context by form.

The question of context is not thereby resolved. It remains unanswered whether these speeches depend upon the context to be properly understood. Are they originally separate units which have no meaningful relationship to the present context? Or, conversely, are they parts of longer poetic compositions? Or are they originally independent utterances which have been given new kerygmatic significance by the careful artistry of a collector? These questions await our consideration in Part Two.

# Chapter Four: Trial Speeches

J. Begrich was the first to undertake a comprehensive form critical analysis of Deutero-Isaiah's trial speeches.[1] Since that time two works by von Waldow and one by Westermann have appeared, as well as a discussion of certain Deutero-Isaianic trial speeches in H. J. Boecker's study of the legal forms in the Hebrew scriptures.[2] They reach different conclusions; thus the question of the nature of Deutero-Isaiah's trial speeches must be posed again. Did Deutero-Isaiah employ legal genres well known in oral tradition, or was he a free literary creator who occasionally used the imagery of the trial? And if the former be true, are the forms used in their original setting? Or are they imitations, now employed in a new realm of life? Ultimately we must explore the relation between form and context: Are Deutero-Isaiah's trial speeches independent units with no relation to their context? Or does he employ his trial speeches as small segments of a larger kerygmatic whole?

## I. THE TRIAL BETWEEN YAHWEH AND ISRAEL

### A. The Problem in Historical Perspective

Begrich and Boecker consider Deutero-Isaiah's trial speeches, along with the trial speeches of other prophets, to be imitations of forms commonly used in legal proceedings in the town gate. The fact that the prophetic trial speeches, particularly those in Deutero-Isaiah, display a variety of forms which correspond to the forms of the various kinds of utterances used in the town gate — i. e., appeal-to-trial speeches of the accuser, appeal-to-trial speeches of the accused, etc.[3] — signifies that the forms of speeches used in the town gate are imitated and transferred to the relationship between Yahweh and Israel.

Von Waldow does not agree that the *Sitz im Leben* for these speeches is the town gate.[4] The fact that Yahweh is both judge and

---

[1] Begrich, Studien zu Deuterojesaja, 1938. 1963, 26—48. Page numbers are from the 1963 edition.

[2] Von Waldow, Anlaß und Hintergrund der Verkündigung des Deuterojesaja, 1953, 37—46, and Der traditionsgeschichtliche Hintergrund der prophetischen Gerichtsreden, 1963; Boecker, Redeformen des Rechtslebens im Alten Testament, 1964; Westermann, Sprache und Struktur der Prophetie Deuterojesajas, in: Forschung am Alten Testament, 1964, 134—144.

[3] Cf. Begrich, Studien, 27.

[4] Von Waldow, Anlaß und Hintergrund, 37—46.

accuser, something inconceivable in the legal life at home in the gate,
means that the prophetic trial speeches are at home in another realm of
life. He believes that they are derived from a cultic lawsuit preserved in
the Covenant Renewal Festival. Von Waldow takes his cue from Würthwein[5] that certain prophetic texts[6] owe their form and content to this
cultic lawsuit genre.[7] Yet von Waldow views the prophetic trial speeches
as imitations of the cultic trial speech form.[8] This is the case with the
prophetic speeches because Yahweh's appearance as accused rather than
accuser in some of them can be explained only if these speeches are
imitations of speech-forms used in the cult.[9]

In my judgment, von Waldow's view that the prophetic trial
speeches are imitations of trial speeches used in the Covenant Renewal
Festival cannot be sustained. To be sure, the imagery of Yahweh in a
court case with his people Israel is at home in the cult rather than trial
in the gate.[10] But even though the content of the prophetic trial speeches
may be influenced by the cult, the fact remains that the forms of the

[5] Würthwein, Der Ursprung der prophetischen Gerichtsrede, ZThK 49 (1952), 1—16.
[6] Cf. e. g., Hos 4, 1 ff. Isa 1, 2 ff.18—20; 3, 13—15 Mal 3, 5.
[7] Würthwein views Ps 50 as one example of this *Gattung*.
[8] Von Waldow seems to adopt Würthwein's conclusion that Ps 50 is a speech
employed at the Covenant Renewal Festival.
[9] The line of argument represented by von Waldow has been expanded by others into
a hypothesis that the prophetic trial speeches are "covenant lawsuits" based on the
structure of the Sinai covenant, which in turn is derived from the pattern reflected
in the Hittite suzerainty treaties. It has even been argued (J. Harvey) that the form
of the prophetic trial speech itself has parallels in the treaty literature. This "school"
of thought is open to severe objections, however. In the first place, it is probable
that the Sinai traditions in Ex 19 ff., which contain the most ancient of the Sinai
traditions, do not fit the treaty pattern (McCarthy), nor do the treaty stipulations
serve as parallels to the covenant commandments (Gerstenberger). Moreover, the
structure of the prophetic trial speeches does not exhibit origins in the sphere of
international law, as Harvey believes; Harvey forces the prophetic speeches into a
structural mold which they do not in fact fit. Cf. the following works: G. Menden-
hall, Law and Covenant in Israel and the Ancient Near East, 1955; K. Baltzer,
Das Bundesformular, 1964. For literature on the "covenant lawsuit," cf. H. Huffmon, The Covenant Lawsuit in the Prophets, JBL 78 (1959), 285—295; G. E.
Wright, The Lawsuit of God: A Form-Critical Study of Deuteronomy 32, Israel's
Prophetic Heritage, edited by B. W. Anderson and W. Harrelson, 1962, 26—67;
J. Harvey, Le 'Rîb-pattern,' réquisitoire prophétique sur la rupture d'alliance,
Biblica 43 (1962), 172—196; H. E. von Waldow, Traditionsgeschichtlicher Hinter-
grund. For criticism of the treaty theory cf. D. J. McCarthy, Treaty and Covenant:
A Study in Form in the Ancient Oriental Documents and in the Old Testament,
1963. 152 ff.; E. Gerstenberger, Covenant and Commandment, JBL 84 (1965),
38—51.
[10] Cf. Pss 50; 81.

prophetic trial speeches do not match the forms of the cultic trial speeches from which they are allegedly derived. Psalm 50, for example, cannot serve as an example of the form which the prophets imitate. This psalm does not contain the pattern of invective and announcement of punishment[11] exhibited by many prophetic trial speeches. *Tôrā* (v. 14—15)[12] and warning (v. 22), followed again by *tôrā* (v. 23),[13] distinguish Psalm 50 quite sharply from the prophetic speeches in question. Moreover, the heavy emphasis on *tôdā* distinguishes this psalm from prophetic speech. Psalm 81 also, another oft-suggested example, does not suffice as an illustration of a cultic form imitated by the prophets. Although it contains invective,[14] there is no announcement of punishment to be carried out in the future. Instead, the dire consequences have already taken place (v. 13). Since the prophetic trial speeches which are allegedly derived from cultic forms announce punishment which is to come in the future, Psalm 81 does not adequately serve as a model which the prophets imitated.

The view of Begrich and Boecker that the prophetic trial speeches are imitations of speech-forms from trial in the gate is somewhat more convincing, for there are a number of similarities in form. For example, Jeremiah 2, 5 ff. displays a form found in I Samuel 24, 10 ff. and Judges 11, 12—27.[15] This form was employed by the accused in appealing for a hearing of his case before a formally-constituted court, and the formal elements are as follows: (1) reproving question concerning the accusation,[16] (2) assertion of the innocence of the accused,[17] (3) counter-accusation by the accused,[18] and (4) call for a decision at a trial.[19] These elements are present in Jeremiah 2, 5 ff.: Member 1 is found in v. 5aα; Members 2 and 3 are woven together in v. 5aβ—8;[20] Member 4 can be recognized in v. 9.[21]

---

[11] The traditional term "threat" *(Drohwort)* should probably be replaced by the term "announcement of punishment." Cf. Westermann, Grundformen prophetischer Rede, 1964, 46—49.

[12] Begrich, Die priesterliche Tora, BZAW 66 (1936), 72—73. Note that Ps 50, 14.15 are in second person singular, in contrast with the plural imperatives discussed by Begrich.

[13] Ibid. 75.

[14] V. 9 ff., particularly v. 12.

[15] Cf. Boecker, Redeformen, 48 ff.

[16] I Sam 24, 10    Judg 11, 12.

[17] I Sam 24, 11—12abα    Judg 11, 15—26.

[18] I Sam 24, 12bβ    Judg 11, 27a.

[19] I Sam 24, 13    Judg 11, 27b.

[20] Member 3 (v. 5aβ—8); member 2 (v. 7a).

[21] Cf. Boecker, Redeformen, 52—54.

The fact that some prophetic trial speeches can be shown to be imitations of speech forms used in legal proceedings in the town gate should not necessarily lead us to generalize that all prophetic trial speeches are therefore derived from that realm of life. Indeed, this is the very question which is the subject of this chapter. Does Deutero-Isaiah in his trial speeches between Yahweh and Israel follow his prophetic predecessors by imitating the speech-forms used in the town gate? If so, does he remain close to the form, or are there significant modifications? Moreover, have we to do with originally isolated and self-contained speeches? Or are they parts of longer literary compositions?

## B. Exegesis of Individual Texts

1. *Isaiah 43, 22—28.* This passage reflects a form of speech used in the legal procedures of the town gate. It is an appeal-to-trial speech of the accused.[22] The form is known from I Samuel 24, 10 ff. and Judges 11, 12 ff.: (1) reproving questions concerning the accusation, (2) assertion of innocence, (3) counter-accusation, and (4) call for decision at a trial. Isaiah 43, 22—28 displays the basic form, although Member 1 is missing. The other members are clearly present, however; Member 2 is present when Yahweh denies the accusation that he has not acted on the behalf of a faithful Israel (v. 22—24a). Indeed, says Yahweh, Israel has not been faithful. Then comes the counter-accusation:

Truly (*'ăk*), you burdened me with your sins,
You wearied me with your iniquities (v. 24 b).

Next appears the summons for decision at a trial (v. 26).[23] Further accusation follows in v. 27—28.

Isaiah 43, 22—28, then, exhibits the appeal-to-trial form, but it is an imitation of the customary form. Yahweh would not be the accused in an actual trial in the town gate. Furthermore, the emphatic statement of Yahweh's mercy in v. 25 would have no place in a real legal proceeding. A trial in the gate was held for the purpose of deciding the validity of an accusation; thus an announcement of mercy by the accused like v. 25 is a sign of an imitation of the original speech-form. Another indication that Isaiah 43, 22—28 is an imitation is the inclusion of language from institutions other than trial in the gate. The accusation against Yahweh which lies in the background and prompts Yahweh's assertion of innocence is not really a legal accusation. The charge which Yahweh answers is rather a complaint *(Klage)* uttered by Israel, sub-

[22]  Cf. Begrich, Studien, 30—33; Boecker, Redeformen, 48—56.
[23]  Begrich, Studien, 33; B. S. Childs, Memory and Tradition in Israel, 1962, 14—15.

stantiated by her claim of having been faithful. The normal setting of such a complaint is the cultic lament psalm rather than the legal realm.[24] In the typical setting of the cultic lament psalm the complaint is not answered by a trial speech but by a salvation oracle.[25] In prophetic tradition, however, the cultic complaint is sometimes treated as if it were a legal accusation against Yahweh. Thus the answering speech of Yahweh takes the form of a legal speech.[26] In Isaiah 43, 22—28 Deutero-Isaiah follows this common prophetic practice by treating Israel's complaint and assertion of righteousness as if it were a legal accusation. The speech of Yahweh takes the form of an appeal-to-trial speech of the accused.

In spite of the continuity of this speech with the practice of Deutero-Isaiah's prophetic predecessors, it is apparent that the poem exhibits the particular marks of Deutero-Isaiah's preaching in the circumstances of the exile. This Deutero-Isaianic stamp is visible both in form and content. Isaiah 43, 22—28 does not function simply to defend Yahweh against a false accusation, as in Micah 6, 1—5, nor is the main thrust of the speech to indict and announce punishment for Yahweh's accusers, as in Jeremiah 2, 5 ff. Although the elements of legal self-defense and counter-accusation are part of the structure of the speech, the main concern of Deutero-Isaiah is disputational — to dispute Israel's right to expect a positive answer to their complaint and plea on the basis of their righteousness. Deutero-Isaiah argues that they have no righteousness; the exile is deserved (v. 22—24a.27—28). Deliverance can come only by forgiveness granted for the sake of Yahweh's name (v. 25). Continuing to employ the trial as a means for carrying out the dispute, Deutero-Isaiah has Yahweh summon Israel that they might refute his assertions argued in v. 22—25 and thus prove that they are a righteous people (v. 26). We can see, then, that Deutero-Isaiah modifies the basic appeal-to-trial form to suit the purposes of his disputation by including v. 25, which has no place in a real trial. The theological dispute concerning the basis for Israel's future deliverance, a characteristic theme of the exilic preaching of Deutero-Isaiah (e. g., 40, 2; 44, 22),[27] can be explained only from the circumstances of the exile. Thus the content of the speech and Deutero-Isaiah's imitation and transformation of the appeal-to-trial form are the result of his own reshaping of traditional material.

---

[24] The cultic complaint lying behind 43, 22—28 is, as Westermann argues, "Du gabest Jakob dem Bann preis und Israel der Schande!" Cf. Sprache und Struktur, 142.

[25] H. Gunkel, Einleitung in die Psalmen, 1966, 246; Begrich, Das priesterliche Heilsorakel, ZAW 52 (1934), 81—92, and Studien, 14—26.

[26] Cf. e. g., Jer 2, 5 ff. Mic 6, 1—5.

[27] Cf. also 48, 1—11, particularly v. 9.10.11.

To summarize: We have discovered that in Isaiah 43, 22—28 the prophet imitates a form known from the legal tradition in the town gate as the mold into which he casts his dispute with the people. He follows his prophetic predecessors by using a trial form as a vehicle for a disputational answer to a complaint whose provenance is the cultic complaint psalm. But his own contribution can be seen, not only in the context of what he has to say, but also in his modification of the form as seen in v. 25.

Despite the fact that the form is to some degree the creation of Deutero-Isaiah, it is not justifiable to draw the conclusion that form critical methodology can no longer provide the proper controls in dealing with the relationship of these verses to the larger context. Even though the stamp of Deutero-Isaiah is evident in both form and content, one must not forget that 43, 22—28 is a trial speech throughout in contrast to the surrounding context, which is cast in the form of salvation oracles.[28] In this sense the speech stands out from its context as a formal unit. A discussion of the relationship of this speech to its context cannot profitably ignore the fact that it can be isolated by form critical methodology.

2. *Isaiah 50, 1—3*. Many scholars, most of whom see this passage as part of a larger poem, regard it as an indictment of Israel throughout.[29] Reacting against the belief of the people that they have been sold for debts and that their mother has been divorced by Yahweh, their God declares that the sin of the people rather than Yahweh's arbitrary acts is responsible for their having been sold and their mother having been sent away. Then follows in v. 2, according to this view, a reproach of the people for their lack of faith. Why did they not believe when Yahweh "came" through his prophet? Did they think he could not save?

Recent form critics have not only viewed these verses as an independent speech unit but also have offered a new interpretation. Begrich and von Waldow (in his second treatment of the problem) view v. 1—2a as an imitation of a speech-form from trial in the gate.[30] It is the form used by the accused in speaking before the court. Begrich outlines the form of the speech of the accused before the court as follows: (1) reproving question to opponents concerning the validity of the charge,[31] and (2) assertion of innocence by the accused, often in the

[28] Isa 43, 14—15.16—21; 44, 1—5.
[29] Cf. e. g., M. Haller, Das Judentum, 1925, 56—57; E. J. Kissane, The Book of Isaiah, II 1943, 139; J. Muilenburg, The Interpreter's Bible, V 1956, 581.
[30] Begrich, Studien, 38—39; von Waldow, Traditionsgeschichtlicher Hintergrund, 42 ff.
[31] Cf. Jer 2, 5.29  Mic 6, 3.

form of a recital of his righteous deeds[32] or in the form of a catalogue
of the unrighteousness of his accuser.[33] Begrich notes that there is considerable variety in the form. All of the elements do not necessarily have
to be present, and they may appear in different sequence. This is because
of the variety of situations which could occur in the town gate.

For Begrich and von Waldow, Isaiah 50, 1—2a displays the
structure of this trial genre. (1) The reproving question appears in v. 1a.
(2) The assertion of the innocence of the accused is in the form of a
counter-accusation (v. 1c). After having presented his case in v. 1, the
accused then finds himself without accusers:

> Why did I come and there was no man?
> Why did I call without anyone answering?

The terms *ba'tî, qara'tî*, and *'onæ* are to be understood as technical legal
terms.[34]

Both Begrich and von Waldow argue, however, that v. 1—3 are not
a slavish imitation of the speech of the accused in the gate. Von Waldow
recognizes that the form is broken in the second part of v. 2 and in v. 3,
but he does not explain the significance of the modification in form.
Begrich, however, views the entire speech (v. 1—3) as a disputation
speech. Only v. 1—2a are cast in the form of a trial speech; v. 2b—3
are a disputation, but without the language of the trial.

The form critics have been correct in viewing v. 1—2a from the
standpoint of the trial. The reproving question followed by the assertion
of the innocence of the accused or the guilt of the accuser has firm roots
in trial language in speeches of the accused.[35] The repeated occurrence in
the Hebrew scriptures of *bô', qara'*, and *'anā* as technical terms from
trial language is reflected here.[36] Finally, the appearance of language
similar to v. 2a in another place in Deutero-Isaiah, in which the trial is
clearly reflected (41, 26b.28), is another indication that 50, 1—2a
draws upon the language of the trial.

I doubt, however, that we can be so precise as to say that we have
before us an imitation of a form used in the gate by the accused in
speaking *before the assembled court*.[37] To be sure, it has been argued
that the lack of an appeal for trial indicates that Deutero-Isaiah is
imitating a speech-form used before an already assembled court. But the

---

[32] Cf. Jer 2, 7a  Mic 6, 4—5.

[33] Cf. Jer 2, 7b—8.29b—30.

[34] Begrich, Studien, 39.

[35] Cf. e. g., Judg 11, 12—27  I Sam 24, 10 ff.  Jer 2, 5 ff.  Isa 43, 22—28.

[36] For statistics, cf. Begrich, Studien, 39. See also A. Schoors, I Am God Your
Saviour: A Study of the Main Genres of Isaiah XL—LV, 1973, 198.

[37] Von Waldow, Traditionsgeschichtlicher Hintergrund, 42.

4*

fact that v. 2b—3 cannot successfully be included within the strict confines of a trial speech makes it doubtful that we can make such fine distinctions. Indeed, we should not expect poetry to be so precise. It is better simply to say that Deutero-Isaiah imitates language used by the accused. Furthermore, it is doubtful that we can say even that Deutero-Isaiah was thinking *particularly* of forms used in the gate. He might simply be following the practice of his prophetic predecessors, who use the reproving question and counter-accusation of the speech of the accused as a vehicle for Yahweh's dealing with the people's complaints.

A closer look at the form of v. 1—3 as a whole indicates that Deutero-Isaiah imitates trial language, but with a great deal of freedom to transform traditional forms of speech. Begrich is correct that v. 1—3 form a disputation speech in which only v. 1—2a imitate trial language. The disputation falls into two parts, each beginning with a question and proceeding to a statement introduced by *hen:*

> Where is your mother's certificate of divorce with which I sent her away?
> Or to which of my creditors have I sold you?
> Behold (*hen*), for your iniquities were you sold, and for your transgressions
>    was your mother sent away.
>
> Is my hand made short, that it cannot save?
>    Or have I no power to deliver?
> Behold (*hen*), by my rebuke I dry up the sea ...

The questions contain the matter which is disputed. In the first half of this speech, the question imitating the reproving question of the accused refers to the complaint at home in the cult, "Yahweh has divorced our mother and sold us to pay his debts." In the second half, the question refers to the contention that Yahweh is powerless to save. The statements introduced by *hen* counter the false view of the people and contain the resolution of the dispute. In the first half of this speech, the reproving question of the speech of the accused demands that the people produce evidence against Yahweh. Since they cannot, Yahweh can state his own claim (v. 1c) without further objection. In the case of the second question, Yahweh appeals to what every Israelite knows from tradition about Yahweh (v. 2b—3). The opponents of Yahweh's claim are left to draw the proper conclusion for themselves.

This double-barreled disputation, the first part of which is an imitation of trial speech, has no setting outside the preaching of Deutero-Isaiah. His free combination of trial forms within the larger framework of the disputation has no roots apart from Deutero-Isaiah's own creativity. Furthermore, the use of disputation to counter doubts both about Yahweh's faithfulness and about his power to save is common throughout Deutero-Isaiah. Thus 50, 1—3 is a disputational poem which

Deutero-Isaiah has created to argue against both doubts, and in so doing, he has freely combined and transformed traditional forms of speech.

The relationship between Isaiah 50, 1—3 and its context is a topic for Part Two. Here it suffices to note that these verses can be isolated as a disputation on the two charges against which Yahweh defends himself. The contrast with v. 4 ff. is striking. In 50, 1—3 *Yahweh* is the speaker of a dispute, while the *servant* utters v. 4—9 as a psalm of confidence. To separate 50, 1—3 from what goes before is more difficult. 49, 14—26 (14—21.22—23.24—26) shares with 50, 1—3 a disputational flavor. Moreover, Yahweh is the speaker in both 49, 14—26 and 50, 1—3. In addition, the theme of the separated mother and children persists throughout both 49, 14—26 and 50, 1—3. Yet 50, 1—3 stands somewhat apart; it differs from 49, 14—26 by using the second masculine plural. Furthermore, the primary intention of 50, 1—3 is disputational; its primary purpose is to overcome the two complaints. The three sections of 49, 14—26, by contrast, despite their disputational flavor, function chiefly to announce the future. Finally, the structure of 50, 1—3 sets it apart. It is a twosided disputation, each part of which is begun by a question and resolved by a statement introduced by *hen*. Thus Isaiah 50, 1—3 stands out from its context by both content and form.

## II. THE TRIAL BETWEEN YAHWEH AND THE NATIONS

### A. The Problem in Historical Perspective

Begrich views the trial speeches between Yahweh and the nations or their gods as imitations of various forms of speech used in the town gate.[38] In his judgment these Deutero-Isaianic speeches betray different forms which correspond to various kinds of speeches used in the gate. Begrich rightly calls these speeches "trial speeches." It seems clear that they reflect the gathering of an assembly for the purpose of making a legally-binding decision.[39] But there are certain difficulties with his position. Almost all of the non-Deutero-Isaianic trial speeches discussed by Begrich have to do with violation of the established order — theft of gods (Gen 31), violence done to the clan mother (Gen 16), and the like. But Deutero-Isaiah's speeches involving Yahweh and the nations or their gods reflect rival claims to deity rather than disruption of the establish-

---

[38] Begrich, Studien, 27.

[39] For example, the nations are summoned to draw near for *mišpaṭ* (41, 1); the gods are summoned to bring near their *rîb* (41, 21); witnesses are to be produced by each side (43, 9.10; 44, 8).

ed order. In these Deutero-Isaianic speeches the court does not restore
the violated order by a verdict of "guilty" or "innocent" or by restitu-
tion of rights which have been violated. Instead, the court determines
which of the opposing parties has proved the validity of his assertion.
To be sure, Begrich is not totally unaware that Deutero-Isaiah's trial
speeches are different, but he views the differences in Deutero-Isaiah as
modifications of the basic form.[40]

The forms of these Deutero-Isaianic texts, however, do not conform
to the forms of speeches known in the town gate as clearly as Begrich
believes. For example, the appeal-to-trial speech of the accuser in the
town gate often contained a question in which the accusation is present:
i. e., "Why have you done this thing?"[41] Sometimes the accuser also
speaks of the punishment which he believes is the proper outcome of the
trial.[42] Or instead of appearing in the form of a question, the accusation
on occasion appears as a statement.[43] Isaiah 41, 1 ff. — in Begrich's view
an appeal-to-trial speech of the accuser — simply is not parallel. To be
sure, v. 1 contains a summons to trial, but there the similarity ends. The
questions in v. 2—4 are not at all like those contained in Jeremiah 26, 9
and I Samuel 26, 15. They are disputational questions rather than
questions for the purpose of making accusation.[44]

Von Waldow views the trial speeches between Yahweh and the
nations as imitations of speech-forms employed in the cult.[45] Form
critically, they can be distinguished from trial in the gate by the fact
that Yahweh is both accuser and judge. They are instead prophetic
imitations of the trial speech form used in the Covenant Renewal Festival, in which Yahweh judges unfaithful Israel. In the Deutero-Isaianic
speeches between Yahweh and the nations, the original cultic form is
modified, however, to a considerable degree. First of all, the role of
Yahweh as judge stands out more in Deutero-Isaiah than it does in the
cult or in imitations of this form by other prophets. This is the result of
Deutero-Isaiah's use of the imagery of the enthronement of Yahweh as
king and judge of the nations. A second modification is that the nations
and their gods are the accused instead of Israel. In the third place,
modification is apparent in Deutero-Isaiah's extensive use of disputation
style.

---

[40] Begrich, Studien, 29.31.35. etc.
[41] Cf. Jer 26, 9  I Sam 26, 15. Boecker, Redeformen, 58—59.
[42] Cf. Jer 26, 8  I Sam 26, 16. Boecker, Redeformen, 58—59.
[43] Cf. Gen 16, 5. Boecker, Redeformen, 59—61.
[44] Note that the disputation style in 41, 1 ff. is for the purpose of arguing to a
conclusion (v. 4b). The conclusion is based on a deduction drawn from a point of
agreement between Yahweh and hearers (v. 4a).
[45] Anlaß und Hintergrund 37—46.

Without doubt the content of Deutero-Isaiah's trial speeches has been influenced by the cult. The Psalms are well acquainted with the court scene involving the nations and their gods.[46] Moreover, Yahweh's appearing as king (Isa 41, 21) is characteristic of the cult, as well as the use of hymn style in the trial speeches. Nevertheless, the Deutero-Isaianic speeches differ markedly from trial language preserved in the cult. In the cult, Yahweh is always sovereign as judge over the nations and their gods. His sovereignty is never questioned; Yahweh's role in the cult is to re-establish the order which has been disrupted. In Deutero-Isaiah, however, the trial is called to determine whether or not Yahweh is God; the possibility that he might not be sovereign is indeed taken seriously. Therefore, the trial in Deutero-Isaiah deals with rival claims to deity rather than violations of the established order.

In addition to these differences in content between Deutero-Isaiah and the cultic material, it is unlikely that the form can be derived from the trial between Yahweh and Israel as preserved in the cult. The modifications which von Waldow postulates change the form so radically that the imitation scarcely resembles the original genre.

H. J. Boecker represents an advance in the study of Deutero-Isaiah's trial speeches. In the Deutero-Isaianic speeches which he discusses,[47] Boecker agrees basically with Begrich in viewing these trial speeches between Yahweh and the nations as imitations of forms used in the town gate. But, unlike Begrich, he recognizes that there is no accuser and accused in the usual sense of the term. Isaiah 41, 1 ff. is not a speech of an accuser summoning to trial those who have transgressed the established order. Instead the trial is called to settle conflicting assertions, which revolve around the question, "Who aroused one from the east...?" Therefore, postulates Boecker, this speech is not an appeal-to-trial speech of the accused in Begrich's sense of the term. It is rather a genre which he calls an appeal speech for a trial to determine the truth of an assertion. It has its own form, which is found also in Isaiah 1, 18—20.[48]

Boecker rightly sees that Isaiah 41, 1 ff. is not the kind of trial genre which Begrich presupposed. But one wonders why Boecker considers it as a speech-form at home in the town gate. Neither Isaiah 1, 18—20 nor 41, 1 ff. reflects the kind of dispute which could be settled in the town gate.[49]

---

[46] Cf. e. g., Ps 75; 82; 96, 10.13; 98, 9. Cf. S. Mowinckel, The Psalms in Israel's Worship, I 1962, 148 ff.

[47] Boecker discusses only 41, 1 ff. and 44, 6—8. Cf. Redeformen, 69—70, 162—163.

[48] Boecker, Redeformen, 68—70.

[49] The former has to do with a dispute between Yahweh and the people over the consequences of sin. The latter is a dispute whether Yahweh is God.

Boecker's arguments for a *Sitz im Leben* in the gate are stronger, however, for Isaiah 44, 6—8.[50] This speech, he argues, can be illuminated by passages such as Ruth 4, 1—12, which portrays a typical situation in which witnesses are called to notarize a legal transaction in the event that their testimony is needed at a future date. Boaz summons the witnesses by means of the following formula: *ʿedîm ʾattæm hayyôm kî qanîtî* ... (v. 9). Isaiah 44, 6—8, Boecker argues, imitates the language from such a setting. Yahweh states the claim which he wants the assembly to confirm as witnesses: "I am the first and the last; besides me there is no God" (v. 6b). Those who oppose this claim are challenged to state their case (v. 7). The challenge goes unanswered, however, so that Yahweh summons the witnesses to validate the establishment of his claim: *wᵉʾattæm ʿedăy* (v. 8).

The presence of the formula *wᵉʾattæm ʿedăy* is without doubt an indication that the prophet is indeed drawing on a *Gattung* from trial in the gate. But this genre from the town gate is not as all-encompassing an influence in 44, 6—8 as Boecker seems to believe. The presence of *ʾal tiphᵉdû wᵉʾal tirhû*[51] is an element which does not fit our trial genre from the town gate. Moreover, the "proof" for Yahweh's claim appears in the form of a disputation which is designed to convince doubters of the validity of Yahweh's claim. In the style of a question introduced by *mî* and assertions in self-praise hymn style,[52] which is typical of both Deutero-Isaiah's disputation and trial speeches,[53] Yahweh appeals to common knowledge that his prophetic word has been effective in the past (v. 8aβ) in order to convince his opponents that he alone is God and thus trustworthy for the future. Since Deutero-Isaiah employs this kind of disputation style in both disputation and trial speeches, we are entitled to question whether this kind of disputation style has any integral relationship with trial language outside Deutero-Isaiah.

The difficulty in showing that Isaiah 41, 1 ff. is an imitation of a genre whose setting is the town gate, coupled with the fact that trial in the gate does not appear to be the only kind of language present in 44, 6—8, forces us to ask whether Deutero-Isaiah's trial speeches are imitations of one genre, as Boecker seems to believe.

Westermann, who is concerned with the question just raised, denies that Deutero-Isaiah's trial speeches between Yahweh and the nations are derived from a genre which has a setting in Israel's life prior to

---

[50] Boecker, Redeformen, 160 ff.; G. Tucker, Witnesses and "Dates" in Israelite Contracts, CBQ 28 (1966), 42—45.

[51] We should probably read the second verb as a form of *yareʾ*.

[52] See my discussion in Chapter Three.

[53] 41, 1 ff.21—29; 43, 8—13; 44, 6—8; 45, 18—21; 46, 5—11; 48, 12—15.

Deutero-Isaiah.[54] A trial to determine whether or not Yahweh is God has no *Sitz im Leben* in Israel; indeed, such a thing, says Westermann, would be unthinkable. Moreover, Westermann believes that the form of Deutero-Isaiah's speeches betrays a stylizing which does not permit the delineation of a structure beyond the following general categories: (1) *Vorladung*, (2) *Verhandlung*, and (3) *Entscheidung*. A more exact imitation of forms from another realm of life is in Westermann's opinion not to be found, for the stylizing is the work of the prophet himself. Although Westermann presumably would not reject the notion that in a very limited sense the prophet borrowed language from trial genres at home somewhere in Israel's life, his concern is to show that the basic form and content is due to the prophet's literary creativity. This stylized structure was created by Deutero-Isaiah, says Westermann, as a response to the need to convince doubting Israel that the emergence of the pagan Cyrus was to be understood as a new event in Israel's salvation history.

The difficulties with the arguments of Begrich, von Waldow, and Boecker make Westermann's view attractive. Why not argue indeed that the form is primarily the result of Deutero-Isaiah's stylization and that the setting is unique to his preaching? Yet we should not too hastily give assent, for Westermann has failed to ask certain important questions: What is the significance of the disputation language in Deutero-Isaiah's trial speeches? Is the incorporation of disputation language into the framework of the trial the work of Deutero-Isaiah himself? Or did he make use of a genre already in existence which combined trial and disputation language? These questions suggest another which is even more basic: Was there in Israel prior to Deutero-Isaiah a trial in which a deity proved before a forum his power as god? With these questions it is obvious that a new form critical analysis is needed.

## B. Form Critical Analysis

The speeches which reflect a trial between Yahweh and the nations or their gods[55] all betray common elements of form: (1) Yahweh's opponents (or witnesses) are summoned to trial,[56] and (2) Yahweh argues his case in a highly stereotyped disputation style. All contain a question (or questions) introduced by *mî*, and the answer to the question is the key to the resolution of the dispute. In Isaiah 41, 21—29, for example, the answer to the rhetorical question, "Who declared from the

[54] Westermann, Sprache und Struktur, 135 ff.
[55] Isa 41, 1—7.21—29; 43, 8—13; 44, 6—8; 45, 18—21; 48, 12—15.
[56] Isa 41, 1.21; 43, 8—9a; 45, 20; 48, 14.

beginning?" makes it possible for the speaker to move from the point of common agreement to resolve the dispute. Or, in 41, 1 ff., the first question introduced by *mî* is the matter under dispute (v. 2), and the answer to the rhetorical question in v. 4a leads the hearers to the proper answer (v. 4b) to the first question. In most of Deutero-Isaiah's trial speeches the utterance is closed by a first-person assertion by Yahweh in self-praise hymn style[57] or by a question in the style of self-praise.[58] Or the speech is sometimes ended by means of statements introduced by *hen*.[59] Differences in structure among the various speeches cannot be ignored, for the various parts are arranged differently in the various speeches; nevertheless, the content and form are stereotyped to the extent normally expected of a *Gattung*.

1. Do Deutero-Isaiah's trial speeches originate in a well-known Israelite practice of holding trials to determine deity? At first glance the contest between Yahweh and Baal on Mt. Carmel (I Kings 18) might suggest that the form of Deutero-Isaiah's trial speeches is derived from such a setting.[60] First of all, a similarity in situation is apparent. Both reflect a crisis in the lordship of Yahweh, and in both an assembly is summoned to determine whether Yahweh is God. In addition, certain structural similarities are apparent. Both have a summons to assembly.[61] In both, each deity is supposed to justify its claim before the assembly — in I Kings 18 by producing fire, in Deutero-Isaiah by demonstrating an ability to utter a word which comes to pass.

---

[57] E. g., 41, 4b; 43, 11—13.

[58] 45, 21.

[59] 41, 29.

[60] The scene at Mt. Carmel was originally a narrative independent from the present context. The drought is not a part of the original Mt. Carmel narrative. The Mt. Carmel narrative is connected with the drought by the collector of chs. 17—19, who uses the drought as punishment for Ahab's sin as a unifying motif in the collection. Even the Obadiah narrative does not belong originally to the Mt. Carmel narrative. It is a connecting link between the calling of the assembly and the motif of drought and rain-making. Cf. the following literature: H. Gunkel, Elias, Jahve, und Baal, 1906; A. Alt, Das Gottesurteil auf dem Karmel, in: Kleine Schriften zur Geschichte des Volkes Israel, II 1964, 135—149; G. Fohrer, Elia, 1957; E. Würthwein, Die Erzählung vom Gottesurteil auf dem Karmel, ZThK 59 (1962), 131—144.

[61] Isa 41, 1.21; 43, 8; 44, 7; 45, 20; 48, 14  I Kings 18, 19. I Kings 18, 19 contains elements that do not appear to be a part of the original Mt. Carmel narrative. The mention of the four hundred prophets of Asherah who eat at Jezebel's table is derived from the larger framework of chs. 17—19; elsewhere in the Mt. Carmel narrative only the four hundred and fifty prophets of Baal are mentioned. Moreover, the command in v. 19 is directed to Ahab, who may have become a part of the narrative only after it was connected with the motif of drought as punishment for Ahab's sin (cf. Würthwein, Erzählung, 132). Finally, the phrase "all Israel"

Without obscuring the difference between I Kings 18 as a narrative
and the Deutero-Isaianic material as speeches of Yahweh as a party in
the trial, can we say that both are derived from a common setting of a
trial between Yahweh and opposing deities (or their people)? If this
should be true, it would be necessary to show that both the Mt. Carmel
narrative and the Deutero-Isaianic speeches are really a trial and that
the trial in each reflects the same basic form. And it is precisely at this
point that we encounter difficulties. Deutero-Isaiah's speeches, as we
have already seen, are clearly trial speeches,[62] but the Mt. Carmel narrative cannot accurately be called a trial. No legal terminology is present,
nor is there any talk of witnesses. In fact, the Mt. Carmel narrative
mirrors a setting more closely related to a contest than a trial. If one
compares I Kings 18 with the narrative about the court-page David and
Goliath in I Samuel 17,[63] certain common elements are apparent. Both
have to do with the performance of certain feats; both have a challenge
to the opposing party as to the nature of the feats to be performed
(I Sam 17, 8.9  I Kings 18, 23—24); both have a statement of the consequences of the contest (I Sam 17, 9  I Kings 18, 24). In both narratives,
the party with whose cause the sympathy of the narrator lies operates at
a clear disadvantage, with the result that his triumph is even more
impressive.

Not only is there no trace of a trial in the Mt. Carmel narrative,
but also there is no indication of a contest in the speeches of Deutero-

---

appears only in this verse, along with the expression "all the people of Israel" in
v. 20, a verse which has perhaps been reworked by the collector of chs. 17—19 in
order to fit Ahab into the narrative. The rest of the narrative speaks of the
assembly as "all the people." There is a strong possibility that v. 19—20 show the
heavy hand of the collector, who inserts Ahab into the narrative and refers to the
people as "Israel." (In 19, 14, obviously dependent traditionally upon 18, 10.22,
and thus the work of the collector of chs. 17—19, the phrase "all the people of
Israel" appears.) Nevertheless, v. 19—20 preserve some elements of the original
narrative. There must have been a summons to assembly and a narration that the
parties were assembled. Moreover, the designation of Mt. Carmel as the place of
assembly and the mention of the four hundred and fifty prophets of Baal seem to
be original to the narrative. Thus it is probable that the Mt. Carmel narrative
originally contained a summons, now reworked by the collector.

[62] Cf. above, footnote 39.

[63] I am following the analysis of H. Gressmann that I Sam 17 is a fusion of two
originally separate narratives — the narrative reflecting David as a shepherd sent
to bring food to his brothers (v. 12—14.17—30.41.48b.50.55—58) and the narrative
of David as a page in Saul's court (v. 1—11.31—40.42—48a.49.51—53; 18, 1.3—5).
Cf. Gressmann, Die älteste Geschichtsschreibung and die Prophetie Israels, 1910,
77 ff.

Isaiah. No feats are performed. Instead, Deutero-Isaiah's speeches present an argument designed to convince doubters that Yahweh is God. To be sure, the opposing side is to demonstrate that the gods can prophesy and have their words come to pass (41, 22; 43, 9; 44, 7), and in one instance there is an explicit invitation to perform a variety of acts that befit deity (41, 22—23). But the performance of these deeds does not actually take place in these speeches. On the contrary, the outcome of the trial is dependent upon an argument which appeals to Yahweh's past record of prophesying the future.

Without doubt Deutero-Isaiah's trial speeches between Yahweh and the nations and the Mt. Carmel narrative draw upon a common motif. There is no evidence, however, for speaking of a common *Gattung*, but simply a motif which can appear in different settings, i. e., the contest, the trial. Thus we cannot establish a trial to determine deity as an already-existing genre which Deutero-Isaiah employed.

2. We have already indicated the importance of disputation language in Deutero-Isaiah's trial speeches between Yahweh and the nations or their gods. Can we discover a trial genre in which this kind of disputation plays an integral role? Or is the combination of trial and disputation language an arbitrary fusion performed by Deutero-Isaiah?

We must recognize at the outset that the disputational language in Deutero-Isaiah's trial speeches is quite similar to the style employed in the prophet's disputation speeches. The pattern consisting of questions introduced by *mî* and of resolution in self-praise hymn style appears in both genres.[64] Indeed, it is sometimes difficult to distinguish between trial speeches and disputation speeches. Isaiah 45, 18 ff. and 48, 12—15 are considered disputation speeches by Begrich and von Waldow,[65] while the former is regarded as a trial speech by Westermann.[66] I view these two poems as trial speeches because of what appears to be a summons to trial in each (45, 20a; 48, 14aα).[67]

Deutero-Isaiah's use of the same style for both trial and disputation speeches suggests that his inclusion of disputation language within the framework of the trial is his own creation. We find no evidence outside Deutero-Isaiah of disputation speech with questions introduced by *mî*

---

[64] Disputation speech: 46, 5—11. Trial speech: 41, 1—7; 43, 8—13; (44, 6—8); 45, 18—21; 48, 12—15.

[65] Begrich, Studien, 49; von Waldow, Anlaß und Hintergrund, 36.

[66] Westermann, Sprache und Struktur, 136 ff.

[67] In 48, 12—15 the shift from singular to plural address probably indicates that Yahweh has turned from Israel to the nations. Addresses to the nations do not occur elsewhere in Deutero-Isaiah's disputation speeches. The imperatives of *qābāṣ* in 45, 20 and 48, 14 (cf. also 43, 9) and *nagaš* in 45, 20 (cf. also 41, 1.21) are probably indications of trial language.

set in the context of a trial. Furthermore, the structure of the disputation language within the trial appears to have been shaped by Deutero-Isaiah. Although Wisdom disputations were sometimes opened by *mî* and concluded with *hen*,[68] Deutero-Isaiah's trial speeches do not betray the Wisdom disputations' almost technical interest in the structure of creation in order to contrast divine and human wisdom.[69] Deutero-Isaiah's disputations, unlike the Wisdom disputations, are concerned with *Heilsgeschichte;* Cyrus is an event in Israel's salvation history.[70] Although appeal is made to Yahweh as creator, Deutero-Isaiah's trial speeches show no interest, as in the Wisdom genre, in cataloguing the structure of the created order. Moreover, there is no attempt to contrast the wisdom of God with that of man. Instead, Deutero-Isaiah's trial speeches try to persuade doubters that Yahweh alone is God and that his word about a new saving deed is trustworthy. Finally, the disputational language of Deutero-Isaiah's trial speeches does not take the form of a long series of questions as is characteristic of the Wisdom genre (Job chapters 38 ff.   Prov 30, 4   Isa 40, 12—17). In Deutero-Isaiah's trial speeches the question introduced by *mî* usually appears only once (41, 26; 43, 9; 45, 21; 48, 14).[71]

3. Deutero-Isaiah also borrowed the language of the temple cult in the formation of his trial speeches. For example, he constantly refers to the Babylonians in general terms like *'iyyîm* (41, 1), *gôyim* (43, 9; 45, 20), and *leʾummîm* (41, 1; 43,9). This is due to the influence of the cult in which Yahweh is depicted in a court scene with the nations (or their gods), who are designated by such general terms (cf. Ps 7, 8; 9, 9; 97, 1; 98, 9). The form of these Deutero-Isaianic trial speeches, as well as the content, is influenced by the cult. We have already observed that the originally-cultic self-praise of the deity has permeated the disputation elements of the trial speeches in Deutero-Isaiah.[72] Another example of cultic influence is the exhortation not to be afraid in 44, 8. The language of that exhortation was not originally at home in the trial but in the cultic salvation oracle.[73] But these cultic elements are not all-embracing

---

[68] Cf. Job chs. 38 ff., especially 40, 25 ff.; also Prov 30, 4   Isa 40, 12—17.

[69] Note the detail in the description of world order in Job chs. 38 ff. and in Isa 40, 12—17.

[70] Isa 41, 1.2.25; 48, 14b.

[71] In 41, 1 ff. the question appears twice (v. 2.4), but even here it is not the same kind of question sequence that we find in the Wisdom genre. In the latter, the entire series piles one rhetorical question on top of another. In Isa 41, 1 ff. the first question is not rhetorical but rather the disputed question which is to be answered.

[72] See the discussion of von Waldow above.

[73] Cf. Begrich, Heilsorakel, 81—92, and Studien, 14—26; von Waldow, Anlaß und Hintergrund, 11—28; Westermann, Das Heilswort bei Deuterojesaja, EvTh 24 (1964), 355—373, and Sprache und Struktur, 117—124.

categories by means of which we can describe the genre of these trial speeches. They are but one of the areas of life from which Deutero-Isaiah drew his language in the formation of the trial speeches between Yahweh and the nations. Basically, the form is his own creation.

4. I have attempted to demonstrate that Deutero-Isaiah's trial speeches between Yahweh and the nations or their gods contain elements of form and content from a variety of settings. The cultically-preserved court scene between Yahweh and the nations or their gods provides much of the imagery. But the trial scene as preserved in the cult is modified by an old motif known also in I Kings 18, so that Yahweh is no longer sovereign judge, but rather a deity who must prove that he is God. In addition, Yahweh argues his case in a disputation style which cannot be shown to be a part of a trial genre with long rootage in oral tradition; instead, Deutero-Isaiah has been the prime factor in the stylization of this disputation language. These elements have been artfully combined by our prophet under the rubric of a trial as a means of convincing Israelite doubters that Yahweh's power is believable even in the crisis of exile. The structure of the trial speeches is the work of Deutero-Isaiah to meet that situation.

I do not intend for one moment to suggest that Deutero-Isaiah did not at any point draw upon real trial genres. Boecker has demonstrated convincingly that Isaiah 44, 6—8 is an imitation of a type of trial speech used in the town gate. Moreover, the fact that there are different kinds of trial speeches in Deutero-Isaiah — i. e., summons to the opposing party, summons to witnesses — suggests that Deutero-Isaiah has in mind different trial speech forms. But even in the case of 44, 6—8, the fusion of Deutero-Isaiah's imitation of trial in the gate with the cultic language of the kingship of Yahweh, as well as the language of disputation and the style of the salvation oracle (v. 8a$\alpha$), prevents the overall form of this speech from being understood as a *Gattung* — real or imitated — which existed apart from Deutero-Isaiah's preaching. The same is true for the rest of the trial speeches between Yahweh and the nations.

The conclusion that the form of these speeches is attributable mostly to Deutero-Isaiah himself must not tempt us to abandon form critical methodology. On the contrary, we find that these speeches separate themselves from their context because they are trial speeches throughout. In this connection a certain structure typically occurs: (1) Yahweh's opponents (or witnesses) are summoned to trial, and (2) Yahweh argues his case in a highly stereotyped disputation style. Admittedly each trial speech has a structure which is somewhat unique; still, they are sufficiently stereotyped that we can understand them collectively as a genre. The common pattern which they all share, though it is without roots in Israel's history, is a *Gattung*, created *de novo* by our prophet from various formal elements to meet a particular crisis in the life of Israel.


### III. CONCLUSION

I have attempted to show that all of Deutero-Isaiah's trial speeches — the trial between Yahweh and Israel and the trial between Yahweh and the nations — are in large measure shaped by the prophet's own hand. To be sure, in some of them we can see the clear imitation of particular forms of speech customarily used in quite definite settings (44, 6—8; 43, 22—28). In others, the form of the speech is shaped less by traditional genres and more by Deutero-Isaiah himself. But in all of them we have seen that the prophet's own hand has played a large role in shaping the form of the speech.

Although the trial between Yahweh and the nations and the trial between Yahweh and Israel can be separated from one another form critically, primarily because of the stereotyped character of the former throughout Deutero-Isaiah, there are certain connections between them. It is noteworthy that Deutero-Isaiah always uses trial speeches for disputational purposes. In the case of the trial between Yahweh and the nations, the purpose is to convince doubters that Yahweh is God. In the trial between Yahweh and Israel other matters are debated. In 50, 1—3, the claim of Israelites that Yahweh has forsaken them and that he is powerless to save is disputed. 43, 22—28 disputes Israel's plea for help on the basis that they are righteous. The fact that all of these trial speeches really function as disputations is no accident, for old forms were radically transformed by the prophet precisely for that purpose. Indeed, in converting the trial from its normal function of dealing with violations of the established order to the purposes of disputation, Deutero-Isaiah has divorced the trial from its traditional moorings. To be sure, he already had the example of his prophetic predecessors in using the trial to counter an accusation made by Israelites (cf. Jer 2, 5 ff., for example) but Deutero-Isaiah went far beyond his predecessors.

For all the creativity of the prophet, our study has consistently shown that Deutero-Isaiah's trial speeches have the capacity to be isolated from their context. Does this mean that they originally stood alone? If so, what is the significance of their present position in the context of Isaiah 40—55? If not, in what sense are they elements of longer compositions? The answers to these questions await our attention in Part Two.

# Chapter Five: The "Servant Songs"

A survey of the form critical studies of the "Servant Songs" reveals widespread disagreement concerning genre; thus a new study is needed. We shall ask in particular whether these poems exemplify genres with a long history of usage in Israelite life or whether the form is primarily the creation of the prophet. No generalizations can be made about the poems as a group; the term "Servant Songs" is but a scholarly convention. Thus each one must be examined separately.

## I. ISAIAH 42, 1—4.5—9

Form critical studies of these verses vary considerably. Otto Kaiser, for example, considers v. 1—4 and v. 5—9 an original unity of two genre units which belong together because of a Near Eastern liturgical pattern.[1] He sees v. 1—4 as an imitation of the liturgical drama in which the deity presents a king before the heavenly council.[2] The imitated liturgy continues in v. 5—9 — an oracle which is directed to the king to inform him of his commissioning.[3] Begrich, however, considers the two texts as originally separate.[4] Moreover, in v. 1—4 the servant is not a king, according to Begrich, but a servant of the king who acts as a herald.[5] V. 5—9 Begrich understands as an oracle commissioning a prophet.[6] Still another view is found in Westermann.[7] He appears to view v. 1—4 as a free literary composition with language reminiscent of the commissioning of charismatic leaders, although speech from royal circles dominates. V. 5—9 are a later expansion of v. 1—4. They are a commissioning genre, but it is not clear just who is being commissioned. With these disagreements, a fresh analysis is needed.

---

[1] Kaiser, Der königliche Knecht, 1962, 16—18.

[2] Kaiser refers to a discussion in G. Widengren, Sakrales Königtum im Alten Testament und im Judentum, 1955, 52 f. Kaiser mentions also II Kings 11, which indicates to him that the enthronement of the king took place in the temple.

[3] Kaiser refers to Egyptian rituals discussed by H. Frankfort in Kingship and the Gods, 1948, 105 f. Cf. also I. Engnell, Studies in Divine Kingship in the Ancient Near East, 1967, 17, for a parallel from Mesopotamia.

[4] Begrich, Studien zu Deuterojesaja, 1938. 1963, 13. Page numbers are from the 1963 edition.

[5] Ibid. 137.

[6] Ibid. 61.

[7] Westermann, Das Buch Jesaja: Kapitel 40—66, 1966, 77 ff.

1. *V. 1—4.* The form of the text is that of a speech by Yahweh *about* his servant. It begins with *hen* followed by phrases indicating Yahweh's election of the servant and endowment with particular gifts:

> Behold my servant, whom I uphold, my chosen in whom my soul delights,
> I have put my spirit upon him.

Next follows a description of the servant's task:

> Justice to the nations will he bring forth;
> He will not cry out, nor lift up nor make his voice heard in the street;
> A crushed reed he will not break, a dimly burning wick he will not quench;
> Faithfully he will bring forth justice;
>   he will not burn out or be crushed[8]
> Until he puts justice in the earth,
>   and the coastlands await his law.

It is quite easy to describe the structure of the text, but more difficult to define precisely the genre with its setting and intention. A study of *hen/hinnē* shows readily that these particles often introduce speeches which proclaim that certain persons have been established in particular offices or functions. But which office is intended in Isaiah 42, 1—4? It appears that the establishment of kings was sometimes announced in this style. II Chronicles 23, 3, though late, suggests a possible setting for such language. During a covenant ceremony with the king in the sanctuary, Jehoida the priest says, "Behold, the king's son will rule just as Yahweh spoke concerning the sons of David." One can imagine too, that when Yahweh says to Samuel regarding Saul, *hinnē ha'îš* (I Sam 9, 17), the narrator has employed language typically used for the enthronement of kings;[9] yet we have no direct evidence from an enthronement liturgy to prove that this phrase was customarily used in such a ceremony. Zechariah 6, 9 ff. might also suggest that Isaiah 42, 1—4 is a royal genre. Unfortunately, the text is in disarray; there is some indication that Zerubbabel as well as Joshua was to be crowned.[10] If the text referred originally to the crowning of Zerubbabel, we have an imitation of the liturgical establishment of a king by means of a speech introduced by

---

[8] Perhaps *yerôṣ* should be read here. See Qoh 12, 6, however, for a parallel usage of the qal.

[9] Westermann mentions this (Das Buch Jesaja 78). The designation of David in I Sam 16 portrays the equipping of the king with the spirit.

[10] MT speaks of the crowning of the high priest Joshua only, yet uses the plural "crowns" (v. 11.14). Moreover, the term "shoot" (v. 12) fits a Messianic figure (cf. Ps 132, 17 Jer 23, 5; 33, 15). In Zech 3, 8 the term seems to apply to one other than Joshua, presumably Zerubbabel. Zech 6, 13b suggests that the text in its original form dealt with both high priest and king.

*hinnē:* "Behold the man whose name is Shoot; he will shoot up in his place and build the temple of Yahweh" (Zech 6, 12).

*Hen* and *hinnē* are used also, however, to introduce speeches in which prophets are commissioned (cf. Jer 1, 9   Ezek 3, 8), though they differ from Isaiah 42, 1—4 in that they are addressed directly to the prophet. *Hen* and *hinnē* appear, too, in speeches which announce the commissioning of certain men as craftsmen (Ex 31, 6). Indeed, the structure of Exodus 31, 1—11 is somewhat similar to Isaiah 42, 1—4; note the parallels to, "Behold my servant whom I uphold . . . I have given my spirit upon him" (Isa 42, 1):

> See (*re'ē*), I have called by name Bezalel son of Uri, son of Hur of the tribe of Judah. I have filled him with the spirit of God, with wisdom, with under-standing, with knowledge, and with all craftsmanship, to make designs, to work in gold, silver, and bronze, in cutting stones for setting, in carving wood for work in every craft. I, behold *(hinnē),* have given to him Oholiab son of Ahisamak of the tribe of Dan, and in the heart of all who are wise in heart I have given wisdom, and they will make everything which I have commanded you. (Ex 31, 2 ff.)

It is obvious that Isaiah 42, 1—4 is not a speech establishing a craftsman in his office, but the reason for including Exodus 31, 1 ff. in the discussion is to show that the style found in Isaiah 42, 1—4 was used in conjunction with several offices in Israel. Thus we cannot determine what kind of figure Deutero-Isaiah had in mind by analysis of form alone.

In addition, we are unable to rely on content to help us define precisely the particular genre and setting. Several of the terms can be applied to more than one figure. *Bḥr* may refer to the choosing of a king or to the people Israel.[11] *Rṣh,* when Yahweh is the subject, does not belong to one particular figure.[12] The divine spirit is given alike to prophets, charismatic warriors, king, and people.[13] *Mišpaṭ* and *tôrā,* too, are ascribed to more than one office. *Tôrā* is the function of priests, wise men, and prophets, but there is no clear indication that it was a part of

---

[11] King: I Sam 10, 24; 16, 8 f.   II Sam 6, 21; 16, 18. Israel: Dt 7, 7   Isa 44, 1   Ezek 20, 5. Cf. Kaiser, Knecht, 21.

[12] Israel: Ps 44, 4; 149, 4   Jer 14, 10 etc. The faithful: Ps 147, 11. Temple: Hag 1, 8. It is used in connection with David (II Sam 24, 23), but not specifically as a sign of his election as king. Cf. Kaiser, Knecht, 21—22, for a more complete discussion of the term.

[13] Prophets: I Sam 10, 6.10; 19, 20.23. Charismatic warriors: Judg 3, 10; 6, 34; 11, 29. King: I Sam 16, 13   II Sam 23, 1 f. People: Num 11, 29 (the people are seen as prophets). Cf. Kaiser, Knecht, 22.

the king's role.[14] *Mišpaṭ* belonged to the king, but the prophets pro-claimed it as well.[15] The ancient traditions ascribing to the king dominion over the nations lend support to the view that bringing forth justice to the nations fits best with a royal figure;[16] nevertheless, the language of Isaiah 42, 1—4 does not clearly indicate that the servant will *rule* over the nations.

Thus a precise identification of the genre with a well-defined setting seems impossible. The style customarily used to announce the establishment of someone in a particular office is clearly employed, but we are unable to be more precise; to try to be more specific would be to overinterpret the text. The prophet employed in general the style customarily used for commissioning various kinds of officials. In that sense v. 1—4 can be isolated from the surrounding context. But the poem is an imitation, torn from any recognizable rootage in a particular function or office. The prophet borrowed from the various genres using this style to create a poem of his own which announces the choosing of Yahweh's servant. We shall have to ask why he used the style without clearly identifying the office. I suspect that the ambiguity is intentional, as I shall argue in the analysis of v. 5—9.

2. V. 5—9. These verses without doubt reflect a commissioning, but what kind? Prophetic or royal? The evidence is ambiguous. In some ways the poem is rather like speeches in which a king is commissioned. One can hardly miss the similarities both in form and content between Isaiah 42, 5—9 and the call of Cyrus in 45, 1—7. Both are oracles addressed to the person commissioned; both employ similar language about the summons.[17] Moreover, Isaiah 42, 5—9 could be understood as parallel to the oracle in Psalm 2.[18] Yet such language was used for the commissioning of prophets as well.[19]

---

[14] That *tôrā* was a function of priests, prophets, and wise men is hardly debatable. Kaiser's contention that it was a function of the king is, however, questionable (Knecht, 30). The parallelism in Lam 2, 9 is not sufficient evidence for arguing that *tôrā* was a royal function. The verse employs a variety of images to show the desolation of Jerusalem. The exile of king and princes and the absence of *tôrā* may be related to the general condition of Jerusalem; it does not necessarily indicate that *tôrā* was the king's prerogative.

[15] King: I Kings 3, 28; 7, 7 Ps 72, 1.2. Prophet: Mic 3, 8. Cf. Kaiser, Knecht, 23 ff.

[16] Ps 72, 1—4.8—11; 2, 7—9. Cf. Kaiser, Knecht, 23—24.

[17] *Weăḥzeq beyadæká/ hæḥᵃᵉzāqtî bimînô* (42, 6; 45, 1); *qr' (bešem)* (42, 6; 45, 3.4).

[18] Like the oracle in Ps 2, Isa 42, 5—9 is directed to one whose task is related to the nations. Note the similarities between "I give the nations as your inheritance" (Ps 2, 8) and "I give you as a covenant of people (?), as a light to the nations" (Isa 42, 6).

[19] Cf. Jer 1, 5.

5*

The content is equally ambiguous. Though II Samuel 23, 4 might seem initially to suggest that 'ôr gôyim signifies the activity of a king, a careful examination of the poems in Deutero- and Trito-Isaiah shows that the problem is rather more complex. On the one hand, the language about the servant "given" as a light to the nations (Isa 42, 6) sounds very much like the Davidic language associated with the witness "given" to the peoples (Isa 55, 4). On the other hand, we find that the city Zion can be a light to the nations (Isa 60, 1 ff.). Thus the language about the servant has affinities both with poems about Zion and poems using images associated with David.

How is the servant poem in Isaiah 42, 5—9 related to the language about David and Zion in Deutero- and Trito-Isaiah? Two things must be kept in mind: (1) in Deutero- and Trito-Isaiah the David and Zion traditions are not characteristically intermingled.[20] None of the Zion poems reflect royal language;[21] neither does the Davidic 55, 4—5 contain anything which belongs uniquely to traditions about Zion. Admittedly in 55, 4—5 the nations will come to David as in the Zion poems they will come to Jerusalem;[22] but other characteristics of the Zion tradition — second feminine singular reference to the mother and children — are absent in 55, 4—5. (2) Nevertheless, in Deutero- and Trito-Isaiah the David and Zion traditions are quite similar in their understanding of the relationship to the nations. The nations run to David; Zion is a light to the peoples.

Thus Deutero-Isaiah and Trito-Isaiah were not tied to one tradition as a vehicle for expressing the "mission" of the covenant people to the nations. Moreover, the ancient traditions are used rather freely: e. g., the Davidic tradition is "democratized" to apply to the whole people.[23] Therefore, we cannot rely on the prophet's use of a fixed tradition which we can then rely upon as a context for interpreting the ambiguities of Isaiah 42, 5—9. The kind of figure commissioned there remains ambiguous. The obscurity is probably intentional. The prophet freely used the images of David and then of Zion to express Israel's mission to the nations; 42, 5—9 is but one more example of his freedom.

---

[20] For a discussion of the David and Zion traditions in Deutero-Isaiah, see E. Rohland, Die Bedeutung der Erwählungstraditionen Israels für die Eschatologie der alttestamentlichen Propheten, 1956, 200—203. 263—265.
[21] It is worthy of note that in Eissfeldt's discussion of the Davidic poem 55, 1—5 no comparisons are made with the Zion poems: The Promises of Grace to David in Isa 55, 1—5. In: Israel's Prophetic Heritage, edited by B. W. Anderson and W. Harrelson, 1962, 196—207.
[22] Cf. Isa 45, 14—17; 49, 22—23; 60, 1 ff.
[23] Roland, Erwählungstraditionen, 264.

Isaiah 42, 5—9, then, imitates commissioning language in general rather than borrowing a particular genre for a specific kind of official. Even v. 8—9 support the contention that we have before us an artistic imitation of the various genres used in the commissioning of a number of different kinds of leaders. V. 8—9 continue v. 5—7,[24] but they are not a part of the commissioning genre. Moreover, they address the hearers of the poem in the plural in contrast to the singular in v. 5—7. Indeed, they reflect the language of disputation. The commissioning of the servant (v. 5—7), then, is an artistic device for an address to the community (v. 8—9). Only if v. 5—9 are a free creation divorced from the original settings of the genres imitated would such a modification in form be conceivable.

To summarize: Both v. 1—4 and v. 5—9 are the result of the creativity of the prophet, although they are based on traditional forms of speech. They are free creations which at the same time do not stray far from the genres which they imitate. Thus they stand apart from their context by form.

## II. ISAIAH 49, 1—6

The form critical discussions of Isaiah 49, 1—6 display no unanimity. Begrich sees the passage as an imitation of the thanksgiving psalm of an individual.[25] Kaiser views it as a confession which includes within it a report of a commissioning modeled on the commissioning of a king.[26] Westermann, too, sees the style of commissioning, but in his judgment the commissioning of king and prophet are combined, with the latter as the dominant category.[27]

These views contain truth, but they are not fully adequate. Begrich was partly right when he saw in 49, 1—6 the genre of the thanksgiving psalm. V. 4 sounds very much like the report of the past situation of need commonly found in the psalms of thanksgiving.[28] Wắ°nî 'amắrtî sometimes introduces the report of what the supplicant had said in the circumstance of need.[29] V. 4a is in the form of a lament, like other

---

[24] See the discussion by Kaiser, Knecht, 39.

[25] Begrich, Studien, 55—56.

[26] Kaiser, Knecht, 54 ff. Kaiser sees the closest parallel in the oracle embedded in Ps 2 (v. 7 ff.); the oracle is in the context of a royal psalm directed to kings and nobles of the nations. Yet Isa 49, 1—6 only imitates enthronement rituals; it functions here as a confession of trust.

[27] Westermann, Das Buch Jesaja, 169.

[28] Cf. e. g., Ps 30, 7—11; 116, 3—4.

[29] Cf. Ps 30, 7 Jon 2, 5.

reports of the supplicant's words in time of need.[30] V. 4b is an "expression of confidence," often a part of laments.[31] But if what follows in v. 5 is the narration of deliverance characteristically found in psalms of thanksgiving, it is a most unusual one indeed. Normally, the thanksgiving psalm narrates what Yahweh has *done*;[32] in Isaiah 49, 5 f. we have a quotation of what Yahweh *said* about the mission of the servant. One wonders indeed whether we have here a pattern typical of the psalm of thanksgiving. If so, we must have a special kind of psalm of thanksgiving — for those who have been given a special task. We have preserved to us, however, no examples elsewhere of such a specialised form of the psalm of thanksgiving. Indeed, from what we have already discovered about Deutero-Isaiah, it is more likely that the overall structure is the creation of Deutero-Isaiah, although elements of traditional genres appear.

The overall form of Isaiah 49, 1—6 is a report of the servant's commissioning. But what kind? King or prophet? In some ways it resembles the commissioning of a king, both in form and content. Like Psalm 2, 7 ff., Isaiah 49, 5 f. is an oracle from Yahweh to his servant. As the king is to have the nations as his inheritance (Ps 2, 8), so the servant is to be a light to the nations (Isa 49, 6).[33] In both, Yahweh has designated his chosen from birth (Ps 2, 7   Isa 49, 1.5). Yet Isaiah 49, 1—6 is much like the commissioning of Jeremiah as well. The servant's confession, "Yahweh called me from the womb" (Isa 49, 1), could be a reference to a prophetic call (cf. Jer 1, 5). We might assume that the reference to the mouth (Isa 49, 2) suggests a prophetic figure,[34] but the mouth played a role in the activities of the king also (cf. Isa 11, 4).[35]

Isaiah 49, 1—6 employs the style of commissioning, but the language is so general that we cannot determine specifically whether it is the commissioning of a king or a prophet. It is probable that the author intended to make no such distinction but was instead simply imitating in general the style of the report of a commissioning.

A study of the opening to the poem adds to the contention that the speech reflects as much Deutero-Isaiah's creativity as it does traditional form. The summoning of the nations in a report of a commissioning appears only here. It was common in Israel's hymns to call the nations to praise;[36] on other occasions the nations were summoned in connection

---

[30] Cf. Ps 30, 9—11; 116, 4.10—11.
[31] Cf. H. Gunkel, Einleitung in die Psalmen, 1966, 232 ff.
[32] Cf. Ps 30, 4; 34, 5; 116, 1—4   Jon 2, 2 ff.
[33] Cf. also Isa 55, 4—5.
[34] Cf. W. Zimmerli, in: Zimmerli and J. Jeremias, The Servant of God, 1957, 27.
[35] Kaiser, Knecht, 58.
[36] E. g., Ps 96, 7—9; 97, 1; 117, 1.

with judgment against Israel,[37] to hear a song,[38] or a wisdom teaching.[39] In Deutero-Isaiah we find the imperative *šimʿû* directed to the nations in a trial speech (48, 14).[40] The closest approximation to the summons to hear in Isaiah 49, 1 is the exhortation to the kings in Psalm 2, 10, which follows the report of the commissioning of the anointed in the verses immediately preceding; but the basic form and intention of Psalm 2 is quite different from that of Isaiah 49, 1—6. In Isaiah 49, 1, Deutero-Isaiah incorporated a summons to the nations into the servant's report of his commissioning because he wanted to emphasize something not conventionally expressed in traditional forms of such reports; he wanted to emphasize that the servant's mission is directed to the nations.

By now it should be apparent that Deutero-Isaiah transformed the traditional language of commissioning reports for his own purposes. Not only did he have the servant address the nations; he also drastically modified the typical commissioning forms by including language from the cult (v. 4) as a response to the call rather than the more typical objection (cf. Jer 1, 6  Ex 4, 10  Judg 6, 15). Deutero-Isaiah made this alteration to express a dynamic native to the psalms, particularly the psalm of thanksgiving: The servant had already experienced failure, but the poet wanted to contrast past and future. Thus he used elements of the thanksgiving psalm to show the relationship of the servant's lament in the past (v. 4a, "I said"), the servant's confidence in Yahweh (v. 4b), and Yahweh's plan for his future (v. 5—6).

The form of Isaiah 49, 1—6 is a Deutero-Isaianic creation, yet it can be distinguished from its context as a report of a commissioning. Neither 49, 7 nor the end of chapter 48 are form critically a part of the commissioning narration.

## III. ISAIAH 50, 4—11

1. *V. 4—9.* Begrich views v. 4—9 as a lament psalm of an individual.[41] V. 4—6 represent the complaint *(Klage)* by showing the painful contrast between the servant's commission and his actual experience. Begrich finds in v. 5—6 the lament psalm's typical assertion of the

---

[37] E. g., Am 3, 9.

[38] Judg 5, 3.

[39] Ps 49, 2.

[40] The imperative of *šamāʿ* is used elsewhere in Deutero-Isaiah to address Israel in disputation speeches (42, 18; 48, 1) or in speeches of salvation (44, 1; 46, 12; 51, 1.7.21).

[41] Begrich, Studien, 54—55.

supplicant's innocence. The expression of confidence follows in v. 7,[42] in which we find language borrowed from legal genres.[43]

As Kaiser and Westermann have observed, however, v. 4—9 lack the plea, which is integral to the lament psalm. It is better, they say, to view v. 4—9 as a psalm of confidence *(Vertrauenpsalm)*.[44] This criticism is fundamentally accurate. Though v. 5—6 resemble the assertion of innocence characteristic of many lament psalms, the most important features of that genre are missing. V. 4—9 are instead a psalm of confidence, but of a special kind. V. 4—5a show that the speaker has a special task; he is to speak with the tongue of *limmûdîm*. We are reminded in many ways of Jeremiah's confessions.[45] Indeed, we appear to have before us a psalm of confidence uttered by one who, like Jeremiah, has encountered opposition to his task.

Is the speaker a prophet? The image of one who knows how to help (?)[46] the weary with a word, one whose ear has been opened by Yahweh, would be appropriate for a prophet. The similarities with Jeremiah's confessions would appear to support this view. Yet the opening of the ear is applied to Israel elsewhere in the Deutero-Isaianic circle of traditions (Isa 48, 8; 35, 5). Have we an imitation of a psalm of confidence in which Israel is personified as a prophet?[47] Perhaps. But the evidence, as in the foregoing "servant songs," is inconclusive.

2. *V. 10—11.* These verses do not continue the genre of the psalm of confidence. Yahweh rather than the servant is the speaker. Yet v. 10—11 do not appear to stand alone.[48] But the precise relationship between v. 10—11 and the preceding psalm of confidence cannot be discussed apart from the problem concerning the translation of the former. V. 10—11 might be translated:

Who among you fears Yahweh, hears the voice of his servant
Who walks in darkness, who has no brightness,
(Yet) trusts in the name of Yahweh, leans on his God?

---

[42] Cf. Jer 20, 11.
[43] Cf. Begrich, Studien, 26 ff., for a discussion of legal language in Deutero-Isaiah.
[44] Kaiser, Knecht, 67—69; Westermann, Das Buch Jesaja, 183—184. K. Elliger also views it as a psalm of confidence, Deuterojesaja in seinem Verhältnis zu Tritojesaja, 1933, 34.
[45] See the parallels with Jeremiah's confessions as listed by Westermann, Das Buch Jesaja, 184.
[46] The meaning of *la'ût* is uncertain.
[47] In Isa 55, 3—5 the prophet personifies the nation as David.
[48] See below.

Or it might be rendered:

> Whoever among you fears Yahweh, hears the voice of his servant
> Who walks in darkness, who has no brightness,
> Let him trust in the name of Yahweh, lean on his God.

The first translation is probably correct. It provides a contrast between the disobedient and the servant by means of an ironic use of the images of darkness and light. The faithful servant walks in darkness, while the unfaithful carry torches! *Mî bakæm* in v. 10, then, introduces a derogatory question which leads to a statement begun by *hen*.

Though v. 10—11 do not continue the genre of v. 4—9 nor do they form a sequel to it which is customarily used in any Israelite liturgical practice known to us, v. 10—11 seem to depend upon v. 4—9. The judgment against the faithless needs the portrayal of the servant as a faithful disciple who teaches God's word. Moreover, a rhetorical pattern involving questions introduced by *mî* followed by assertions begun by *hen* is shared by v. 4—9 and v. 10—11 (v. 8b.9.10.11). Either v. 10—11 were added later by someone who employed a similar style, or v. 4—11 were an originally unified poem, the first part of which is an imitation of a psalm of confidence. I suspect the latter is true; the stylistic similarities, together with Deutero-Isaiah's tendency to fuse and transform conventional genres, combine to suggest an originally unified poem. In any event, in the present form of the text they must be taken together.

## IV. ISAIAH 52, 13—53, 12

Begrich saw the text as composed of two Yahweh speeches (52, 13—15; 53, 11—12) with a song of a group in between. The song of the group is profoundly influenced by the speech-patterns of the psalm of thanksgiving. V. 2—3 are a narrative closely related to the utterances of the lament psalm and the narration of need in the psalm of thanksgiving, except that the sufferer himself does not speak but is spoken about. V. 4—6 continue the style of narration. The speakers' changed evaluation of the significance of the servant's suffering is expressed in suffixes, prepositional expressions, and genitives, with the style of narration remaining predominant. The narration, says Begrich, continues to be patterned after the complaint and the narration of need in the psalm of thanksgiving. V. 7—9 return to pure narration of need, still modeled on the psalm of thanksgiving. V. 10 is derived from the narration of deliverance, again with the exception that the one saved is here not the speaker but the one spoken about.[49]

---

[49] Begrich, Studien, 62—65.

The analysis of Begrich is excellent but not fully satisfactory. First of all, it is not certain whether the second Yahweh-speech begins with v. 11.[50] 'Ămmî in v. 8 suggests that Yahweh's address might begin in v. 7;[51] at the same time, Yahweh is referred to in third person in v. 10. Normally 'ammî refers to Yahweh's people,[52] though there are instances in which this is not the case.[53] Lacking introductory formulae, it is doubtful whether the problem can be resolved.

A more important criticism of Begrich is that his emphasis on the poem as an imitation of the psalm of thanksgiving is misleading. Without doubt the poem is influenced by the language of the lament psalm and its related forms.[54] Possibly the narrative style of the psalm of thanksgiving was a factor in the structure of the poem. But all of this forms scarcely more than the background.[55] The structure of the poem is basically the prophet's own creation.

The opening speech of salvation (52, 13—15) has a typical beginning (hinnē), but it is formed rather uniquely. Everything in it points to the paradox of the servant's exaltation. There is such a contrast between the servant's appearance (v. 14) and his exaltation that the nations express surprise at what they see and understand (v. 15). What follows (53, 1 ff.) is a confession by the nations in a manner unprecedented in Hebrew literature. The typical language of the cult is converted into a narration by the nations concerning their deliverance through the suffering of the despised servant. The poem ends with a promise of the triumph of the servant. He will "see offspring," "lengthen days," and, indeed, Yahweh's desire will prosper in him. Yet even in the promise of triumph his victory is explicitly connected with his bearing the iniquity of "many."[56]

Thus we have a poem whose structure is the creation of Deutero-Isaiah. Basically it functions as a speech of salvation,[57] but it differs from most speeches of that type in that even the announcement of salvation proper sees the deliverance directly connected with the servant's suffering. Nevertheless, the poem stands apart from its context both by form and content.

[50] Cf. Kaiser, Knecht, 87.
[51] 1QIsaᵃ has 'ammô.
[52] Isa 1, 3; 3, 15; 10, 24; 19, 25; 40, 1; 43, 20; 47, 6; 51, 4.16; 52, 4.5.6; 58, 1; 63, 8; 65, 22.
[53] Cf. e. g., Ps 59, 12; 78, 1  Lam 2, 11; 4, 3.6.10. In all these cases "my people" refers to the relationship of a *human* speaker and people.
[54] Begrich, Studien, 62—65.
[55] Westermann, Das Buch Jesaja, 207.
[56] 53, 12.
[57] Kaiser, Knecht, 88.

Part Two: The Arrangement of Genre Units

# Chapter Six: The Problem of a Suitable Method

## I. THE BACKGROUND OF THE PROBLEM

Our form critical study of the major genres in Deutero-Isaiah has led us to conclude that "units" may be isolated from the context by form. In most instances we are not dealing with genres with a long history in Israel's oral tradition but rather with poems whose form, though influenced by traditional genres, is basically the creation of Deutero-Isaiah. Nevertheless, many of the poems are quite stereotyped in structure and thus capable of standing alone both by form and content. Since they possess this kind of autonomy, it might seem logical to conclude that the Deutero-Isaianic corpus is a collection of originally independent units. Had the genres betrayed a long history in oral tradition, our supposition would be doubly reinforced. But since most of Deutero-Isaiah's speech-forms are his own creation, we must entertain another possibility — that the poet created longer poems out of several "units." Thus our basic question is: What is the nature of the relationship of genre units to one another?

A number of studies growing out of form criticism have dealt with the arrangement of units in Deutero-Isaiah. One of the most controversial was the study by Sigmund Mowinckel.[1] He argued, as we saw, that originally independent units of tradition were arranged by means of a loose association of catchword and, to some extent, theme. Hardly anyone has completely agreed with him; few have been able to imagine that the arrangement had no kerygmatic intention.[2] Moreover, various technical difficulties have been discerned.[3] Yet the weaknesses of Mowinckel's arguments should not be allowed to obscure the significance of his contribution. The fault lies, not in having argued that verbal repetition was important in the association of units, but rather in having assumed that it was merely a mechanical means of arrangement. He ought to have asked: What is the *significance* of the repetition of words and phrases?

---

[1] Mowinckel, Die Komposition des deuterojesajanischen Buches, ZAW 49 (1931), 87—112. 242—260.

[2] E. g., K. Elliger, Deuterojesaja in seinem Verhältnis zu Tritojesaja, 1933, 219 ff.; O. Eissfeldt, The OT: An Introduction, 1965, 338.

[3] Elliger notes a number of difficulties in Mowinckel's method (Deuterojesaja 223 f.). Other objections are scattered throughout the latter portion of Elliger's book.

At the opposite pole, Karl Elliger argued that the units were arranged in terms of their content — progression in thought.[4] His thesis is quite plausible, as almost any example from his work will show. In his discussion of chapter 41, for instance, he argues that 41, 1—5 specifies what was expressed quite generally in the promise in 40, 27—31; Yahweh's salvation is in Cyrus — to the astonishment of the world. 41, 8 ff. continues the thought by expressing the needlessness for fear. The *Stichwort* "Fear not" (v. 10.13.14) is but the means for carrying the main thought. Even v. 17—20 continue the thought of the foregoing; corresponding to the "worm" (v. 14) are the poor (v. 17).[5]

Whether or not one agrees with every detail of Elliger's work, one can see that this is not a totally improper way to proceed. The weakness lies, not in the use of the method, but in failing to recognize its limits. To concentrate almost exclusively on progression in *thought* is to rely on a method which is more suitable for a discursive mode of presentation. In poetry the forms and images are at least as important as the thought. By means of these the poet calls into being certain feelings and attitudes and associations which are not, strictly speaking, "thoughts." Elliger's method, then, needs to be supplemented by methods which are more sensitive to the artistry of the literature.

Eva Hessler also finds significance in the structural patterns of the Deutero-Isaianic corpus.[6] First of all, she finds that 40, 1—11 and 55, 1—13 reflect the structure of chapters 40—55. The similarity of 40, 1—11 and 55, 1—13 indicates to her that they were positioned intentionally as prologue and epilogue for the chapters in between.[7] Furthermore, she notes that the first part of the corpus, which is dominated by references to Jacob-Israel, is separated by a hymn (48, 20—21) from the second section, which speaks of Zion-Jerusalem.[8] Another hymn (44, 23) further divides the corpus, separating the section concerning Israel as Yahweh's witnesses (chapters 41—44) from the part that follows (44, 24—48, 19).[9] In a similar way the large section consisting of chapters 49—55 is divided by a hymn (52, 7—10).[10] This structure appears to be the result of careful planning.

---

[4] Ibid. 225 ff.

[5] Ibid. 229—233.

[6] Hessler, Gott der Schöpfer: Ein Beitrag zur Komposition und Theologie Deuterojesajas, 1961. In Hessler's view, the author imitated and transformed *Gattungen* from various realms of life, and he combined them according to the structure of the trial.

[7] Ibid. 98, 102, 253 ff.

[8] Ibid. 82.

[9] Ibid. 82.

[10] Ibid. 83.

Beyond the overall patterns of arrangement which Hessler sees, we find in her work a particular approach to the juxtaposition of individual genre "units." The author imitated various genres, argues Hessler, and arranged them in such a way that we may perceive a kerygmatic unity in the arrangement. The unity is based, not on progression in thought, but rather on a structure which imitates the form of a legal proceeding.[11] After the prologue (40, 1—11) and the questions which follow it (40, 12—31), speeches are juxtaposed to simulate a trial. First come the preliminaries to the trial (41, 1—42, 9),[12] which include in particular the challenge of opponents to come to trial (41, 1 ff.21—29).[13] Then the trial proper takes place (42, 10—48, 22).[14] It begins with a hymn (42, 10—13) and salvation oracle (42, 14—17). Then comes the introduction of witnesses (42, 18—43, 21), followed by their *Begegnung* (43, 22—44, 22). After this the salvation of the remnant by Cyrus is announced (44, 24—46, 13), concluding with the legal decisions promulgated by the court (47, 1—48, 16).[15]

Although Hessler regards chapters 49—55 also as an imitation of legal proceedings, it is not important for us to illustrate in greater detail. Our concern in this chapter is rather with method. What is important about Hessler's approach is that a speech need not continue the thought of the foregoing speech; it is necessary only that it follow as the next element in the trial process. In 42, 18 ff., for instance, the blindness of Israel is reviewed as the witnesses are introduced (42, 18—25), followed by the promise of a new future in which witnesses may take up their true task (43, 1—7). Having been prepared for their work by exhortation and promise, the witnesses are now confronted by the gathered forum (43, 8—13) and challenged to testify for Yahweh. V. 14—15 continue in this vein, serving as the *content* of the affirmation which the witnesses are supposed to make in Yahweh's behalf. Israel, however, does not make this testimony; the witnesses, unfortunately, have a fixation on the "former things" and lack conviction about Yahweh's saving acts in the future. Therefore, v. 16—21 are added to urge the witnesses to shift their attention from the "former things" to the new deeds which Yahweh is about to perform.[16] A close examination of this treatment of Isaiah 42, 18—43, 21 reveals that none of the transitions between units indicated above are actually stated in the text. They need not be supplied

---

[11] Ibid. 15—17, 28, 98—102, 107.
[12] Ibid. 99, 254—259.
[13] Ibid. 99, 254, 256—257.
[14] Ibid. 99, 259 ff.
[15] Ibid. 99 ff.
[16] Ibid. 260—263.

purely by imagination, however. In Hessler's view, one makes these transitions because the structure of the trial prompts him to do so.

Though Claus Westermann does not use the legal proceeding for the overall pattern of arrangement, we can see in his analysis the influence of Hessler.[17] He, too, recognizes Jacob-Israel and Zion-Jerusalem sections surrounded by prologue and epilogue. The Jacob-Israel block begins with a disputation (40, 12—31) and ends with a call to leave the city (48, 20—21) in the style of the hymn of praise *(Loblied)*. The Zion-Jerusalem section, too, begins with a disputational poem (49, 14—26) and concludes with the hymn of praise (52, 9—10) and call to leave the city (52, 11—12). Chapters 54—55 constitute a third major section with their own distinctive theme.

The first block (chapters 40—48) is subdivided by the hymn in 44, 23. 41, 1—44, 23 is composed of independent poems identifiable by genre.[18] It is in this subsection that we find the basic genres of Deutero-Isaiah — the *Gerichtsrede,* the *Heilsorakel,* and the *Heilsankündigung.* Indeed, only here do we find the *Heilsorakel* or *Heilszusage* in pure form. Chapters 45—48[19] begin something new with the Cyrus oracle (45, 1—7) and its introduction (44, 24—28). This segment of chapters 40—55, dominated by the theme of the victory of Cyrus and the fall of Babylon (chapter 47) and her gods (46, 1—2), is made up of longer poems rather than independent genre units. Chapters 49 ff., too, are composed of longer poetic compositions.

Thus Isaiah 40—55 is not simply a collection of single speeches, argues Westermann, but a meaningful whole growing out of the major genres.[20] It is not accidental that the structure of the prologue (40, 1—11) corresponds to the structure of the collection; the prologue takes its shape from the various genres: v. 1—2 from the *Heilsorakel,* v. 3—5 from the *Gerichtsrede,* v. 6—8 from the *Disputationsrede,* v. 9—11 from the *"eschatologische" Loblied.*[21]

This careful plan did not originate, however, when the poetry was first created. Isaiah 40—55 is instead a collection. Moreover, the collection in its present form represents various stages of redactional activity. Although the basic pattern or arrangement is the result of one major, intentional act of compilation, Westermann does see later accretions: e. g., the exhortation to return to Yahweh in 44, 21.22b, the woe sentences (45, 9—10), additions to chapter 48 (v. 1c.4.5b.7b.8 ff.18 f.), and

---

[17] Westermann, Sprache und Struktur der Prophetie Deuterojesajas, in: Forschung am Alten Testament, 1964, 161 ff.
[18] Ibid. 164. Cf. also Das Buch Jesaja: Kapitel 40—66, 1966, 26.
[19] More accurately, 44, 24—48, 21.
[20] Westermann, Sprache und Struktur, 167.
[21] Ibid. 166.

certain "Amen glosses."[22] Of particular importance is Westermann's hypothesis that the "servant songs" were added after the basic collection had been made.[23] 42, 1—9 and 49, 1—12 each form a complex of tradition ending with a *Loblied* (42, 10—13; 49, 13).[24] Westermann suggests a reconstruction of the text so that 50, 4—9 is also concluded by a hymn of praise.[25]

I have discussed Hessler and Westermann at length because their description of the overall structure of chapters 40—55 is a step in the right direction. It is surely not accidental that the first part of the collection addresses the people as Jacob-Israel while the latter half is dominated by Zion-Jerusalem. Moreover, their belief that hymns are used to mark turning points in the collection is a step forward. Finally, I agree that Isaiah 40, 1—11 and the closing verses of chapter 55 constitute prologue and epilogue.

Nevertheless, Hessler's attempt to view the whole as a literary replica of a trial cannot be supported by the text. Although we find both trial genres and legal language in non-forensic genres,[26] there is no reason why we should consider genres such as the cultic salvation-assurance oracle as part of the trial. The arranger provides no clue to direct us to do so, nor does the overall structure of chapters 40—55 conform so closely to the patterns employed in the town gate that we are compelled to see the whole as a trial.[27]

Westermann's approach, too, is not without problems. In particular, I should like to pose two crucial questions: (1) Is Westermann correct that a collector worked mostly with longer poems rather than independent genre units? Our form critical analysis has led us to the conclusion that many "units" have a greater capacity to stand alone by the twin criteria of form and content than Westermann suggests. My hunch that the collector dealt basically with independent units, identifiable by genre analysis, will be tested thoroughly in the ensuing chapters. (2) I am skeptical of Westermann's attempts to distinguish various layers in the growth of the collection. If the *Loblieder* 44, 23, 48, 20—21, and 52, 9—10 were hymnic responses in the *original* collection, how can we be sure that the use of similar forms in 42, 10—13 and 49, 13 served as markers for segments of the collection which were added *later*? Why should we not just as readily presume that at the earliest stage of growth

---

[22] Westermann, Das Buch Jesaja, 25—28.
[23] Westermann, Sprache und Struktur, 162—163; Das Buch Jesaja, 26—27.
[24] 42, 1—4 are reinterpreted by v. 5—9, and 49, 1—6 is reinterpreted by v. 7—12.
[25] Westermann, Sprache und Struktur, 162—163.
[26] Cf. e. g., the legal language (50, 7—9) in the liturgical *Gattung* (50, 4 ff.).
[27] For a discussion of the speech-forms used in the town gate, cf. H. J. Boecker, Redeformen des Rechtslebens im alten Testament, 1964.

41, 1—42, 9 were closed by 42, 10—13, 42, 14—44, 22 by 44, 23, and
44, 24—48, 19 by 48, 20—21? Only in the case of the hymn 49, 13 do I
find Westermann's arguments at all convincing; when one compares the
brevity of 49, 1—13 with the usual lengths of sections concluded by
hymns, one could easily imagine that the shorter block originated at a
different stage in the process of collection. Nevertheless, even this
argument can scarcely attain the status of probability.

My purpose is not to doubt that Isaiah 40—55 underwent several
stages of growth. Indeed, I would argue that we can occasionally see
later stages of development.[28] But in most instances the collectors did
not leave distinctive footprints by which we may retrace their respective
paths. We are therefore by and large unable to reconstruct the history
of the redaction. We can deal only with the final form of the text in its
relationship to the individual genre unit.

To summarize: Hessler and Westermann have laid a proper
foundation for discussing the larger patterns in the arrangement of
Isaiah 40—55. What is needed now is an understanding of the precise
relationships between the placement of individual units side by side and
the larger scheme of organization. Have we some kind of progression
with kerymatic significance? In order to place this question in perspective we first need a systematic outline of the overall structure of chapters
40—55; then we can turn directly to the methodological issues in the
juxtaposition of individual units.

## II. THE BASIC STRUCTURE OF ISAIAH 40—55

### A. The Form of the Prologue and the Structure of the "Book"

Hessler and Westermann argued that 40, 1—11 reflects the structure of the entire corpus in miniature and was intentionally employed as
the prologue to the collection. We shall now discuss this matter in
detail. Immediately we are confronted with the question of the form of
these eleven verses.

Usually these verses, though not always regarded as a unity,[29] have
been regarded as a reflection of a prophetic commission. Westermann

---

[28] The repetition of 48, 22 in 57, 21 probably indicates, for example, that 48, 22 was
included after the basic collection of chs. 40—55 had already taken shape.

[29] Gressmann, Köhler, and Mowinckel see four units: v. 1—2.3—5.6—8.9—11. Von
Waldow thinks of v. 1—8 as one unit in three parts. Gressmann, Die literarische
Analyse Deuterojesaja, ZAW 35 (1914), 264; Köhler, Deuterojesaja stilkritisch
untersucht, 1923, 102—104, 106, 125; Mowinckel, Komposition, 88—89; von Waldow, Anlaß und Hintergrund der Verkündigung des Deuterojesaja, 1953, 50.

sees v. 1—11 as a unified account which is related to the call,[30] while Begrich believes that v. 1—8 are composed of three separate "units", each of which reflects an element of the experience of commissioning.[31] For Begrich, v. 1—2 and v. 3—5 are words from divine beings to divine beings; v. 6—8 reflect the voice of the prophet. V. 9—11 are an imitation of a command given to a messenger of good tidings and have nothing to do with the prophet's call.[32]

I shall argue that v. 1—8 are a unity, and that their unity is rooted in language which reminds us of a particular kind of prophetic commissioning. Despite the fact that these words are not cast in the customary narrative style, we are reminded of the kind of prophetic commissioning which we find in Isaiah 6 — a form of commissioning which is closely related to the prophetic vision of judgment in the heavenly council.[33] In both I Kings 22 and Isaiah 6 the prophet is transported by vision into the realm of the heavenly council where Yahweh is seated on his throne in the presence of the members of the council (I Kings 22, 19 Isa 6, 1—2).[34] The prophet hears Yahweh ask by means of a question introduced by *mî* who will perform a certain task (I Kings 22, 20 Isa 6, 8). Isaiah appropriated the kind of vision of judgment found in I Kings 22 to portray his commissioning as a prophet of judgment.[35]

Although Isaiah 40, 1—8 is not a narrative like Isaiah 6, it is based on the imagery of the commissioning of a prophet by means of a vision of the heavenly council. The plural imperatives in v. 1—2 and v. 3—5 indicate that the prophet is not the addressee. One might suppose that these imperatives are directed to members of the heavenly council.[36] Our guess becomes probability in the realization that just as Isaiah of Jerusalem heard the "voice" of Yahweh "speaking," (*qôl* plus the participle *'omer*), so also Isaiah 40, 3 reports that a "voice is calling" (*qôl qôre'*). In 40, 6—8 the "voice" speaks to the one addressed (*qôl*

---

[30] Westermann, Das Buch Jesaja, 29—41. Although Westermann sees the language of the commissioning of the messenger as an element in 40, 1—11, the poet has transformed it and combined it with other kinds of speech, so that it no longer serves the original purpose of the commissioning genre.

[31] Begrich, Studien zu Deuterojesaja, 1963, 61.

[32] Ibid. 58—59.

[33] R. Knierim, The Vocation of Isaiah, VT 18 (1968), 50—54, 57—60. Cf. also W. Zimmerli, Ezechiel, 1956—, 16—21; H. Wildberger, Jesaja Kapitel 1—12, 1972, 234—238.

[34] "I saw the Lord sitting upon a throne" (Isa 6, 1 cf. I Kings 22, 19).

[35] Knierim, Vocation, 57—60.

[36] Cf. F. M. Cross, Jr., The Council of Yahweh in Second Isaiah, JNES 12 (1953), 274—277.

'*omer*). Instead of a question introduced by *mî* we find the command, "Cry!" In response to this imperative the recipient of the command objects, "What shall I cry? All flesh is grass . . ."[37] Just as Isaiah of Jerusalem had responded with uncertainty to the message he was given to proclaim (6, 11), so the "I" in Deutero-Isaiah is taken aback by his commission. His problem, however, is not "how long" he must utter a terrifying message, but whether he can proclaim anything at all. In the exile the cultic affirmation that man is "grass" which withers[38] became intensified to the extent that the "I" in Isaiah 40, 6—8 doubts that any human can proclaim a message of hope. His objection is met, however: "The grass withers, the flower fades, but the word of our God stands forever."

V. 1—8 are without doubt a unity. The transactions in the heavenly council (v. 1—5) cannot be separated from the summons to the "I" (v. 6—8). The function or intention of these verses is, however, somewhat ambiguous. Though it reminds us of the type of prophetic commissioning found in Isaiah 6, we can at the most infer that it is a prophetic call. The setting of the poem is not clear, nor are we given a referent for the plural imperatives.[39] Even the identity of the "I" in v. 6—8 must be inferred: is it the prophet or the people? The similarities with Isaiah 6 suggest a prophet, but the language of doubt with which the "I" responds reminds us of Israel's complaints (40, 27; 49, 14). Indeed, the ambiguity of the "I" is bound up with the lack of clear setting which characterizes the entire corpus and makes the problem of the "servant songs" so difficult. We must eventually ask why the prologue does not provide us with a concrete setting to give a well-defined context for interpretation. For the moment we content ourselves with the recognition that the poet uses the images of a prophetic commissioning but that the identity of the *personae* is ambiguous. The equivocation, doubtless, is intentional; the "I" is at once prophet and people.

Now we must inquire whether v. 9—11 continue v. 1—8. Begrich correctly views v. 9—11 as an imitation of instructions given to a messenger who bears news concerning a battle.[40] Although the content of the message draws upon cultic language,[41] the form of the speech reflects instructions to a messenger. Not only is the addressee named as a messenger, but the imperatives indicate that the messenger is being told

---

[37] *W'mr* should be read as first person singular. Cf. 1QIsaᵃ.

[38] Cf. Ps 90, 5; 103, 15.

[39] The conclusions of Cross (Council of Yahweh) are probable; nevertheless, they are a reconstruction.

[40] Begrich, Studien, 58—59.

[41] V. 10—11 betray the style and content of the hymn.

what to say. Moreover, the imagery is military. Yahweh will come in strength; he will bring his booty with him. Thus v. 9—11 are not a continuation of the "prophetic" commissioning in v. 1—8. It is likely, then, that v. 1—8 and v. 9—11 were originally separate. Other considerations reinforce this contention: the shift to the second feminine singular (v. 9), the change from imagery of a highway in the desert as a revelation of Yahweh's glory and a manifestation of the efficacy of the divine word (v. 1—8) to the imagery of Yahweh's rule in Zion as a shepherd-like king (v. 9—11).

The juxtaposition of v. 1—8 and v. 9—11 is not accidental, however, nor is it fully explained by the catchword qôl.[42] Instead, it reflects the structure of chapters 40—55 in miniature. 40, 1—8 is a microcosm of chapters 41—48. First of all, the image of the highway through the desert (v. 3—5) is a recurring theme in chapters 41—48. Indeed, it is the theme of the new Exodus: Yahweh will create an oasis in the desert (41, 17—20), a "way" in the desert (43, 19.20).[43] When the people of Israel are commanded to leave Babylon (48, 20—21), they are reminded that they did not thirst when they went through the desert. Chapters 49, 14 ff. do not contain this theme. To be sure, the theme of return home is present, as well as Exodus imagery, but the image of the way through the desert is restricted to chapters 41—48. The same is true as well of the theme of Yahweh's gracious acts in the desert.[44]

Another major theme shared by 40, 1—8 and chapters 41—48 is that Yahweh will deliver that his glory "may be made known" (40, 5; cf. 42. 8.12; 43, 7; 48, 11).[45] This theme is absent in 49, 14 ff.[46] The theme of the reliability of Yahweh's word is common to 40, 1—8 and chapters 41—48,[47] but totally absent in 49, 14 ff.[48] Finally, the tense structure of 40, 1—2 corresponds to the tense sequence of the salvation-assurance oracles, a genre which is pivotal in chapters 41—48[49] and relatively unimportant in the latter part of the book.[50]

40, 9—11 corresponds to 49, 14 ff. The second feminine singular address anticipates the last half of the collection.[51] Except for 45, 14—17, chapters 41—48 consistently use Jacob-Israel. Other features in

42 Mowinckel, Komposition, 89.
43 "Way" is also mentioned in 42, 16.
44 49, 14 ff. do not speak of Yahweh's merciful acts on the way home through the desert.
45 Cf. also 42, 21; 43, 20.21.23.25.
46 Except in the epilogue 55, 13b.
47 Particularly in the trial and disputation speeches.
48 Except in the epilogue (55, 10—11).
49 Westermann, Sprache und Struktur, 164, 166.
50 In 51, 7—8 and 54, 4—6 the form is considerably modified.
51 49, 14—26; 51, 9—52, 12 ch. 54. 50, 1—3 also uses the image of the mother.

40, 9—11 correspond to 49, 14 ff.: the image of messengers announcing
the return of Yahweh as ruler in Zion (40, 9—11; 52, 7—10), the
"voice" of the messengers (40, 9; 52, 8), and the victory of Yahweh's
"arm" (40, 10; 51, 5.9; 52, 10; 53, 1).

## B. The Epilogue in the Context of Chapters 40—55

Isaiah 55, 6—13 corresponds to the beginning of the corpus.
Following a discussion of the formal structure of 55, 6—13 the correspondence with 40, 1 ff. will be shown.

Form critical studies of 55, 6—13 have led to different results as
to the number of units and their nature.[52] Thus a new attempt is
necessary. V. 6—7 constitute what has generally been called prophetic
imitation of priestly *tôrā*.[53] The passage begins with masculine plural
imperatives — exhortations to "seek Yahweh" and "to call upon him"
(v. 6). The imperatives are followed by jussives (v. 7).[54] Here, as
elsewhere in prophetic literature,[55] the utterance is a word of the prophet
rather than a word of Yahweh.

V. 8—9 appear to serve as the substantiation for the exhortation
in v. 6—7; yet Yahweh rather than the prophet is the speaker. Does
this mean that we have before us a new unit of speech, as Begrich and
others claim? V. 8—9 do not stand alone very well; moreover, the close
association of *dæræk* and *măḥšæbæt* in v. 8—9 is rather similar to their
relationship in v. 6—7. V. 8—9 seem indeed to have a disputational
function — to explain why the exhortation in v. 6—7 is trustworthy.
Yahweh will forgive because his ways and thoughts are different from
those of man. Whether v. 6—7 and v. 8—9 were originally uttered
together or whether v. 8—9 were added later as a disputational reflection is not clear. The shift from prophetic to divine speech suggests the
latter. In any event, v. 8—9 are dependent upon v. 6—7; thus in the
present form of the text they cannot be separated.

In v. 10 the subject matter changes. No longer are we dealing with
the question of Yahweh's mercy or the ways and thoughts of Yahweh
compared to man, but rather with the reliability of Yahweh's word.
Moreover, the text does not clearly suggest how the meanings of v. 6—9
and v. 10—11 are related. Still, the introductory *kî* appears to connect
v. 10—11 with the preceding verses as a second substantiation of the

---

[52] Cf. e. g., Gressmann, Analyse, 264; Mowinckel, Komposition, 111; Begrich, Studien,
13; Westermann, Das Buch Jesaja, 230—235.
[53] Cf. Begrich, Studien, 58.
[54] For this style elsewhere in prophetic literature, cf. Am 5, 4.5.6.23  Isa 1, 16.17.
Cf. Begrich, Die priesterliche Tora, BZAW 66 (1936), 73.
[55] Cf. e. g., Am 5, 6.

exhortation in v. 6—7. Furthermore, v. 10—11 are similar stylistically to v. 8—9; an introductory *kî* clause followed by *ken*, similar in structure to v. 8—9, functions as a disputation to convince doubters that Yahweh's word is dependable. Whether v. 8—9 and v. 10—11 were originally joined may be debated, but in the present text they both substantiate v. 6—7.

V. 12—13 take the form of an announcement of salvation.[56] Those who hear are promised that they will go out from Babylon with rejoicing (v. 12a). The announcement is extended by the promise that creation will be renewed (v. 13a). The salvation speech ends with an assertion of the purpose of Yahweh's action (v. 13b). Not only are v. 12—13 distinguishable from their context by form, but by content as well; they could easily stand alone. Yet they are joined to the context by an introductory *kî*.

It is unlikely that the question of original unity versus secondary juxtaposition can be settled definitively with regard to the "units" in 55, 6—13. We are able, however, to understand that the structure of these verses is closely related to the collection as a whole. Isaiah 55, 6—13 — the end of the Deutero-Isaianic corpus — is quite similar to the beginning. The theme of returning to Yahweh who is merciful in 55, 6—7 corresponds to the announcement in 40, 1—2 that Jerusalem's sins are accepted. The promise of exodus from captivity in 55, 12—13 is also present in 40, 3—5. The assertions about the radical differences between Yahweh and man in 55, 8—9 and about the reliability of Yahweh's word (v. 10—11) may be perceived also in 40, 6—8.[57]

## III. THE JUXTAPOSITION OF INDIVIDUAL GENRE UNITS

The overall pattern of arrangement seems clear. But what are the precise means by which each genre unit is placed in its particular context? We have considered merely a mechanical catchword pattern inadequate. At the same time we have not deemed progression in thought a fully satisfactory model. Nor do we find evidence that a traditional formal pattern widely used in Israel, such as Hessler's trial proceedings, explains the arrangement of units. We have also been unable to reconstruct the history of the growth of the collection; thus we cannot explain the arrangement in terms of the developing needs of the community, which, stage by stage, produced Isaiah 40—55.

As an alternative to these approaches I suggest a basic working hypothesis: that we assume that there might be an analogy to the

---

[56] Note the influence of hymn style in v. 12b.
[57] Both 40, 6—8 and 55, 10—11 function to some extent for disputational purposes.

artistic use of language *inside* the genre unit and the way in which units are related to their context. In the individual genre unit language is not used discursively. We cannot speak primarily of development of "thought." In poetry, meaning is conveyed by images, word-plays, repetition of sound, and the like. The form of the poem, too, contributes significantly to its meaning. Indeed, the progression within a unit is to be seen, as Muilenburg teaches us,[58] by observing the rhetorical features of the text, e. g., repetition of words, phrases and images, development of theme, contrasting words and images, change in tone. I differ with Muilenburg primarily in that I think the basic unit is the genre rather than the strophe. The following chapters, when compared with Muilenburg's commentary, should illustrate the differences between using "rhetorical criticism"[59] with the genre unit as the starting point for analysis of the arrangement of Isaiah 40—55 and the use of similar methodology with the strophe as the basic unit.

Isaiah 41, 1—7 is a good illustration of the use of the method within a genre unit. The form of the speech conveys immediately a partial understanding of the meaning of the unit. The poet gives us a mental picture of a summons to trial: "Listen to me ... let them approach, let them speak, let us all draw near *(niqrabā)* for judgment." The mocking tone of the summons to trial undergoes development in the description of the nations' coming to trial (v. 5—7). The repetition of *qrb* (v. 1.5) is one of the means by which progression in the poem takes places; a broader mode of development is the repetition of other language about assembling for trial (v. 1.5).

Likewise in Isaiah 46, 1—4 repetition of words and images is the means by which the poem progresses. The roots *nš'* (v. 1.3.4), *'ms* (v. 1.3), and *mlṭ* (v. 2.4) are repeated to show the contrast between the gods who must be carried and Yahweh who carries and delivers. The mental picture of impotent gods who must be delivered by beasts and are themselves a burden contrasts sharply with Yahweh who bears the burden and delivers.

Similar phenomena serve as vehicles for associating genre units. E. M. Good has suggested that units in Hosea were arranged by:

> 1) Verbal association, i. e., congruences in terminology between two poems which could be the means by which the second poem would be called to mind by the recitation of the first; 2) image association, i. e., congruence of metaphors, similes, and other figurative terms between two poems serving the same func-

---

[58] J. Muilenburg, The Interpreter's Bible, V 1956, 389, and Form Criticism and Beyond, JBL 88 (1969), 1—18.

[59] This is a term which through Muilenburg's prestige is being introduced into biblical criticism.

tion; 3) thematic association, i. e., congruences of subject matter between two poems; 4) aural association, i. e., conjunctions of sounds between two poems, consistency of various kinds of paronomasia, similar sounding words, similar assonances, etc.[60]

I see patterns of this kind in the arrangement of units in Deutero-Isaiah. In the juxtaposition of Isaiah 43, 22—28 (a trial speech) and 44, 1—5 (a salvation-assurance oracle), for instance, Westermann sees a connection between units in the phrase, "but now" (44, 1).[61] I shall argue in Chapter Seven that the images of extinction of ancestors (43, 27—28) and promise of posterity (44, 3—5) are rhetorical features which the arranger uses to serve his kerygmatic purposes. Or, to use another example, I shall contend that the juxtaposition of Isaiah 42, 14—17 (a salvation oracle), 42, 18—25 (a disputation speech), and 43, 1—7 (an assurance of salvation) uses various rhetorical devices to lend a significance to the whole richer than the meaning of each individual unit. The repetition of the image of Israel's being burned — once as an image of punishment (42, 25) and once as an image of affliction in the face of which Yahweh will graciously protect (43, 2) — is a means of juxtaposing units in order to express a particular theology concerning the relationship between past and future.[62] Moreover, as we shall see, the image of "walking in the way" (42, 16.24, implied in 43, 2) and the terms *lo' yada'û/šam<sup>e</sup>'û* (42, 16.25), *'iwwer* and *ḥereš* (42, 16.18.19) are repeated in order to show the collection's theology of the relationship between past and future.

I find distinct advantages in this method. It does not necessitate hypothetical reconstructions of the history of redaction or of a formal archetype which the arranger imitated. The method relies instead on discovering patterns which are actually in the text. Moreover, the method assumes the likelihood that the arranger,[63] sharing something of the spirit of the poet, understood that he was dealing with the language of poetry and arranged his material in artistic fashion also.

---

[60] E. M. Good, The Composition of Hosea, SEA 31 (1966), 224.
[61] Westermann, Sprache und Struktur, 142—143, and Das Buch Jesaja, 109.
[62] See my discussion of this text in Chapter Seven.
[63] Or arrangers.

## Chapter Seven: Isaiah 40, 12—44, 23

The larger patterns in the first major block of the Deutero-Isaianic corpus we have already seen:[1] the people addressed as "Jacob-Israel," the "way" in the desert, the revelation of Yahweh's glory, the trustworthiness of Yahweh's creative word. Within chapters 40—48 we find smaller sections: an introductory group of disputations (40, 12—31),[2] and three sections, each of which concludes with a brief hymn (41, 1— 42, 13; 42, 14—44, 23; 44, 24—48, 21).[3] We turn now to inquire precisely how the individual units were arranged.

### I. ISAIAH 40, 12—31

1. *Form Critical Analysis.* As we saw,[4] Isaiah 40, 12—31 is composed of four genre units (v. 12—17.18—24.25—26.27—31). Each stands apart from its context by form. But what should we conclude about the process of composition? Have we a collection of originally separate units?[5] Or is it an originally unified poem each of whose parts displays a certain type of disputation speech?[6]

2. *Arrangement of Genre Units.* I have written elsewhere on this passage, so that I shall largely repeat the arguments made there.[7] We discovered[8] that only v. 12—17, a Wisdom genre, can be identified as a conventional genre with usage in tradition prior to Deutero-Isaiah. All the others were given their form through Deutero-Isaiah's creativity.

---

[1] Cf. above, Chapter Six.

[2] See my discussion below.

[3] See my analysis below for a more accurate form critical analysis of the "hymn" in 48, 20—21 (Chapter Eight, I, E, 1, e).

[4] Cf. above, Chapter Three, II, 1. 2. 3.

[5] L. Köhler, Deuterojesaja stilkritisch untersucht, 1923, 111; K. Elliger, Deuterojesaja in seinem Verhältnis zu Tritojesaja, 1933, 225 ff.; J. Begrich, Studien zu Deuterojesaja, 1963, 49; H. E. von Waldow, Anlaß und Hintergrund der Verkündigung des Deuterojesaja, 1953, 36.

[6] This is not precisely the position of Westermann, but his arguments for the unity of v. 12—31 have led me to consider this possibility. Cf. Westermann, Sprache und Struktur der Prophetie Deuterojesajas, in Forschung am alten Testament, 1964, 127—132.

[7] R. F. Melugin, Deutero-Isaiah and Form Criticism, VT 21 (1971), 326—337.

[8] See my analysis above in Chapter Three, II, 1. 2. 3. and in Deutero-Isaiah and Form Criticism, 330—335.

Even so, v. 18—24 and v. 25—26 are stereotyped much like a conventional *Gattung*. It appears that Deutero-Isaiah originated a new form of disputation which has life apart from its particular context.[9]

Nevertheless, it is clear that the arrangement is not without significance. All four units share a common theme; the entire passage is a series of arguments for faith in Yahweh. Moreover, an interrogative style persists throughout, particularly with questions introduced by *mî* (v. 12.13.14.18.25).[10] Despite this, we find signs indicating that Isaiah 40, 12—31 is a collection. Each section is distinctive both in form and content; thus each has a kind of internal unity. In v. 12—17 the disputation argues that no one can compare with Yahweh's size and his wisdom as creator; hence the nations are nothing. In v. 18—24 the subject is not the nations but rather the gods. The tone is different as well. One is led to laugh at the gods who are made by men and subject to being moved when one contrasts them with Yahweh who creates and disposes the men whom he has made. V. 25—26, though similar in form to v. 18—24, are quite different in subject matter and tone. The sarcasm of v. 18—24 has disappeared. Instead we find a quite straightforward argument. "Lift your eyes above and see who created these . . ." V. 27—31, too, can stand alone as a disputation on the complaint, "My way is hid from Yahweh . . ."

The recognition that each section of this passage is distinct in form and content is not by itself sufficient to make the case that they were originally separate utterances; one could just as easily argue that this reflects the artistry of the poet. But when one adds to this certain other factors, evidence for a collection builds. It is quite noticeable that changes in speaker correspond to shifts from one genre unit to another. In v. 18—24 the prophet is the speaker, while Yahweh is the speaker in v. 25—26. The prophet again speaks in v. 27—31. The most plausible explanation for the change in speaker is that a collector has placed originally separate utterances side by side. Moreover, the sudden shift to singular address in v. 27—31 at the beginning of a new formal unit is more likely the sign of a collection than an originally unified poem. Two additional factors suggest that Isaiah 40, 12—31 is a collection of separate utterances: (1) The Wisdom genre in v. 12—17 stands out as quite different from the rest of the passage. (2) Progression in thought does not seem to occur in v. 12—31. Admittedly, one theme embraces the whole. But the argument progresses only within each disputation; thus each appears to be a self-contained argument.

---

[9] Cf. above, Chapter Three, II, 2. 3.
[10] J. Muilenburg, Interpreter's Bible, V 1956, 434; Westermann, Sprache und Struktur, 127—132.

Isaiah 40, 12—31, then, is a mosaic arranged by a collector. But it is obvious that he arranged the units quite carefully. First of all we find verbal repetition: questions introduced by *mî* (v. 12.13.14.18.25), *h⁽ᵃ⁾lổ ted⁽ᵉ⁾û/yadā̔ta* (v. 21.28), *br̉* (v. 26.28), and *byn* (v. 14.21). But the verbal repetition is but one of the means by which units have been associated. The juxtaposition of disputations in Isaiah 40, 12—31 parallels the arrangement of speeches in chapters 41—44. In these chapters one sometimes finds trial speeches between Yahweh and the nations or their gods placed immediately before speeches of salvation (41, 1—7.8 ff.; 43, 8—13.14 ff.). As far as we know, this kind of juxtaposition has no setting outside Deutero-Isaiah. Why, then, did the collector choose this arrangement? The doubt about Yahweh's power occasioned by the exile provides the key. Traditionally the lament psalm and its answering assurance of salvation were not concerned with Yahweh's *ability* to deliver.[11] The lament psalms and the answering oracles assume that Yahweh *can* save; the issue is whether he *will*. But the exile had raised doubts about Yahweh's power, against which Deutero-Isaiah directed his disputation and trial speeches. In chapters 41—44 the argument that Yahweh *can* save sometimes is followed by the traditional assurance that he *will* save.[12] Isaiah 40, 12—31 displays a similar structure: v. 12—26 contend that Yahweh is able to deliver; v. 27—31, based on the "expression of confidence" of the lament psalm, emphasize his willingness to save.[13] Thus Isaiah 40, 12—31, a collection of speeches once existing separately, is molded into an introduction for the opening chapters of the collection. Just as in the lament psalm the "expression of confidence" normally preceded the oracle of salvation, so also in Isaiah 40—55 we find a similar pattern; 40, 12—31, based partly on the "expression of confidence,"[14] precedes the section of the collection which is dominated by the salvation-assurance oracle.

V. 27—31 set the stage for what is to follow in the collection. These verses attempt to persuade Israel that her way is not hidden from Yahweh, nor has he overlooked her *mišpaṭ* (v. 27). The collection proclaims that Israel's "way" is not "hidden;" Yahweh will lead them in the "way" (42, 16). Though Israel is "hidden" in prisons (42, 22),[15]

---

[11] Even lament psalms which appear to reflect the direst of need (e. g., Ps 74) show no doubt of Yahweh's ability to save.

[12] Cf. Isa 41, 1—7 and v. 8 ff.; also 43, 8—13 and v. 14 ff. Isa 41, 1—7; for example, argues that Yahweh *can* save, while the assurance of salvation in v. 8 ff. gives the traditional cultic assurance that he *will* deliver.

[13] Westermann, Sprache und Struktur, 128 ff.

[14] V. 27—31. Cf. the discussion of the basic structure in Chapter Three, II, 3.

[15] Different terms are used in 40, 27 and 42, 22, but essentially the same meaning is expressed.

her way is not ultimately concealed from Yahweh. Quite the contrary; it is Yahweh who has hidden Israel "until now" (49, 2.5—6). Indeed, 49, 1—6, at the end of the Jacob-Israel segment of the collection, recapitulates what 40, 27—31 at the beginning says about Israel's *mišpaṭ* and concerning those who are weary and without strength. In 49, 1—6 Israel no longer needs persuasion; the servant Israel overcomes the lament that he is "weary" and has spent his "strength" for nought by the affirmation that his *mišpaṭ* is with Yahweh. Thus 40, 27—31 and 49, 1—6 begin and end a section. What goes between (chapters 41—48) builds upon 40, 27—31 and leads to 49, 1—6.

## II. ISAIAH 41, 1—42, 13

This segment of the collection, which ends with a hymn (42, 10—13), is made up of two trial speeches (41, 1—7; 41, 21—29), each of which is followed by genre units which concern themselves with Yahweh's servant (41, 8 ff.; 42, 1 ff.). We address ourselves now to the precise arrangement of units.

### A. 41, 1—7.8—13.14—16.17—20

1. *Form Critical Analysis.* The trial speech in v. 1—7 has the basic elements typical of Deutero-Isaiah's trial speeches between the nations or their gods, yet the structure of this particular text is somewhat unique.[16] Only here in Deutero-Isaiah's trial speeches have we anything like v. 5—7. Yet these three verses are integral to the structure and intention of the poem.[17] The mental picture of the nations' "drawing near" fits perfectly with the summons to trial in v. 1. There the nations are called to "draw near for judgment" and to "renew strength." A derisive tone is implied in v. 1;[18] we suspect as the summons is uttered that the nations cannot "renew strength." V. 5—7 carry the mockery a step farther, in part through repetition of the verb *qārăb* (v. 1.5). The nations "draw near and come," not in strength, but in fear and trembling, desperately encouraging each other as in futility they manufacture gods who cannot hold firm unless they are made secure by hapless men.

---

[16] Cf. the discussion above in Chapter Four, II.

[17] The transfer of v. 6—7 behind 40, 19 is arbitrary, as well as the assumption that v. 5 is secondary. Moreover, it is unlikely that we should repoint the verbs as imperatives and jussives. Cf. e. g., B. Duhm, Das Buch Jesaia übersetzt und erklärt, 1922, 303; Begrich, Studien, 36, 53.

[18] For a comprehensive study of the mockery of the gods in ancient Israel, see H. D. Preuss, Verspottung fremder Religionen im Alten Testament, 1971, especially 192 ff.

Like others of Deutero-Isaiah's trial speeches, the intention is to
persuade doubters that Yahweh is responsible for Cyrus' victories.[19]
V. 1—7 share, too, with the other trial speeches an intent to deride the
gods. Yet the structure and language of 41, 1—7 give to that intent a
special coloration: The nations and their gods are not merely impotent
before Yahweh's creative word; they are fearful, helping each other in
sheer desperation. They say of their hopeless craftsmanship, "Be strong"
(v. 6) or, "it is good" (v. 7), while *Yahweh's* words "summon the
generations." How appropriate that the summons should begin, "Be
silent before me, O coastlands!" They might as well be silent, for their
words, compared to Yahweh's speeches, are but the chatter of frightened
men.

V. 8—13 and v. 14—16 both exhibit the typical structure of the
salvation-assurance oracle.[20] But each has particular features as well.[21]
V. 8—13 begin with an emphatic $w^e$'$att\bar{a}$[22] and a greatly expanded
direct address.[23] At the end (v. 13) we find a substantiation which
recapitulates in a degree unknown to other examples of this genre the
general expressions of the assurance of salvation.[24] The emphatic
$w^e$'$att\bar{a}$ seems to have the particular intention of connecting the text with
with something which precedes. Though it seems to be original to the
genre,[25] in its present context in Isaiah 41 it appears to play a role in
connecting units. The emphatic pronoun addresses Israel as if she were
to be singled out, perhaps in contrast with someone else. Furthermore,
the text goes out of its way to emphasize that Israel is "chosen" (v. 8.9)
and "strengthened" (v. 9.13). Finally, this text more than most examples
of the genre emphasizes the exhortation, "Fear not;" it appears both
at the beginning and the end of the genre unit (v. 10.13).

V. 14—16 appear to be a new genre unit.[26] Israel is addressed in
second feminine singular (v. 14—15a); the subject matter of v. 14—16
differs substantially from v. 8—13 as well. Moreover, the form of

---

[19] 41, 21—29; 48, 12—15.

[20] Cf. above, Chapter Two, I.

[21] For a study of the poetic structure and style of v. 8—13, see L. Boadt, Isaiah
41, 8—13: Notes on Poetic Structure and Style, CBQ 35 (1973) 20—34.

[22] Muilenburg, Interpreter's Bible, V 453.

[23] E. Hessler, Gott der Schöpfer: Ein Beitrag zur Komposition und Theologie
Deuterojesajas, 1961, 37—38.

[24] In other examples of this genre the general verbs in the perfect tense and the
associated nominal clauses occur near the beginning of the unit, prior to the more
concrete announcement of the future in the imperfect (cf. Isa 41, 14—16; 44, 1—5
Jer 46, 28; this is true also of 43, 1—7).

[25] Cf. Jer 30, 10; 46, 27.28.

[26] Cf. e. g., Begrich, Studien, 13.

v. 14—16 has all the elements necessary for a complete unit.[27] In addition to this, v. 14—16 has certain peculiarities which contribute to our sense of its independence from its context. The entire oracle revolves around the assurance that Yahweh has turned to help the lowly "worm" Jacob; the impotent worm will become a mighty threshing sledge. The major intention of this oracle is indeed related to the contrast between the present powerlessness of Israel with the mighty nation of the future. A complete reversal of present conditions will take place; the oppressing nations will become chaff,[28] while the downtrodden Israel will become a potent instrument of destruction.

V. 17—20 reflect the form of a cultic genre apparently used as an answer to communal laments.[29] The particular setting in which Deutero-Isaiah used it cannot be clearly identified.[30] Nevertheless, we have no difficulty distinguishing it from its context both by form and content. The entire oracle, in contrast with the preceding oracles, is in third person plural. It begins with a reference to the complaint that Yahweh has not answered his thirsty poor and needy (v. 17a). The announcement of the future which follows is dominated by the image of an oasis created in the desert. The purpose of Yahweh in answering the needy, says this oracle, is that "they" may know that it is Yahweh who has done this (v. 20). In no way does this oracle need those which precede to be understood.

2. *Arrangement of Genre Units.* a. Although each of the four genre units (v. 1—7.8—13.14—16.17—20) is capable of standing alone both by content and form, it is apparent immediately that they are connected by verbal repetition: e. g., $q^e d\hat{o}\check{s}$ $yi\acute{s}ra'el$ (v. 14.20), *'al tîra' (î)* (v. 10.13. 14), *'zr* (v. 6.10.13.14), *ḥzq* (v. 6.7.9) and *bqš* (v. 12.17).[31] The units are joined in other ways as well: We see here the kind of juxtaposition of trial speeches and speeches of salvation found elsewhere in chapters 41—44.[32] Moreover, the theme of Yahweh as creator binds the units together. At the beginning the trial speech argues for Yahweh's power to save on the basis of his ability as creator (v. 4); his work as creator is the theme of the final unit as well (v. 17—20).

---

[27] "Fear not" plus direct address (v. 14a), the substantiation in perfect tense and participle (v. 14b), announcement of the future mostly in the imperfect (v. 15—16a), and the purpose of Yahweh's intervention (v. 16b).

[28] Cf. Isa 40, 23—24.

[29] Cf. the discussion above, Chapter Two, II, 1.

[30] It is questionable whether the oracle was actually uttered in the cult.

[31] Mowinckel mentions some but not all of these connections, Die Komposition des deuterojesajanischen Buches, ZAW 49 (1931), 91.

[32] Cf. above on the arrangement of 40, 12—31.

If we look more carefully at the structure of units, we find an intricate pattern of arrangement. The ties between the trial speech (v. 1—7) and the first salvation-assurance oracle are particularly close. The way in which the nations receive help in the trial contrasts sharply with the manner in which Israel receives help from Yahweh. The contrast is made in large part through the repetition of the verbs *ḥazăq* (v. 6.7.9.13) and *'azăr* (v. 6.10.13). A word play on *qara'* is apparent as well (v. 4.9): By juxtaposition Yahweh's power to "call the generations" (v. 4) is connected with his having called Israel (v. 9). A further relationship between v. 1—7 and v. 8—13 is expressed by the repetition of *yr'*. The nations' frantic fear (v. 5) is in dramatic opposition to the admonition to Israel, "Fear not" (v. 10.13). Finally, the phrase *'anšê rîbæka* (v. 11) reminds us of the nations in v. 1—7 who appear in the trial against Yahweh (and, by implication, his people).

We may add to these verbal associations the relationship achieved by the particular structure of v. 1—7 and v. 8—13. Though these two units exhibit respectively the stereotyped features of the Deutero-Isaianic trial speech and the cultic salvation-assurance oracle, each unit is somewhat unique in structure as well. We saw above that the description in v. 5—7 is unique to the trial speeches; likewise the unusually expanded introduction to v. 8—13 is not found in other salvation-assurance oracles. These two structural modifications contribute to the unity between v. 1—7 and v. 8—13. These modifications contrast the nations' frantic "strengthening" one another's courage on the one hand through the manufacture of idols and "strengthening" them with nails and, on the other, Israel's being "strengthened" by Yahweh. Even the close of v. 8—13 contributes to the unity of v. 1—7 and v. 8—13. No other salvation-assurance oracle ends with such an emphatic re-affirmation of the major theme of the oracle as does this one (v. 13). Thus the close of v. 8—13 emphasizes that *Israel* is not to fear; in contrast with the nations in the trial[33] Israel is strengthened and helped by Yahweh.

V. 14—16 relate more loosely to the context than we saw in the relationship of v. 1—7 and v. 8—13 to each other. Nevertheless, the placement of v. 14—16 is not accidental. In addition to the verbal repetitions mentioned above,[34] v. 14—16 and v. 8—13 are related thematically. In v. 8—13 those who do battle against Israel will be nothing (v. 12); v. 14—16 portray Israel as an instrument of battle. Thus the images which portray the demise (v. 11) and scattering (v. 15—16) of Israel's enemies are a means of associating the two genre

---

[33] Note the transition (*we'ăttā* — v. 8).

[34] *'ăl tîra' (î)* (v. 10.13.14); *'zr* (v. 13.14); *qedôš yiśra'el* (v. 14.20).

units.[35] Finally, v. 8—13 and v. 14—16 are held together by common stylistic features. In both, the announcement of salvation is introduced by *hen* or *hinnē*.[36] In both, *weʿāttā* makes a contrast between Israel and the nations (v. 8.16).

V. 17—20, too, are part of the pattern beginning in v. 1 ff. We find not only the verbal associations discussed above but also a stylistic parallel; the self-predication of Yahweh in v. 4 is similar to v. 17b. Moreover, the parallel between v. 16 b and v. 20 reflects a two-fold emphasis of the collection: Yahweh delivers so that both Israel and the nations may know and worship him.[37] Most important of all, v. 17—20 recapitulate the creation theme of v. 1—7. Thus the "enlarged poem" (41, 1—20) begins and ends with the portrayal of Yahweh's saving deeds in acts of creation.

It is probable that the association of these four genre units is the product of a collection of originally separate poems. V. 14—16 and v. 17—20 are not so tightly bound to the context that they could not easily at one time have existed apart from each other. V. 1—7 and v. 8—13, however, are so closely intertwined that one can imagine that they might originally have belonged together, or at least that they were reworked to relate more closely.

b. Isaiah 41, 1—20 relates to the foregoing context in several ways. We find repetition of words and phrases: *qeṣôt haʾaræṣ* (40, 28; 41, 9), *mišpat* (40, 27; 41, 1), *ʾiyyîm* (40, 15; 41, 1), *keʿāyin nægdô keʿāyin ukeʿ ʾæpæs* (40, 17; 41, 12). The repetition of *yaḥᵃlîpû koᵃḥ* (40, 31; 41, 1) is used ironically as a transition between 40, 12—31 and 41, 1 ff. 40, 27—31 proclaims that "those who hope in Yahweh will renew strength." In 41, 1 the phrase is used in the summons to trial. Read without the foregoing context, this phrase in 41, 1 is straightforward enough, but in the context of 40, 27—31 the summons is ironic. We know in advance that this potentially hopeful word to the nations will come to nought. They will be unable to renew their strength.

Legal images and terms abound in 40, 12—31 and 41, 1—20: the term *rîb* (41, 11), the term *mišpat*, the trial speech form (41, 1—7). The collector[38] uses these terms and images to express his own message:

---

[35] It may also be the case, as Westermann suggests, that the "double-wish" of the lament psalm is a factor in the association of v. 8—13.14—16 — that is, the wish for the supplicant's deliverance and the wish for calamity upon his foes. Westermann, Das Buch Jesaja: Kapitel 40—66, 1966, 63.

[36] Muilenburg, too, recognizes the significance of this particle in the arrangement of the text. Cf. Interpreter's Bible, V 447.

[37] Isa 40, 5; 45, 3.6.22.23; 49, 23.26; 52, 10.

[38] We use the singular term "collector" for convenience. It was admitted toward the end of Chapter Six that there were probably several stages in the compilation of the collection. Since we can deal only with the final stage, we shall indulge ourselves in the simplification, "collector."

Israel's complaint that Yahweh has ignored her legal rights (40, 27) is ultimately unjustified; Yahweh helps her in the trial against her adversaries (41, 11); indeed, the nations have no case to make (41, 1—7).

### B. 41, 21—29; 42, 1—4.5—9.10—13

1. *Form Critical Analysis.* The trial speech in Isaiah 41, 21—29 exhibits the features typical of Deutero-Isaiah's trial speeches between the nations or their gods:[39] summons to trial (v. 21), challenge to the opposing party to demonstrate its claim (v. 22—23), and the argument in the style of questions introduced by *mî* (v. 26 ff.). This typical pattern is manipulated by the poet, however, into a two-fold structure which is unique to this pericope: (1) The trial begins with a mocking challenge to the gods (v. 21—23). Then follows the assertion, "Behold *(hen)*, you are nothing, and your deeds are naught" (v. 24).[40] (2) In the second part of the poem Yahweh argues his own case, first by the assertion that he is responsible for Cyrus' victories (v. 25) and then by asking which god "announced it from the beginning" (v. 26a). After contending that he alone has done that (v. 26 b—28)[41] Yahweh concludes his argument with a statement parallel to v. 24 in form and content (v. 29). The structure is unique in that the movement of the trial aims toward the two statements introduced by *hen* (v. 24.29). This is not accidental, for the intent of this unit it to persuade hearers that the gods are nothing.

The form of 42, 1—4 and 42, 5—9 has already been discussed.[42] V. 1—4 announce to others that Yahweh has established his servant in a particular role. Whether the genre is royal or prophetic we cannot be certain.[43] Indeed, it is probable that the language is deliberately ambiguous, as is characteristic of Deutero-Isaiah from the very beginning.[44] Similarly the commissioning oracle directed to the servant (v. 5—9) does not permit precise identification. We must content ourselves with the recognition that the style used in commissioning oracles for various kinds of officials has been imitated here.

V. 10—13 exhibit the form of an "eschatological hymn."[45] There is a call to praise in imperative style, expanded by jussives (v. 11—12).

---

[39] Cf. above, Chapter Four, II.

[40] Read *me'apæs*.

[41] V. 27a should be emended to read, "at the beginning I declared it to Zion," as parallelism suggests.

[42] Cf. above, Chapter Five, I.

[43] See my discussion in Chapter Five.

[44] The identity of the "I" in Isa 40, 6—8 is impossible to determine without ambiguity. Cf. above, Chapter Six, II, A.

[45] Cf. Westermann, Sprache und Struktur, 157 ff.

The substantiation of the summons to praise, most often in the perfect,[46] appears here in the imperfect (v. 13). The hymn is eschatological in the sense that hearers are summoned to praise Yahweh for deeds which he is to perform in the future.

2. *Arrangement of Genre Units*. a. Each of the units is capable of standing alone, both by form and content, but careful study shows that the pattern of arrangement is by no means haphazard. First of all, the juxtaposition of 42, 1—4 and 42, 5—9 is significant. In both the servant is chosen for his task. At the same time, each unit portrays his mission differently. In v. 1—4 the servant's basic task is to bring justice to the nations. V. 2—4 depict that task with a number of images. The servant "will not cry out, will not lift up or make heard in the streets his voice." *Ṣaʿăq* usually means "to cry in distress," often a lament.[47] Given Deutero-Isaiah's proclivity for the language of the psalms, *lo' yiṣʿăq* surely means that the servant will not utter lamentation. *Yiśśaʾ . . . qôl*, here in parallelism, undoubtedly means the same.[48] V. 3—4 are a word play on *rṣṣ* and *khh*. The servant who will neither "break a crushed reed nor quench a dimly-burning wick" will not "burn dim" or "crush out."[49] The precise significance of v. 3a is difficult to ascertain. Most often it has been seen as the servant's non-violent approach,[50] but little or no evidence has been cited in support of the contention. In my judgment these images should be studied from their usage in tradition, particularly the Isaianic tradition. In the Isaianic tradition *qānæ* is closely associated with Egypt (Isa 19, 6; 36, 6 = II Kings 18, 21). The image "crushed reed" seems clearly to have been associated with Egypt (Isa 36, 6).[51] The image of the quenched wick (flax) appears also to be associated with Egypt (Isa 43, 17).[52] In both Isaiah 36 and Ezekiel 29[53] the reed which crushes and breaks is a symbol of Egypt's inability to provide security; when Israel leans upon the reed it breaks. Thus Isaiah 42, 3a is in my judgment drawn from traditional language about security: the servant will not rely on a crushed reed and thus break it; nor will he depend upon and thus extinguish a dimly-burning wick.

---

[46] Isa 44, 23; 48, 20; 49, 13; 52, 9—10.

[47] Ex 8, 8; 14, 10.15; 15, 25; 22, 22.26   Num 12, 13; 20, 16   Dt 26, 7   Jos 24, 7   Judg 4, 3; 10, 12   Isa 19, 20; 46, 7   Ps 77,2; 88, 2. Cf. O. Kaiser, Der königliche Knecht, 1962, 26. 27.

[48] Cf. Gen 21, 16   Num 14, 1   Judg 2, 4. But cf. also, e. g., Isa 24, 14 or 52, 8, where the phrase refers to a cry of joy.

[49] Cf. Qoh 12, 6. Or perhaps the verb should be read as niph.

[50] See the commentaries.

[51] Cf. also Ezek 29, 6.

[52] See also the association of both flax and reed with Egypt in Isa 19, 6.9. Cf. also Ex 9, 31.

[53] Isa 36, 6   Ezek 29, 6.

Isaiah 42, 1—4, then, is an announcement of the servant's faithfulness. He will not cry out in lamentation, nor will he put his reliance upon the reed which breaks or quench the flickering wick. He will let nothing stand in his way "until he puts justice in the earth, and the coastlands await his *tôrā*."

V. 5—9 complement v. 1—4. As in v. 1—4, the servant has a mission to the nations; he is a *bᵉrît ʿam*, a "light to the nations," one who opens blind eyes and releases from prison.[54] Nevertheless, the intention of v. 5—9 is somewhat different. In v. 1—4 the emphasis is on the servant's faithfulness. He will be unlike the Israel without hope in 40, 27. In v. 5—9 the focus is rather on *persuading* the community (v. 8—9). Although the unit begins with commissioning language (v. 5—7), the central purpose is not to announce to the servant his commission. Indeed, the commissioning of the servant does not exhibit a well-defined genre and *Sitz im Leben*;[55] the commissioning language instead serves a larger disputational purpose as the prophet addresses the community (v. 8—9)[56] with the typical argument about the "former things" and the "new things."[57] V. 5—9 differ from v. 1—4, too, in emphasizing Yahweh's motivation in sending the servant to the nations: "My glory to another I will not give." The juxtaposition of these two genre units enriches the understanding of the purpose of the servant's commissioning; the juxtaposition brings together the respective emphases of each unit concerning the servant's mission.

The trial speech in 41, 21—29, too, contributes to the larger unity of 41, 21—42, 13. The use of *hen* (41, 24.29; 42, 1) gives a sense of stylistic unity.[58] Moreover, the juxtaposition of 41, 21—29 and the two "servant songs" gives us a contrast between the gods on the one hand (41, 21—29) and Yahweh and his purposes for the servant on the other (42, 1—4.5—9). 41, 21—29 and 42, 1—9 share the contention that Yahweh alone can declare the future and make it come to pass (41, 26—28; 42, 9). Only Yahweh can "declare" and "make heard" the events of history (41, 26; 42, 9). The gods are *rûᵃḥ watohû* (41, 29), while the servant is endowed with Yahweh's *rûᵃḥ* (42, 1). The gods are "chosen" by men (41, 24), whereas Yahweh chooses the servant (42, 1).[59] The legal sphere of life, connoted by the term *mišpaṭ* (42, 1.3.4), binds

---

[54] Parallelism suggests that *bᵉrît ʿam* refers to the nations. But cf. Kaiser, Knecht, 34 ff. Kaiser's arguments rest too much, however, on evidence external to this passage.
[55] Cf. above, Chapter Five, I.
[56] Note the plural *ʾetkæm* (v. 9). Cf. Kaiser, Knecht, 39.
[57] Cf. Isa 41, 22.23; 48, 1—11.
[58] Muilenburg, Interpreter's Bible, V 447—464.
[59] Cf. also v. 6.

42, 1 ff. with 41, 21—29: in the legal proceedings between Yahweh and the gods, the nations can take no comfort; their gods are impotent. Instead, it is Yahweh's *mišpaṭ* that will prevail, and it will come to the nations through his servant.

The hymn in v. 10—13 is bound to the preceding verses by verbal repetition. But these are more than mechanical devices. In the present arrangement of the text Israel is summoned in familiar hymn style to sing a "new song" (v. 10) to Yahweh, who proclaims the "new things" (v. 9). They are exhorted to sing "praise" to the ends of the earth (v. 10) to the God who will not give his "praise" to idols (v. 8). They are to "glorify" Yahweh (v. 12), who will not give his "glory" to another (v. 8). They are to "declare" the praise of Yahweh (v. 12), the God who "declares" the future (41, 26; 42, 9).[60] The kerygmatic significance of the juxtaposition is clear. The hymn responds to the foregoing context[61] by repeating the language of what precedes.

It is difficult to be certain whether Isaiah 41, 21—42, 13 is a long poetic composition or a collection of originally separate units, particularly since each genre unit[62] owes its form to Deutero-Isaiah rather than to long usage in Israel's oral tradition. Each unit can nevertheless stand alone; each can be distinguished by form, and each one has its own particular intent. Moreover, as we shall see, most of Isaiah 40—55 seems to have taken its arrangement by the process of collection. In all likelihood this is true also of 41, 21—42, 13.

b. A few remarks are needed now concerning the entire section begun by 41, 1 and ended by 42, 13. Most noticeable is the pattern of juxtaposing trial speeches with speeches concerning Yahweh's servant.[63] We find other connecting features as well: the whole section is dominated by language associated with the legal realm, i. e., trial forms of speech (41, 1—7.21—29), terms like *mišpaṭ* (41, 1; 42, 1.3.4) and *rîb* (41, 11. 21).[64] Also we find language associated with battle (41, 11—13.15—16; 42, 13), in particular the assertions concerning the victories of Cyrus (41, 2.25). Moreover, the repetition of the Hiph'il of *'ûr* is a unifying feature of 41, 1—42, 13; Yahweh, who "stirred up" Cyrus (41, 2.25), has "stirred up" his jealousy (42, 13).

The juxtaposition of the trial speeches (41, 1—7; 41, 21—29) with the speeches about Yahweh's servant (41, 8 ff.; 42, 1 ff.) reflects one of

---

[60] Hiph. of *ngd*.

[61] Westermann, Sprache und Struktur, 160 ff.

[62] With the exception of the hymn in v. 10—13.

[63] 41, 1—7 with 41, 8 ff.; 41, 21—29 with 42, 1 ff.

[64] Muilenburg rightly sees the strong influence of trial language here (Interpreter's Bible, V 447 ff.), but he errs in viewing everything, including the salvation oracles and "servant poems," as literary imitation of the trial process.

the basic theological tensions of the collection. The first cluster (41, 1—7.8—13.14—16.17—20) promises deliverance for the servant Israel and the defeat of the nations; in the second cluster (41, 21—29; 42, 1—4.5—9), the servant is commissioned with the task of bringing justice and *tôrā* to the nations. We cannot resolve the tension by taking refuge in arguments about the non-genuineness of the "servant songs." Whatever their origin, they are now to be judged from the perspective of their meaning in the collection. The collection makes no explicit distinction in the identity of the servant between 41, 8—13.14—16 and 42, 1—4.5—9; therefore, we must assume that the collector regards the servant in 42, 1—4.5—9 as Israel. Thus the tension between the two pictures of the servant must be understood as a paradox within the collection rather than a contradiction. The hymn at the close of this section of the collection (42, 10—13) reinforces the tension imposed by the collection: the picture of the servant with a mission to "save" the nations (42, 1—4.5—9) is counter-balanced by a hymn extolling Yahweh's victory in battle. The arrangement of genre units in 41, 1—42, 13 holds together the images of the servant Israel who through Yahweh defeats the nations in battle and the servant who brings light to the nations. As we shall see, this paradox appears again in the collection.

The larger unity 41, 1—42, 13 builds upon 40, 12—31. The language about the nations and the gods is quite similar (40, 17 and 41, 24.29; 40, 23—24 and 41, 15b—16a). The term *mišpaṭ* and the associated legal imagery in 41, 1—42, 13 respond to 40, 27—31. In 40, 27—31 Israel laments that Yahweh has "passed over" her *mišpaṭ*. This complaint is without foundation, says 41, 1—42, 13. When the nations are summoned for *mišpaṭ* (41, 1), they are found wanting; Israel will discover that the *'anšê rîbæka* are nowhere to be found (41, 11). And that is not all. The servant Israel is an *agent* of justice; through him justice will come to the nations. This section of the collection, then, answers the complaint in 40, 27, and its structure is twofold: a promise of justice for Israel and a promise of justice for the nations.

### III. ISAIAH 42, 14—44, 23

#### A. 42, 14—17.18—25; 43, 1—7

1. *Form Critical Analysis.* a. I argued above that Isaiah 42, 14—17 exhibits the form of a kind of salvation oracle genre used in the cult as an answer to the communal lament.[65] The structure of v. 14—17 is as follows: (1) reference to the complaint (v. 14a), (2) statement of Yah-

---

[65] Cf. above, Chapter Two, II, 1.

weh's intervention, expressed in the imperfect (v. 14b), and (3) elaboration on the statement of Yahweh's intervention (v. 15—16), concluding with the summary statement, "These are the things I will do to them..." Although Isaiah 42, 14—17 exemplifies a genre with stereotyped features,[66] the structure of v. 14—17 has unique as well as typical characteristics. Only here do we have Yahweh engaged in disputation; he argues against the complaint that he has been silent. Admittedly Yahweh was silent, so the argument goes, but the time of silence is past; Yahweh will now act (v. 14—15a). The summary statement (v. 16c—17), too, is unique to this example of the genre.

We cannot ascertain precisely the setting in which this oracle was originally spoken, but the unique structural features instruct us about the intention of the oracle. Deutero-Isaiah could not rest content with announcing the deliverance which Yahweh was planning to execute; the doubt occasioned by the exile led him to feel the necessity of persuading his hearers. Thus he argues that Yahweh's silence was only for a time.

The summary statement, too, reflects the particularity of the prophet's intention in his use of the genre. It appears to be a modification of the traditional summary-appraisal,[67] originally at home in Wisdom literature but passed along to Deutero-Isaiah by First Isaiah. In its original form it contains a demonstrative which introduces a summary statement which functions as a general appraisal, usually about what has just been said: i. e., "Such is the fate of all who forget God ..." (Job 8, 13),[68] or "This is the plan which is formed concerning the whole earth ..." (Isa 14, 26).[69] Deutero-Isaiah modifies the typical form, in which Yahweh was originally spoken *about*,[70] so that Yahweh is the speaker. In so doing, he transforms what was originally a summary observation into an integral part of the oracle. Indeed, it is no longer a summary statement but rather a point of transition from promise to announcement of doom. It is not quite certain who is included in the group to whom promise is directed and the group destined for doom, but we can see that Deutero-Isaiah clearly intends to distinguish between those whom Yahweh will deliver and those who trust in idols.

b. V. 18—25 begin a new genre unit, a disputation rather than an oracle. We have already discussed its form,[71] so that only the most

---

[66] Cf. Isa 41, 17—20 and Ps 12, 6 for examples of the genre.

[67] For a complete discussion of the form see B. S. Childs, Isaiah and the Assyrian Crisis, 1967, 128—136; J. W. Whedbee, Isaiah and Wisdom, 1971, 75—79.

[68] Cf. also Job 18, 21; 20, 29; 27, 13   Prov 1, 19   Ps 49, 14. Childs, Assyrian Crisis, 132. 133.

[69] Cf. also Isa 17, 14b; 28, 29.

[70] Cf. Job 8, 13; 18, 21; 20, 29; 27, 13   Isa 28, 29.

[71] Cf. above, Chapter Three, II, 7.

important conclusions will be stated here. The purpose of the disputation
is to convince Israel that their plight is a result of their sin. They, rather
than Yahweh, are blind and deaf; they have been unwilling to walk in
the way. The purpose of the disputation is not, however, primarily to
indict, but to provide the possibility of a new future: "Who among you
will give ear to this, will incline and hear for the future?" (v. 23). The
intention of the disputation is, then, redemptive. Yahweh offers the
hope that his activity in the future will not be, as in the past, punitive;
what he will do is contingent upon the behavior of the blind and deaf.

c. The form critical problems associated with 43, 1—7 have in the
history of research proved difficult indeed. Since Begrich, form critics
have generally believed that the form of the text has been decisively
influenced by the salvation-assurance oracle genre. The appearance of
'ăl tîra' and the substantiations kî gᵉʾāltîka (v. 1b) and 'ittᵉka 'ănî
(v. 2.5) demonstrates that.[72] But the overall structure of these verses has
produced significant disagreement. Begrich views v. 1—7 as one speech
in two parts (v. 1—3a.3b—7).[73] Von Waldow,[74] by rearranging the text,
arrives at another scheme consisting of two complete oracles (v. 1—3a.
5a.3b—7).[75] Westermann suggests that we have one speech in two parts
(v. 1—4.5—7).[76] In v. 1—4, following the exhortation, "Fear not," and
the nominal-clause and perfect-tense substantiations (v. 1b),[77] the concrete announcement of the future (Heilsankündigung) appears. In
v. 5—7, he argues, the same structure is evident.

None of these solutions is wholly satisfactory. The omissions and
rearrangements of the text by Begrich and von Waldow are arbitrary.
Westermann's assumption that we have two formally-complete oracles
in one unit of tradition is unsatisfactory because v. 3b—4 do not fit the
normal structure of the salvation-assurance oracle. Thus a fresh analysis
is needed.

V. 1—3a correspond to the structure found in other examples of
the genre: (1) "Fear not," followed by substantiating clauses containing
perfect-tense verbs with generalized meaning (v. 1b),[78] and (2) the
elaboration of Yahweh's intervention expressed by verbs in the imperfect (v. 2), followed by another substantiating clause (v. 3a).[79] The

---

[72] See my discussion of the form in Chapter Two, I.
[73] V. 5a is deleted as a variant. Begrich, Studien, 20.
[74] Von Waldow, Anlaß und Hintergrund, 15.
[75] V. 1—3a: v. 1a—1b (introduction and intervention); v. 1b (substantiation); v. 2 (elaboration); v. 5a.3b—7; v. 5a (introduction); v. 3b (intervention); v. 4a (sub-stantiation); v. 4b.5b—7 (elaboration).
[76] Das Buch Jesaja 95.
[77] I refer here to the assurance of salvation proper (Heilszusage).
[78] Member 1 follows the introduction in v. 1a.
[79] Cf. 41, 13 for another example of a substantiating clause at the end

elaboration of Yahweh's intervention is an announcement of Yahweh's protective presence while Israel passes through fire and water. In v. 3b—4 the language shifts radically to a promise that Egypt, Ethiopia, and Seba will serve as a ransom for Israel (v. 3b). This promise is accompanied by its own substantiating clause (v. 4). In none of the other examples of the salvation-assurance oracle do we have anything like v. 3b—4 at the end of the announcement of salvation. Moreover, a comparison of 43, 3a with 41, 13 suggests the possibility that 43, 3a marks the end of a formal unit.

It is better to think in terms of three parts rather than two. V. 1—3a, as we saw, display the form of the salvation-assurance oracle. The same is true of v. 5—7: "Fear not" and the substantiating clause expressing Yahweh's intervention appear in v. 5a, and the elaboration of that intervention may be seen in v. 5b—6. The purpose of Yahweh's intervention is found in v. 7. This leaves v. 3b—4 yet to be explained. By form, v. 3b is a statement of Yahweh's intervention and v. 4 is its substantiation. Even though v. 3b is in the perfect tense, the picture of the divine activity is more specific than we characteristically find in the verbs in the perfect tense which substantiate the exhortation, "Fear not." Furthermore, we have examples elsewhere which show that the perfect tense can sometimes be used in the *announcement of salvation*.[80] The structure of 43, 3b—4 is in fact quite similar to that of 43, 14—15. In both the *announcement of salvation* is expressed in the perfect;[81] both have a statement giving a reason for the announcement.[82] Thus there is some evidence that 43, 3b—4 is sufficiently stereotyped to have a degree of independence from its context.

The separation of v. 1—7 into three parts is reinforced by an examination of the content. In v. 1—3a Israel is promised that Yahweh will be with her during the ordeal of fire and water. This complex of images comes to an end, however, with the substantiation in v. 3a; v. 3b—4 use completely different images in the announcement that Egypt, Ethiopia, and Seba are given as a ransom in exchange for Israel's life. Again in v. 5 the imagery shifts; now we are told that Yahweh will gather Israel from the four directions.

Despite the fact that v. 1—7 can be isolated into three parts on the basis of both form and content, we must not assume that the text is not a unity. The way in which qara' b°šem, bara', and yaṣär are used in v. 1 and 7 shows that all seven verses must be taken together. Moreover, v. 1—3a and v. 5—6(7) are held together by formal similarities, such as

---

[80] Isa 41, 15; 51, 6.

[81] The perfect tense is augmented by *waw* plus the perfect in v. 14.

[82] V. 4 substantiates v. 3b. In v. 14—15 l°mä'ánkæm substantiates the following announcement of the future.

the repetition of *'ăl tîra'* and *'itt^eka 'anî*. In addition, v. 1—3a and
v. 3b—4 are linked by the common promise of redemption.[83] Finally,
the promise of the return home (v. 5—6) and the announcement of
Israel's deliverance through the ransom of Egypt, Ethiopia, and Seba
(v. 3b—4) were easily associated with one another; in Deutero-Isaiah
nations such as these play a role in connection with the return home.[84]

It is uncertain whether Isaiah 43, 1—7 is the work of a collector
or an originally unified poem. The overbalanced line in v. 7 suggests that
we have to do with a collector who tried to relate the end to the
beginning, but the evidence is not clear enough for certainty. In the
present form of the text, however, it may be read as a unified poem.

2. *Arrangement of Genre Units.* a. A rapid survey informs us that
a kind of progressive chain of repetition of words and images binds the
units to each other and to the foregoing context: *'iwwer*, usually in
plural form, first appears in 42, 5—9 (v. 7) and is repeated in 42,
14—17 (v. 16) and in 42, 18—25 (v. 18—19).[85] *'Ôr* is seen first in 42,
5—9 (v. 6) and reappears in 42, 14—17 (v. 16). *Kælæ'*, appearing initially in 42, 5—9 (v. 7), occurs again in 42, 18—25 (v. 22) and 43, 1—7
(v. 6).[86] *Tôrā* makes its first appearance in 42, 1—4 (v. 4), and is repeated in 42, 18—25 (v. 21.24). The image of a people who "do not know"
is a means of linking units (42, 16.25), as well as the image of "walking
in the way" (42, 16.24).

It is unlikely that this kind of repetition is accidental, but is the
pattern of arrangement of units the work of an author or a collector?
42, 14—17 and 42, 18—25, as we saw, are associated through the
repetition of *'iwwer* (v. 16.18.19), *lo' yadă'* (v. 16.25), and the image of
"walking in the way" (v. 16.24).[87] The two genre units use *'iwwer* in
quite different ways, however. In v. 14—17 only the blind are mentioned, while v. 18—25 speak of both blind and deaf. Moreover, in
v. 14—17, "blind" is not a pejorative term; Yahweh will save his un-
fortunate blind. In v. 18—25, however, being blind and deaf is equated
with disobedience. The use of *yadă'* in v. 14—17 and v. 18—25 is quite
different as well: Israel's "not knowing" in v. 16 refers merely to
Yahweh's deliverance of a people who "do not know" in the sense that
they are utterly dependent upon him; v. 14—17 do not appear to direct
a polemic against their not knowing. In v. 18—25, however, their "not
knowing" is a refusal to "put it on the heart" (v. 25). The image of
"walking in the way," too, is not used in the same way in both genre

---

[83] *Ge'ăltîka* (v. 1); *kåpr^eka* (v. 3b).
[84] Isa 45, 14—17; 49, 22—23. Cf. also 60, 1 ff.
[85] Cf. Mowinckel, Komposition, 96. 97.
[86] In 43, 6 it appears in the form of a verb.
[87] Cf. also *'aḥôr* in v. 17.23.

units. Nothing disparaging is intended in v. 14—17, but in v. 18—25 (v. 24) it is an image of disobedience. These differences suggest that v. 14—17 and v. 18—25 were not originally uttered together. The former is an oracle of salvation to comfort a needy people in the face of doubt and despair. The latter is polemical, an argument to persuade Israel that their sin rather than Yahweh's blindness is the cause of their plight and that they must hear this for the sake of the future. Finally, the fact that v. 14—17 and v. 18—25 are not consistent in having both genre units use the two terms "blind" and "deaf"[88] suggests that their juxtaposition is the work of a collector rather than an author.

The juxtaposition of the disputation 42, 18—25 and the salvation-assurance oracle(s) 43, 1—7 cannot be accounted for from traditional association in customary usage in Israel. The salvation oracle was used to answer the individual lament and was not customarily employed in connection with disputation speech. The most prominent linkage between these two units, then, is the image of fire and burning (42, 25; 43, 2). The way in which each unit uses this image suggests that we have to do with a collector. In 42, 18—25 only burning is mentioned, while both fire and water appear in 43, 1—7. In the former, moreover, the burning is a result of Yahweh's wrath and appears in connection with battle imagery. In addition, the burning is seen as a destroyer of Israel. In 43, 1 ff., by contrast, both fire and water are mentioned with no indication that they are punishment for Israel's disobedience. Indeed, 43, 2 indicates — in opposition to 42, 25 — that Israel will not be burned. Another discontinuity between the two passages is in theme. Everything in 43, 1—7 is related to the theme of Israel as created and named by Yahweh. 42, 18—25 makes no mention of this but concentrates rather on the blindness and deafness of Israel. Finally, the term "servant" is of great importance for 42, 18—25 (v. 19), so that one might expect it to reappear in 43, 1—7 if 42, 18—43, 7 were an original unity, particularly since salvation-assurance oracles characteristically address Israel as servant.[89] Thus it is probable that the juxtaposition of 42, 18—25 and 43, 1—7 is the work of a collector.

b. The collector arranged the three units (42, 14—17.18—25; 43, 1—7) very carefully. As we saw, he used a progressive chain of verbal repetition and similarity in images and theme. This stair-step progression is used to express a particular understanding which the collector exhibits concerning the relationship between past and future. 42, 14—17 contains within itself a definite understanding of the relationship between past and future. In the past, Yahweh was silent and Israel was allowed to fall into her present plight. In the future, however, Yahweh will lead

---

[88] V. 14—17 mention only "blind."
[89] Isa 41, 8.9; 44, 1.2   Jer 46, 27—28 = 30, 10.

the blind through the desert in a "way" or "path" which they "do not know," while putting to shame those who trust in idols.

When 42, 18—25 and 43, 1—7 are placed side by side we find a theology of the relationship between past and future. The disputation in 42, 18—25 was uttered that Israel might profit — that the people of God might see (v. 18) and hear for the sake of the future (v. 23). When the collector juxtaposed 42, 18—25 and 43, 1—7, he joined them with the particle $w^{e\,c}\bar{a}tt\bar{a}$ (43, 1)[90] in order to show a relationship between past and future. In this way the collector makes a theological affirmation about the relationship between Israel's punishment in the exile and the hope for the future. The burning came as punishment (42, 25), yet in the midst of fire and water Yahweh's redeeming presence can be seen (43, 2).

The repetition of words, phrases, and images contributes in other ways to the kergymatic significance of the arrangement of these three genre units. When 42, 18—25 repeats words, phrases, and images found in 42, 14—17, a larger significance for both units emerges. The image of deafness takes on an enlarged meaning. Yahweh was indeed deaf (v. 14), yet ultimately the problem, says the collector, is that *Israel* is deaf and blind (v. 18.19). The enlarged "poem" says: Yahweh has been deaf only because Israel was deaf! Yahweh was deaf to Israel's outcry only to punish her for her own deafness. The image of walking in the "way" also takes on a larger significance when 42, 14—17 and 42, 18—25 are juxtaposed. The image now has a double meaning: Yahweh will lead in the way (v. 16) those who were unwilling to walk in the way (v. 24). Ironically, in the future Israel will be led in the way which she in the past refused to walk. The juxtaposition of v. 14—17 and v. 18—25 gives to Israel's "not knowing" a double significance as well. The promise that Yahweh will lead Israel in a way she "does not know" (v. 16) in the context of v. 14—17 connotes nothing negative about Israel; it merely expresses Israel's total dependence upon Yahweh. Yet Israel's "not knowing," when read in the context of v. 25, enriches the meaning.

---

[90] Cf. Muilenburg, Interpreter's Bible, V 480. Westermann, too, sees a close relationship between the two units: Das Buch Jesaja, 94. H. E. von Waldow and A. Schoors, however, argue that $w^{e\,c}\bar{a}tt\bar{a}$ belongs to the terminology of the genre of the assurance of salvation and is not merely a connecting particle supplied by the collector. Cf. von Waldow, "... denn ich erlöse dich." Eine Auslegung von Jes 43, 1960, 15; Schoors, I Am God Your Saviour: A Form Critical Study of the Main Genres of Isa XL—LV, 1973, 68. Von Waldow's argument depends upon the appearance of $w^{e\,c}\bar{a}tt\bar{a}$ in 44, 1 and 49, 6. In 44, 1, it could be argued that it is the work of a collector. 49, 6 is not a salvation-assurance oracle. Thus it is not certain whether the particle belonged originally to the genre of the assurance of salvation. In any event, the collector uses the particle for the purpose of expressing a relationship between past and future.

The phrase becomes at once a sign of Israel's helplessness *and* her disobedience.

When 43, 1—7 is added to 42, 14—17.18—25, the image of walking in the way takes on an even larger meaning. When Israel walks through fire and water, Yahweh will protect her. In the larger "poem" Israel's "walking" through fire and water (43, 2) makes the image of walking in the way (42, 16) take on a connotation of Yahweh's presence[91] through trial and danger. Furthermore, walking in the way under Yahweh's protection means, as the collector sees it, obedience to *tôrā*.[92]

c. Isaiah 42, 14—43, 7, as we saw, is related to the context which precedes it by repetition of words and images. This repetition gives to 42, 14 ff. and the passages which go before it a significance which they do not possess when each unit is taken by itself. Of particular importance is the picture of the servant. In 42, 1—4 the servant is faithful; in 42, 18—25 he is disobedient (v. 19.20). In 42, 18—25 he is unwilling to hear *tôrā* (v. 24); in 42, 1—4 he brings *tôrā* to the nations. In 42, 18—25 he is blind, deaf, and imprisoned; in 42, 5—9 he opens the eyes of the blind and releases those who are in prison. The servant in 42, 18—25 is Israel in the past; in 42, 1—4.5—9 he is Israel in the future. Thus in the enlarged context, the collector presents the faithful servant as one who was in the past disobedient.

The juxtaposition of the blind, deaf, and imprisoned servant of 42, 18—25 with the servant who opens blind eyes and delivers from prison (42, 5—9) creates a certain ambiguity in the message of the collection. As we saw above, the blind and imprisoned in v. 5—9 appear in the context of that genre unit to be the nations. Yet in 42, 18—25 those images clearly refer to the servant Israel. The ambiguity is in my judgment intentional and is related to the theology of the collection. As we shall see in 49, 1—6,[93] the servant Israel is both to restore Israel and to be a light to the nations. In chapter 42 the collection anticipates the two-fold task by creating ambiguity in the images.

A final comment about the relation of 42, 14—43, 7 to the foregoing context: The collection gives qualified support to Israel's complaint, "My way is hidden from Yahweh" (40, 27). To be sure! says the collection. Israel is indeed hidden — in prison (42, 22) but for her sins! Nevertheless, Yahweh's silence was but for a time; soon he will act (42, 14—17).

---

[91] Cf. "I am with you" (43, 2.5).
[92] The parallelism in 42, 25 shows the relationship between hearing *tôrā* and walking in the way.
[93] Cf. Chapter Eight, II.

### *B. 43, 8—13.14—15.16—21*

1. *Form Critical Analysis.* a. We have here three genre units: a trial
speech (v. 8—13) and two speeches of salvation (v. 14—15.16—21).
V. 8—13 display the typical features of the Deutero-Isaianic trial
between Yahweh and the nations or their gods:[94] (1) Yahweh's opponents (or witnesses) are summoned to trial (v. 8—9a), and (2) Yahweh
argues his case in the usual Deutero-Isaianic disputation style. Beginning
with a question introduced by *mî,* Yahweh sets forth the conditions by
which the dispute is to be resolved: "Who among them can declare this
and can tell us the former things?" Yahweh then challenges the gods
to produce witnesses to verify their ability to declare the "former
things" (v. 9b. c). They cannot; thus Yahweh's claim to be God, expressed in the typical self-praise style of Deutero-Isaiah's disputations,
stands (v. 11—13).

The typical Deutero-Isaianic pattern is given certain features
peculiar to this poem. Nowhere else are witnesses summoned in order
that the witnesses themselves will understand that Yahweh alone can
deliver (v. 10). How strange for witnesses in a trial to be summoned for
their own benefit! Yet the prophet has structured the poem precisely
this way to emphasize that Yahweh acts in order that men may know
him.[95] Thus this trial speech, in contrast with others in Deutero-Isaiah,
is concerned explicitly with the subjective act of faith on Israel's part
as the goal of the trial itself. Israel is more than an observer of the trial
proceedings; she is incorporated into the trial because her witness of the
past will give her faith in the ambiguity of her present situation in
the exile.

b. V. 14—15 can be distinguished from the surrounding context
by form. The passage begins with a messenger formula expanded in
hymn style (v. 14a). Then follows a promise: "For your sake I have
sent to Babylon, and I will bring down the fugitives[96] — all of them."
The unit closes with an asyndeton substantiating clause (v. 15).[97] The
form differs from that of the salvation-assurance oracle. "Fear not" is
absent. Moreover, it is addressed to a masculine plural audience.
Whether it is a complete oracle or a fragment is not clear, partly
because it cannot be translated with certainty.[98] However that may be,

---

[94] Cf. above, Chapter Four, II.

[95] Notice the verbs in v. 10b.

[96] Or perhaps "bars" (cf. 45, 2). No satisfactory solution has been found for the
reading of this text.

[97] Cf. 41, 13 and 43, 3a for closing substantiating clauses.

[98] It has been suggested that something between v. 14 and v. 15 has dropped out.
Cf. Westermann, Das Buch Jesaja, 102. 103.

the formal similarity with 43, 3b—4 noted above indicates that it is complete form critically. The original setting of this form of speech is far from certain,[99] but the similarity between 43, 3b—4 and 43, 14—15 shows that the latter has a degree of independence from its context.

c. V. 16—21 also stand apart from the context by form. The passage opens with a messenger formula, which is expanded by clauses in hymn style which refer to the Exodus (v. 16—17). Following an exhortation not to remember Yahweh's saving deeds of the past (v. 18), the prophet has Yahweh announce the future events of deliverance (v. 19—20a.b). The unit closes with an expression of the purpose of Yahweh's action (v. 20c—21).

The fact that this speech begins with a messenger formula, closes with the purpose of Yahweh's intervention, and contains the announcement of the future by Yahweh indicates that this speech is complete form critically. The unity of content, reflected in the Exodus-wilderness imagery, serves as additional support for isolating this speech from the surrounding context. But what kind of genre is it? Is its structure traditional, or is it the result of Deutero-Isaiah's creativity?

On the broadest level we find a structure typical of salvation speech: messenger formula, announcement of salvation, and purpose of Yahweh's action. A closer scrutiny, however, reveals a structure somewhat unique. The messenger formula is expanded by participial phrases which refer to a mighty saving deed in the past, namely, the Exodus. Thereupon the audience is told:

Remember not the former things; the things of old consider not;
Behold, I am doing a new thing; now it springs forth, do you not know it?

The structure of this passage is related to its intent: Yahweh, who in days of old delivered Israel from Egypt, exhorts hearers not to focus on the past but to perceive the future creation (Exodus). They should not be fixed on the past in the belief that Yahweh no longer delivers.[100] Yahweh argues that he is indeed acting now if they will but perceive it.

The structure of this unit is for the most part Deutero-Isaiah's creation. Beyond the influence of the general structure characteristic of salvation speech, we find little that is typical. Everything seems to have been shaped for Deutero-Isaiah's specific purposes.[101] Despite the fact

---

[99] Was it cultic? Or did it have a long tradition of usage in prophetic circles? Or is its form a creation of Deutero-Isaiah?

[100] Cf. Ps 77, 4.7 for an instance in which a cleavage between past and present is felt. In this connection, see the discussion by B. S. Childs, Memory and Tradition in Israel, 1962, 60—63.

[101] If Begrich is correct that "remember not" is a modification of the usual "fear not," this alteration is additional evidence for the role of the prophet's creativity in the structure of this speech. Cf. Studien 21.

that the structure is not traditional, v. 16—21 stand out from the context by both form and content.

2. *Arrangement of Genre Units.* a. Isaiah 43, 8 ff. continues the kind of progressive chain of repetition which we have seen before. The terms "blind" and "deaf," which we met already in 42, 14—17.18—25 (v. 16.18.19), reappear in 43, 8—13 (v. 8).[102] The verb *yadă'*, important in the foregoing context (42, 16.25), is quite significant in 43, 8—13 (v. 10) and is repeated again in 43, 16—21 (v. 19). The terms *dæræk* and *n$^e$tîbā*, which we discussed above (42, 16.24), are significant in 43, 16—21 (v. 16.19). A repetition of the term *'æbæd* is also a feature in the relationship of 43, 8 ff. to the foregoing context (42, 19; 43, 10). The same is true of *yaṣăr* (43, 1.7.21), *ga'ăl* (43, 1.14), and *q$^e$dôš yiśra'el* (43, 3.14).[103] Moreover, within 43, 8—21, the repetition of *ri'šonôt* seems to be a factor in the arrangement of units.[104] Thus the arrangement is not accidental. But is it the work of an author or a collector?

In our search for patterns of arrangement we are struck immediately by the importance of *ri'šonôt* in both 43, 8—13 and 43, 16—21. When we ask whether the repetition of this word is the sign of an author or a collector, we find an important clue in the arrangement of chapters 41—44. In several instances we find a salvation speech (or speeches) preceded by an utterance which functions as a disputation; in three cases the speech of salvation follows a trial speech (41, 8 ff.; 43, 14 ff.; 44, 1—5), and in one instance a disputation speech (43, 1—7). In one of these speech complexes the creation theme is a major unifying factor (41, 1—7. 8—13. 14—16. 17—20);[105] in another it is the image of fire (42, 18—25; 43, 1—7);[106] in still another, as I shall presently argue, it is the polarity between ancestors and posterity (43, 22—28; 44, 1—5). In 43, 8—21, the term *ri'šonôt* is an important factor in the arrangement of genre units.

The pattern of arrangement in chapters 41—44 helps us understand how the emphasis on the "former things" in both 43, 8—13 and 43, 16—21 caused this particular trial speech to be joined with no other salvation speech than this. But how do v. 14—15 fit into the context? At first glance, no obvious connection appears, unless *l$^e$mă'ăn/l$^e$mă'ănkæm* (v. 10.14) and the self-predications (v. 11—13.15) should suffice. A closer look, however, suggests that the root *g'l* may provide a clue to the position of v. 14—15 in the larger context of v. 8—21. Just as in

---

[102] Cf. Mowinckel, Komposition, 98.
[103] Ibid. 98.
[104] Ibid. 98.
[105] Cf. above in this chapter, II, A, 2, a.
[106] Cf. above in this chapter, III, A, 2, a.

42, 18—43, 7 the salvation speech introduces Yahweh as Israel's "redeemer" (43, 1), so also the salvation-speech portion of 43, 8—21 begins with a similar introduction (43, 14).

It is probable that the arrangement is the work of a collector rather than an author. The placement of v. 14—15 appears to be a rather loose juxtaposition of units based on a pattern used elsewhere rather than a tightly integrated poem. Another sign that we have to do with a collector is the difference in the use of the term *ri'šonôt* in v. 8—13 and v. 16—21. In v. 8—13, the "former things" serve as a point of agreement between speaker and hearers; it is a base from which to demonstrate that Yahweh is God. V. 16—21, by contrast, show no hint of a dispute about Yahweh's relationship to the gods. Instead, Deutero-Isaiah attempts to overcome the fixation of the people on the past and their inability to perceive a new saving event before their very eyes.

b. It appears, then, that v. 8—13.14—15, and 16—21 were arranged through the process of collection. We must inquire now about the significance of the arrangement. As we saw, the progressive chain of repetition is an important factor in the arrangement of units. The trial speech in v. 8—13, with its use of *yadā'*, *'iwwer*, and *her°šîm*, could not have appeared before this point in the process of repetition. More important than this, however, is the collector's understanding of the relationship between past and future. The juxtaposition of these three units is based upon the relationship between Israel's knowledge of the past and her knowledge of the future. In the trial speech (v. 8—13), the people of God are summoned in order that they might "know" and "have faith" and "understand" (v. 10) on the basis of their remembrance of his activity with regard to the "former things." Yet v. 16—21 say, "Remember not the former things." The arrangement of units manifests a larger view of past and future than each unit taken separately. To serve as witnesses that Yahweh did the "former things" may provide "knowledge" and "faith" that Yahweh is God (v. 10); but to "remember" and "understand" Yahweh simply in terms of the past is to misunderstand his activity (v. 18). The past is a model for the future — an archetype (v. 16—17) for the creation-exodus soon to occur (v. 18—21). The memory of Yahweh's past acts proves his deity; yet memory, says the arranger of v. 8—21, must go beyond being mere memory. Memory must be transcended by hope.[107]

---

[107] For an excellent bibliography see C. Stuhlmueller, Creative Redemption in Deutero-Isaiah, 1970, 135. Cf. also Schoors, I Am God Your Saviour, 94—95, 215—217, 224—225, 231, 275—276, 287, 291—292.

A theology of Yahweh's purpose is also expressed in the arrange-
ment of units.[108] The repetition of $l^e m\breve{a}'\bar{a}n/l^e m\breve{a}'\bar{a}nk\ae m$ does just that
(v. 10.14). In the trial (v. 8—13), Yahweh's purpose is that Israel will
be witness *so that* she would "know" and "have faith," i. e., that she
would have faith in Deutero-Isaiah's prophetic word uttered in the
despair of the exile (v. 10). V. 14—15, in the collector's theology, spell
out concretely Yahweh's purpose for the future: "*For your sake* I will
send to Babylon . . ."
   c. The use of words and images in 43, 8—21 is related to the
foregoing context as well. Blindness and deafness, "knowing" and "not
knowing," and images of the way or path in 43, 8—21 take on richer
meaning when read in the light of 42, 14 ff.[109] The blind and deaf, who
"do not know" (42, 16.25) are in 43, 8 ff. summoned as witnesses in
order that they may know (43, 10). The blind and deaf, who have eyes
and ears (42, 20; 43, 8), are called to be witnesses.[110] This paradox
which the collector emphasizes reinforces a similar paradox between the
faithful and sinful servant (42, 1—4.18—25).
   The repetition of the image of the way and the term *yad\breve{a}'* also
reflects a similar tension in the collection's understanding of God's
people. Israel, who in 42, 16 does not "know" the "way," is exhorted in
43, 16—21 to "know" the future in which Yahweh will provide a "way"
through the desert. The helpless, sinful Israel of the past, the Israel who
does not know, is to become the Israel who knows and has faith in
Yahweh's redemption to come.
   The image of the "way" or "path" in the desert is understood by
the collector in connection with the tradition of deliverance from Egypt.
Admittedly, in 42, 14—17 by itself the image would not necessarily
have to be understood as a reference to the traditional Exodus-wilderness theme;[111] in 42, 18—25, when standing alone, *d\ae r\ae k* (v. 24) was
certainly not a reference to the tradition of Exodus and wandering in
the wilderness. But in the context of 43, 16—21 (cf. v. 16), all references
to the "way" or "path" in 42, 14—43, 21 must be understood in terms
of the Exodus-wilderness theme of the collector's theology. Even the
promise in 43, 2, though not in itself clearly a reference to the deliver-

---

[108] Cf. Muilenburg, Interpreter's Bible, V 488.
[109] Cf. K. Elliger, Deuterojesaja, 238, 239; Muilenburg, Interpreter's Bible, V 485.
[110] Cf. Elliger, Deuterojesaja, 238.
[111] Important works on the Exodus theme in Deutero-Isaiah: E. Rohland, Die Bedeu-
     tung der Erwählungstraditionen Israels für die Eschatologie der alttestamentlichen
     Propheten, 1956, 94 ff.; W. Zimmerli, Der „neue Exodus" in der Verkündigung
     der beiden großen Exilspropheten, Gottes Offenbarung, 1963, 192—204; B. W. An-
     derson, Exodus Typology in Second Isaiah, Israel's Prophetic Heritage, edited by
     B. W. Anderson and W. Harrelson, 1962, 177—195; C. Stuhlmueller, Creative
     Redemption, 59 ff.; D. Baltzer, Ezechiel und Deuterojesaja, 1971, 12 ff.

ance at the Sea,[112] should in the context of the collection be understood in terms of the Exodus.

To summarize: Our study indicates that 43, 8—21 is a complex of three units which have been carefully arranged both in terms of each other and in relationship to the foregoing context. The arrangement is kerygmatic. Indeed, each unit takes on an enriched meaning when interpreted in its context.

## C. 43, 22—28; 44, 1—5

1. *Form Critical Analysis.* This section of Isaiah 40—55 is composed of a trial speech (43, 22—28) and a salvation-assurance oracle (44, 1—5). Form critical analysis of the trial speech has already been done.[113] The particular intention of Deutero-Isaiah in the trial speech is to dispute Israel's claim that she has called on Yahweh. Her plight is instead quite deserved (v. 26—27). Deliverance is an act which Yahweh performs purely for his own sake (v. 25).

The oracle in 44, 1—5 conforms to the general structure of the salvation-assurance oracle as discussed in Chapter Two. Yet Isaiah 44, 1—5 particularizes the genre: After an introduction which includes the particle $w^{e'}\ddot{a}tt\bar{a}$ and imperative $\check{s}^e m\check{a}^c$, which are in turn followed by vocatives and a messenger formula expanded by the appositives, "your maker, the one who formed you from the womb, your helper" (v. 1—2a), we find the exhortation, "Fear not" and the direct address (v. 2b). The typical substantiating clause which consists of nominal sentences and verbs in the perfect tense does not appear,[114] probably because the essence of that genre element is included already in the introduction.[115] The future, as is usually the case with this genre, is depicted concretely in the imperfect (v. 3—5). As is sometimes found in this genre, the announcement of the future begins with $k\hat{i}$.[116]

2. *Arrangement of Genre Units.* a. Both 43, 22—28 and 44, 1—5 distinguish themselves from their context by form. Moreover, neither requires its context in order to be understood. Nevertheless, the arrangement of the text is not haphazard. The repetition of "Jacob-Israel" (43, 22; 44,1), *zkr* (43, 18.25.26), *zærǎ<sup>c</sup>* (43, 5; 44,3), *yoṣærka* (43, 1;

---

[112] The language is much too general to be identified clearly as a reference to the Exodus.

[113] Cf. above, Chapter Four, I, B, 1.

[114] Cf. Isa 41, 10.14b; 43, 1b.

[115] The phrases, "your maker" and "your helper," appear here as expansions of the messenger formula in contrast to their role elsewhere as substantiations for "fear not." Cf. Isa 41, 10.14.

[116] Isa 43, 2; 44, 3 Jer 30, 10b = 46, 27b.

44, 2), and *qara' bᵉšem* (43, 1; 44, 5) is immediately apparent.[117]
Furthermore, the juxtaposition of the trial speech and the speech of
salvation is part of a larger pattern of arrangement.[118] The trial speech
(43, 22—28) argues that Yahweh was perfectly justified in the extinction of Israel's sinful ancestors (v. 26—28). Past and future are contrasted, however, when 43, 22—28 and 44, 1—5 are placed side by side:
The annihilation of ancestors in the past contrasts with the abundance
of posterity in the future. The particle *wᵉ'attā* (44, 1) makes the connection between these two texts,[119] expressing a relationship between past
and future.

The juxtaposition of 43, 22—28 and 44, 1—5 is probably the work
of a collector. First of all, each unit is capable of standing alone. In the
second place, we know of no conventional setting in which these two
forms of speech were customarily juxtaposed. Finally, the images associated with the destruction of ancestors in 43, 22—28 and those connected with the fruitfulness of the barren land in 44, 1—5 function
primarily *within* the genre unit; the images of the two units are not
closely intertwined. In 43, 22—28 the assertion of the extinction of
ancestors appears for one purpose — as a part of the argument to convince Israel that her punishment was deserved. The element of hope in
v. 25 is subordinate to the disputational intention of the speech. Isaiah
43, 22—28 does not set out to address the relationship between punishment in the past and redemption in the future; it is at best only implied.
Thus v. 27—28 do not point forward to 44, 1 ff. Moreover, the promise
of posterity in 44, 1—5 makes no direct connection with the images in
43, 27—28. The promise of descendants is here but a part of the general
imagery of fertility in v. 3—5, albeit the most important part. Fertility
imagery is totally lacking in 43, 27—28. Furthermore, 44, 5 emphasizes
that Jacob's posterity will be "called" by Yahweh's name;[120] nothing
of the kind is to be found in 43, 22—28. Admittedly, the verb *qara'*
is used in both 43, 22—28 and 44, 1—5,[121] but the meaning is quite
different. Nothing in 44, 1—5, other than *wᵉ'attā*, explicitly indicates
a contrast between the two units. Thus no organic relationship between
the two units and their image clusters can be established. It is probable,
then, that a collector juxtaposed them in the light of his theology of
past and future.

b. The collector's theology of past and future is a significant
reason for associating these two units. The repetition of words and

[117] Cf. Mowinckel, Komposition, 98.
[118] Cf. above on the discussion of the juxtaposition of 42, 18—25 and 43, 1—7.
[119] Cf. Muilenburg, Interpreter's Bible, V 492, 501.
[120] Also by the names "Jacob" and "Israel".
[121] 43, 22; 44, 5.

images contributes also to the kerygmatic significance of the juxtaposition of these two speeches in relationship with the foregoing context. In 43, 16—21 Yahweh promises a way in the desert and water to "give drink to my chosen people whom I formed for myself *that they might tell my praise*" (v. 20—21). In the context of the present arrangement of units, v. 22 ff. follow from v. 20—21: "And upon me you did not call, O Jacob."[122]

The repetition of *lᵉmǎʿǎn* also contributes to the kerygmatic significance of the arrangement of units. We find in the association of units that all of Yahweh's activity is for a purpose: The God of Israel, who magnified *tôrā* "for the sake of his righteousness" (42, 21), summoned Israel to trial "in order that they might know" (43, 10), and promised to send to Babylon for Israel's sake (43, 14), now removes Israel's transgressions for his own sake (43, 25). Yahweh's purpose has various dimensions as it appears in the collection, and the repetition of *lᵉmǎʿǎn* is a vehicle for conveying to us the richness of Yahweh's purpose.

The multifold nature of Yahweh's purpose is presented as an unfolding drama in the collection's juxtaposition of units. Yahweh's purpose was to magnify "his righteousness and *tôrā*" (42, 21), but his people refused to obey his *tôrā* (42, 24). Yahweh's response to their blind disobedience, as the collection presents it, is to make them his witnesses *in order that* they might become faithful (43, 10). Their act of faith, moreover, will not be in vain, for Yahweh will indeed act *for their sake* (43, 14). But why? Not because they declared his praise — they didn't! — but rather for his own sake (43, 25). This particular theology of Yahweh's purpose is in no sense the original intention of any unit; it is rather the kerygma of the collection.

The repetition of *zkr* also connects 43, 22 ff. with what precedes it and contributes to the larger unity of the message of the collection. The collection portrays God's remembering and Israel's remembering in parallel fashion. Just as Israel must not remember the past but look to Yahweh's acts in the future (43, 18), so also Yahweh will not remember what happened in the past (43, 25).

The image of water (44, 3) is also significant in the collector's pattern of arrangement. It is a continuation of an image pattern found in the foregoing context. In 43, 16—21 the poet's use of water is closely related to the Exodus: Yahweh made a way in the sea (v. 16); in the future he will put water in the desert (v. 20).[123] As we saw, in the context of the collection 43, 2 must be seen as an Exodus image.[124] Although the image of water in 44, 3 by itself would not necessarily imply the

---

[122] Cf. G. A. F. Knight, Deutero-Isaiah: A Theological Commentary, 1965, 105.
[123] Cf. Ex 17, 6.
[124] See above.

Exodus-wilderness theme, in the context of the collection it does. Just as Yahweh will perform a "new Exodus"[125] by creating in the desert an oasis for a thirsty people (43, 20), so also he will pour out fertility-giving water to create offspring for a decimated nation (44, 3—5).

Finally, the repetition of zærǎ' and qara' bᵉšem (43, 1.5; 44, 3.5) is a factor in the arrangement of this section of the collection. The repetition of these terms takes what was a minor note in 43, 1—7 and makes it into something important. In 43, 1—7, zærǎ' is of little significance; the emphasis is on the return home. In 44, 1—5, however, Israel's having "seed" is the central element in the promise. Thus when 44, 1—5 is placed after 43, 1—7, the return of Israel's "seed" to their homeland (43, 5) is enriched by the images of the blessing and growth of the seed (44, 3—5). Likewise the phrase qara' bᵉšem, only one of several in 43, 1—7 used to indicate Yahweh's relationship with Israel,[126] is in 44, 1—5 an expression of the main theme of the oracle; everywhere Israel's seed will sprout, each claiming identity with Yahweh and his covenant people (v. 5). Indeed, the collection, by placing 43, 1—7 and 44, 1—5 in close proximity, indicates that the return home (43, 5—6) will be a time of such fertility and blessing that offspring will sprout literally everywhere and call themselves by the names appropriate to the people of Yahweh (44, 3—5). I see no reason to assume that 44, 3—5 must necessarily be interpreted as a specific reference to the incorporation of foreigners into Israel. It could just as well portray the growth of a remnant[127] made small by exile. In the context of the collection it means just that. Verbal repetition connects 43, 1—7 with 44, 1—5, and the emphasis of the former on the return of the scattered exiles suggests that the collector understood the latter in terms of the gift of offspring to returned exiles.

## D. 44, 6—8.9—20

1. *Form Critical Analysis.* The typical structure of the Deutero-Isaianic trial speech is present in 44, 6—8,[128] though the particular structure of this poem is somewhat unique. Yahweh begins with the claim that he alone is God, stated in self-praise hymn style (v. 6). The issue under dispute becomes apparent in the question introduced by mî: "Who is like me?" (v. 7). A summons to trial follows, in which Yahweh challenges his opponents to present their case by declaring what is to come (v. 7).[129] Thus Yahweh appeals to common Israelite belief con-

---

[125] See the bibliography in footnote 111.
[126] Cf. 43, 1.
[127] Cf. Isa 46, 3.
[128] Cf. above, Chapter Four, II.
[129] Read mî yašmîᵃᶜ meᶜôlam 'ôtiyyôt. Cf. Schoors, I Am God Your Saviour, 230.

cerning his ability to declare the future as they have experienced this power in the past. Indeed, it is to their experience of the effectiveness of his word that they are summoned as witnesses (v. 8).

Isaiah 44, 6—8, as we saw in Chapter Four, is an imitation of a legal situation in which witnesses are summoned to validate a claim. But this imitation of speech from trial in the gate represents only one of the structural features of the poem. Language which is unrelated to the trial is a major component of these verses. The typical Deutero-Isaianic disputation style forms the core of Yahweh's argument. Moreover, v. 8aα, a word of comfort resembling the language of the salvation oracle,[130] introduces a cultic element into this trial speech. We can find no other setting for the combination of these elements besides the preaching of Deutero-Isaiah. Thus the genre is, as we argued, his own creation for the purpose of dealing with the doubt occasioned by the exile. The intention of 44, 6—8 is even more specific: The use of both disputation and cultic language in the same unit is the result of the need both to persuade and to announce hope. The people Israel are Yahweh's witnesses; as witnesses they can be persuaded and thus open to hear the word of hope.

Although the genre is the creation of Deutero-Isaiah, the genre is sufficiently stereotyped that Isaiah 44, 6—8 can be set off from the context because it reflects the trial. The previous verses are a salvation-assurance oracle. But how should the relationship between v. 6—8 and v. 9—20 be understood? Are v. 9—20 to be viewed as a continuation of v. 6—8, in analogy with the relationship of v. 1—4 and v. 5—7 in Isaiah chapter 41?[131]

Let us begin by comparing Isaiah 44, 9—20 and its relation to v. 6—8 with other instances of sarcastic description of idol-making in relation to their context. In 46, 5—11 the inanimate idols cannot be compared to Yahweh because they are made by men.[132] Yahweh, by contrast, is the creator; instead of having been created, he utters event-creating words. The idol does not speak (46, 7), but Yahweh's speech creates the future. Thus the mocking description in 46, 6—7 is integral to its context; it cannot be considered secondary. In 41, 1—7 the same is true: the description of idol-making (v. 5—7) is directly related to the nations' "fearing" and "trembling" as they come to the trial. In 40, 18—24, too, the idols made by men are the opposite of the Creator who deposes "princes and judges."[133] In a word, these three examples of

---

[130] In v. 8 1QIsaᵃ reads *wᵉʾăl tîrᵉʾû*, which is probably the correct text.
[131] See the form critical discussions of those texts above in this chapter.
[132] Cf. above, Chapter Three, II, 2.
[133] This text is discussed also in Chapter Three, II, 2.

description of idol-making can be shown to play an integral role in their respective poems.

A close examination of 44, 9—20, however, reveals that the description of the manufacture of idols is not as closely related to v. 6—8 as we found in the three texts discussed in the preceding paragraph. In v. 6—8 the trial speech is a response to the hearers' doubt that Yahweh is God, and the purpose of the arguments in the trial is to persuade them of it on the ground that only he can declare the future. In v. 9—20, however, not a word is said about the power to declare the future. Instead, the idols are ridiculed because they "do not profit" (v. 9). Moreover, the emphasis in v. 9—20 is to heap scorn on the idol-*worshippers* rather than to deal with their deities' power to declare the future.[134] Even though the emphasis shifts to the idols themselves in v. 18, attention swiftly returns to those who make and worship them.

Another indication that v. 9—20 are not an integral part of v. 6 ff. is the looseness of the verbal repetition. The "witnesses" in v. 6—8 are to *testify* to Yahweh's ability to declare the future. In v. 9—20, by contrast, emphasis on the legal function of the witnesses is lacking (v. 9). In the case of the repetition of *phd* (v. 8.11), the verb appears in v. 6—8 as a word of comfort for doubting Israel because she knows from her past history that Yahweh's word is trustworthy. In v. 9—20, the term is used in connection with a summons to appear for "dread and shame." The summons to assemble in v. 11 is probably drawn out of a trial background, but the subject matter of the trial differs from that of v. 6—8. In v. 6—8 Yahweh and the nations (or the gods) are opponents in a trial composed of arguments to prove that Yahweh is God; v. 9—20 are not, properly speaking, arguments at all. Indeed, all these connections are so loose that it is unlikely that v. 6—8 originally included v. 9—20.

2. *Arrangement of Genre Units.* a. Since it appears that v. 6—8 did not originally include v. 9—20, we may inquire about the significance of their present relationship. In the present context v. 9—20 add a new dimension to v. 6—8. When one reads or hears v. 9—20 and thinks of v. 7, the somewhat sarcastic summons to trial becomes a derisive taunt; one can hardly help laughing at the irony of calling to trial the gods described in v. 9—20. A relationship between v. 6—8 and v. 9—20 appears also in an implied contrast in the role of the witnesses. In v. 6—8 Yahweh "declared" and caused his witnesses to "hear" (v. 8), while in v. 9 ff. the witnesses who make idols "do not see or know" (v. 9). A contrast is implied, too, in the repetition of the verb *phd*. In the first unit Israel is exhorted, "Tremble not" (v. 8), while the craftsmen in v. 9—20 can but tremble when they are summoned to trial

---

[134] Note that the subject of the sentences is for the most part the idol-worshippers.

(v. 11). Whether v. 9—20 originally stood alone or were composed as a later interpretation of v. 6—8 is not certain; but there is little doubt that v. 6—8 can stand alone and that the relations between the two units simply enrich a speech independent both by form and content.

b. Isaiah 44, 6—8.9—20 relate to the foregoing context through the repetition of *ʿed(îm)* (43, 10; 44, 8.9). The collection implies a contrast between Yahweh's witnesses who will "know" (43, 10) and the idols' witnesses who do not see or know (44, 9). Moreover, Yahweh chooses Israel as his witnesses "in order that" *(lᵉmăʿăn)* they may "know", "have faith," and "understand" (43, 10); the witnesses of the idols do not see or know "so that" *(lᵉmăʿăn)* they will be put to shame (44, 9). Finally, it is apparent that 44, 6—8 relates to the preceding context by accomplishing within itself what the collection normally does by juxtaposition — the association of trial and salvation speech.

## E. 44, 21—22.23

1. *Form Critical Analysis.* V. 21—22 are an exhortation.[135] If the form of speech originated in priestly *tôrā*,[136] Deutero-Isaiah's use of the form here is not a direct imitation. Instead, he employs a type of speech which enjoyed widespread usage in prophetic circles.[137] Considerable variety in structure is characteristic: Sometimes it is prophetic speech;[138] sometimes Yahweh is the speaker.[139] There is a tendency for the exhortation to "return" to be closely tied with the language of promise,[140] but sometimes it is joined with other forms of speech.[141]

Deutero-Isaiah structures this rather flexible prophetic genre in his own way. He begins with the exhortation, "Remember these things..."[142] But the imperative is followed by the typical style of the assurance of salvation through nominal clauses and clauses with verbs in the perfect. Thus the structure is shaped as much by Deutero-Isaiah as by tradition. Nevertheless, these two verses stand out from their context as an exhortation.

---

[135] Begrich, Studien, 58.

[136] Begrich, Die priesterliche Tora, BZAW 66 (1936), 63—88.

[137] Hos 14, 2  Isa 31, 6  Jer 3, 12.14.22  Ezek 14, 6; 18, 30; 33, 11  Joel 2, 12  Zech 1, 3.4  Mal 3, 7. Cf. H. W. Wolff, Das Thema „Umkehr" in der alttestamentlichen Prophetie, ZThK 48 (1951), 129—148.

[138] Isa 31, 6  Hos 14, 2.

[139] Jer 3, 12.14.22  Ezek 14, 6; 18, 30; 33, 11  Zech 1, 3.4  Mal 3, 7.

[140] Wolff, Umkehr, 140 ff. Isa 31, 6  Jer 3, 12.14.22  Zech 1, 3  Mal 3, 7. Hos 14, 2 ff. is somewhat more complex, for the exhortation to return is embedded in a prophetic liturgy.

[141] Particularly in Ezekiel. Cf. Ezek 14, 6; 18, 30; 33, 11; also Joel 2, 12.23.

[142] Cf. Jer 51, 50  Mal 3, 22. Childs, Memory and Tradition, 50.

V. 23 is a brief hymn. Its similarity with basic hymn form can readily be seen.[143] There is a call to praise in imperative style with substantiations introduced by *kî* and followed by clauses with verbs in the perfect tense which proclaim what Yahweh has done.[144] Thus v. 23 is independent from its context by form.

2. *Arrangement of Genre Units.* The hymn in v. 23 possibly was originally joined with v. 21—22, but its pivotal place as a close of a major section of the collection[145] makes it more likely that the collector juxtaposed the two passages, using the hymn as he did elsewhere as a response to the entire section which precedes. In any event, v. 21—22 and v. 23 are positioned as a summary exhortation and hymn to respond by means of verbal repetition to the foregoing context. *Zkr* in v. 21 recalls 43, 18; v. 22a recapitulates 43, 25. The style of the salvation-assurance oracle in v. 22a reminds us that 42, 14—44, 23 are influenced by the salvation-assurance oracle.[146] The hymnic celebration of Yahweh's redemption *(g'l)* in v. 23[147] rounds out a major theme of chapters 43—44.[148]

We have seen that the collector has placed the units in 42, 14—44, 23 in association with one another by means of repetition of key words, phrases, and images. In so doing he expresses a kerygma concerning Yahweh's *purpose* in the relationship of past and future. The imagery of the Exodus-wilderness experience serves as the basic theme for this section of the collection; the images of water, walking in the way, and the picture of Yahweh's transformation of the wilderness are understood by the collection as a new Exodus. We have seen other connections as well, but all are related to Yahweh's movement from silence (42, 14) or punishment (42, 18—25; 43, 27—28) in the past to his deliverance in the future Exodus.

---

[143] Cf. H. Gunkel, Einleitung in die Psalmen, 1966, 32 ff.; Westermann, Sprache und Struktur, 157 ff.

[144] The second verb in the second substantiation is in the imperfect, but it is in parallel with a verb in the perfect.

[145] Cf. above, Chapter Six, I.

[146] Cf. 43, 1—7; 44, 1—5.

[147] Cf. also v. 22.

[148] 43, 1.14; 44, 6.22.23.

# Chapter Eight: Isaiah 44, 24—49, 13

In this chapter we shall explore the arrangement of genre units in the last half of the Jacob-Israel section of the collection. Using hymns as responses to segments of the collection, we find two of them between 44, 24 and 49, 13 (48, 20—21 and 49, 13).[1] Thus we have two blocks of text to consider in this chapter (44, 24—48, 22 and 49, 1—13). The first opens with the Cyrus speeches (44, 24—28; 45, 1—7(8); 45, 9—13), continues with poems related to the eschatological battle during which Babylon will fall (45, 14—47, 15), and concludes with an intricately related set of poems in chapter 48. The second block, beginning with a "servant song" (49, 1—6), is a response to 40, 27—31, so that 41, 1—48, 21(22) are encapsulated by 40, 12—31 and 49, 1—13.

## I. ISAIAH 44, 24—48, 21

### A. 44, 24—28; 45, 1—7(8).9—13

1. *Form Critical Analysis.* The form of Isaiah 44, 24—28 was sufficiently discussed in Chapter Three.[2] Although it employs the self-praise style of the hymn, it functions as a disputational promise[3] which argues that Yahweh will use Cyrus to rebuild Jerusalem.

45, 1—7, as we argued,[4] is not form critically a part of 44, 24—28. Indeed, 45, 1—7 exhibits the genre of an oracle to a king. In particular, it is a kind of oracle which promises the king victory over enemies. It reminds us of the oracles in Psalm 2, 7—9 and in Psalm 110, as well as the prophecy of Nathan in II Samuel 7.[5] We also find examples of oracles of this type from Egypt and Mesopotamia:

> ... One of these days it happened that the King's Son Thut-mose came on an
> excursion at noon time. Then he rested in the shadow of this great god. Sleep

---

[1] I am leaving out of consideration for the moment the hymn in 45, 8. It will be discussed below.

[2] Chapter Three, II, 5.

[3] Note the messenger formula in v. 24.

[4] Cf. above, Chapter Three, II, 5.

[5] Cf. also Ps 89, 4—5.20 ff. (*'amărtî* in v. 3 should perhaps be read as second masculine singular.) See the form critical discussion of C. Westermann, Sprache und Struktur der Prophetie Deuterojesajas, in: Forschung am Alten Testament, 1964, 148—150.

took hold of him, slumbering at the time when the sun was at (its) peak. He found the majesty of this august god speaking with his own mouth, as a father speaks to his son, saying: "See me, look at me, my son, Thut-mose! I am thy father, Harmakhis-Khepre-Re-Atum. I shall give thee my kingdom upon earth at the head of the living. Thou shalt wear the southern crown and the northern crown on the throne... *Approach* thou! Behold, I am with thee; I am thy guide...[6]

Isaiah 45, 1—7, apparently an oracle commissioning a king, is not an oracle actually delivered. Rather an imitation of that genre functions here as a promise to Israel.[7] Its intention is both to announce deliverance to Israel (v. 4) and to express Yahweh's purpose in so doing: "in order that they may know from the rising of the sun and from the west that there is none like me . . ." (v. 6).

45, 9—13, as we saw,[8] is a disputation speech of the "handler-handled" variety. The intention of this oracle is to persuade the prophet's Israelite hearers that they lack the prerogative to question the creator. Although Deutero-Isaiah formulated a traditional form of speech in his own particular way,[9] it stands apart from its context as a disputation.

*2. Arrangement of Genre Units.* a. Is the juxtaposition of these genre units the work of an author or of a collector? The ties between 44, 24—28 and 45, 1—7 are quite close. Both mention Cyrus by name as the agent by which Yahweh will deliver his people. Both use the style *'anokî/'°nî yhwh*. Both see Yahweh's use of Cyrus as an act of creation. Still, both seem to be self-contained genre units.[10] Moreover, they speak of the Cyrus event quite differently. In 45, 1—7 the intent of the imitation of the royal oracle is to announce that Yahweh will deliver Israel in a most unexpected way. The oracle takes great pains to show that Cyrus, who does not know Yahweh, is nevertheless chosen for the sake of Israel (v. 4). That Cyrus does not know Yahweh is reaffirmed throughout the oracle (v. 4.5). In 44, 24—28 the emphasis lies elsewhere — to convince despairing Israel that Yahweh is indeed God ("Who was with me?") and that Jerusalem will be rebuilt. Indeed, Cyrus is only an incidental part of v. 24—28. These differences in intention, along with the differences in genre, suggest that the juxtaposition of 44, 24—28 and 45, 1—7 is the work of a collector.

---

[6] ANET 449. See also the Akkadian oracles on 449—450.
[7] Begrich was right that its function is that of a salvation oracle, though he apparently did not recognize that its form is that of an oracle to a king. Cf. Studien zu Deuterojesaja, 1938. 1963, 14. Page numbers are from the 1963 edition.
[8] Cf. above, Chapter Three, II, 4.
[9] This is argued in detail in Chapter Three, II, 4.
[10] Cf. my discussion in Chapter Three.

45, 9—13 has close affinities with both 44, 24—28 and 45, 1—7. First of all, we find similarities in language and theme. Yahweh will "make straight" Cyrus' way (45, 2.13).[11] The rebuilding of Jerusalem is Yahweh's goal (44, 26.28; 45, 13). The phrase *noṭæ/naṭû šamăyim* appears in both 44, 24 and 45, 12. Furthermore, the use of the pronoun *hû'* in v. 13 suggests that we might expect an antecedent, which 45, 1 would admirably provide. In addition, the disputation in v. 9—13 relates closely to the issues in v. 1—7. In contrast with most of Deutero-Isaiah's disputation speeches, v. 9—13 do not try to persuade doubters of the superiority of Yahweh over the gods. Instead, the disputation is precisely on the subject of v. 1—7 — the hard-to-believe plan of Yahweh to use the pagan Cyrus to accomplish his purpose. Indeed, v. 9—13 seem to presuppose 45, 1 ff. The fact that v. 9—13 has connections with both 44, 24—28 and 45, 1—7 might be an indication that 45, 9—13 was composed after the preceding two poems had been joined. We may not be certain of that, however.

V. 8, like the hymns in 42, 10—13 and 49, 13, is a response to an utterance about Yahweh's chosen. More specifically, 45, 8, like 42, 10—13, follows a commissioning oracle.[12] Indeed, one may wonder whether v. 8 was originally a part of v. 1—7, serving as a hymnic close to a commissioning oracle. If it was originally separate, it was connected by verbal repetition: *ptḥ* (v. 1.8), *br'* (v. 7.8), and the self predication (v. 6.8). Still, the fact that only here in Deutero-Isaiah do we find an entire hymn[13] in self-praise style[14] suggests that v. 8 originally belonged to v. 1—7.

b. The arrangement of these genre units is not accidental. Structurally we have two disputations (44, 24—28; 45, 9—13) framing an oracle to a king. This structure contains its own inner logic. Though 44, 24—28 by itself is only incidentally an oracle about Cyrus, in the present context, 45, 1—7(8) amplifies 44, 28a. The participial phrase, "saying to Cyrus, 'My shepherd, all my *purpose* he will fulfill,'" is quite unspecific. But when followed by 45, 1—7(8), its meaning takes on concrete significance. Yahweh's *purpose* is that Cyrus may know "I am Yahweh who calls you . . ." (v. 3b), that Israel may be delivered (v. 4), and that *all* may know that Yahweh alone is God (v. 6). The disputation in v. 9—13 answers the doubt that Yahweh would use a pagan to free his people.

---

[11] The meaning of *ḥᵃdûrîm* in MT (v. 2) is not clear. LXX and 1QIsaᵃ read *ḥᵃrarîm*. In any case, the context makes it plain that Yahweh is preparing the way for Cyrus.

[12] Isa 49, 13 also follows the report of a commissioning (49, 1—6).

[13] As opposed to self-praise hymn style in disputation and trial speeches.

[14] 42, 10—13; 44, 23; 48, 20—21; 49, 13; 52, 7—10 are not in self-praise style.

c. These three genre units (44, 24—28; 45, 1—8.9—13) introduce
a section of the collection which emphasizes the defeat of the nations at
the eschaton (chapters 45—48).[15] Moreover, chapters 45—48 focus on
Cyrus as the agent of Yahweh's purpose *(ḥḗpæṣ)*.[16] Another important
theme of chapters 45—48 — introduced by 44, 24—45, 13 — is the
knowledge and confession of Yahweh made by the nations (45, 14—17.
18—21.22—25). Finally, the "woe" in the disputation (45, 9.10) anticipates the emphasis on Israel as sinner (46, 5—11.12—13; 48, 1—11.
17—19).

44, 24 ff. is related to the context which precedes it by verbal repetition: *g'l* (44, 22.23.24),[17] *yṣr* (44, 21.24),[18] *'śh* (44, 23.24). Also the
phrases *wa'æqra' lᵉka biśmæka* and *'ᵃkǎnnᵉka* (45, 4), employed in connection with Cyrus, remind us of the similar phrase in 43, 1 concerning
Israel, as well the language of 44, 5. Such phrases, undoubtedly familiar
when used to refer to Israel, must have appeared strange when directed
toward the commissioning of Cyrus. The collection senses the offense in
so doing by surrounding the Cyrus oracle with disputations. Indeed, for
the first time in the collection we have a hint that the "light and *tôrā*
and *miśpaṭ*" for the nations (42, 1—4.5—9) involves the election of
Cyrus as a means by which the whole world may know that only
Yahweh is God (45, 6). We should not go so far as to say that Cyrus
becomes one of Yahweh's covenant people. He is not called by Yahweh's name;[19] Yahweh instead calls *his* name for a very special but
limited purpose.

### B. 45, 14—17.18—21.22—25

1. *Form Critical Analysis.* a. Begrich viewed Isaiah 45, 14—17 as
an imitation and transformation of the cultic salvation oracle form from
which he believed all of Deutero-Isaiah's salvation speeches were derived.[20] In his opinion, member *a*, the intervention of Yahweh, is missing.
Only the consequences of Yahweh's intervention are present.[21] Indeed,
the confession in v. 14d—15, in his view, is a transformation of the

---

[15] Particularly 45, 14—17.18—21.22—25; 46, 1—4.
[16] 44, 28; 46, 10; 48, 14.
[17] More precisely, "your redeemer" (43, 1.14; 44, 6.22.24). Cf. S. Mowinckel, Die Komposition des deuterojesajanischen Buches, ZAW 49 (1931), 99.
[18] The phrase, "the one who formed you from the womb," appears both in 44, 2 and 44, 24. Mowinckel, Komposition, 99.
[19] Cf. 43, 7.
[20] See my discussion of Begrich in Chapter Two.
[21] Cf. Begrich, Studien, 16, for an outline of the basic structure of the oracle form.

usual phrase, "that they may know that I alone am God."[22] In light of Westermann's critique of Begrich's derivation of all the Deutero-Isaianic salvation speeches from one cultic speech-form, the absence of both "Fear not" and the substantiating nominal and verbal clauses suggests that this speech is not an imitation of that genre. Moreover, the fact that it is addressed to Zion (2nd feminine singular) rather than Jacob-Israel is not typical of the salvation-assurance oracle. In addition, the confession speech of the nations is not characteristic of the assurance of salvation. Thus it is probable that we are dealing with a different kind of salvation speech.

This speech is an example of a type of salvation speech addressed to Zion, where we find a traditionary complex in which, among other things, the nations come to Zion bringing home the exiled Israelites (Isa 49, 22 ff.; 60, 1 ff.) and the treasuries of these nations (Isa 45, 14—17; 60, 1 ff. Hag 2, 7—8). The nations will bow down before Israel (Isa 45, 14 f.; 49, 23; 60, 14) or before Yahweh (45, 23).[23] Certain typical formal features belong to this type of oracle. As already mentioned, Zion is the addressee.[24] Often the nations make confession to Zion or to Yahweh, and the words of the confession are quoted (Isa 45, 14—17.24—25; 60, 14).[25] To be sure, the form is flexible; yet these formal features tend to recur. Since we have no examples of this type of speech in the cult, or for that matter, outside Deutero- and Trito-Isaiah, we must assume a prophetic, or perhaps even Deutero-Isaianic, *Sitz im Leben*. At any rate, the formal features of promise of the nations' pilgrimage followed by their confession sets this speech off from its context.

b. V. 18—21 is not a disputation speech, as Begrich and von Waldow argue.[26] It is rather a trial speech like several others in Deutero-Isaiah.[27] The summons to trial (v. 21) is parallel to the summons to trial found elsewhere in Deutero-Isaiah's trial speeches.[28] Yet this speech has distinctive structural features.[29] The summons to trial is not at the

---

[22] Ibid. 23.

[23] Cf. G. von Rad, Old Testament Theology, II 1965, 239—240, 293 ff.

[24] Isa 45, 14 ff.; 49, 22—23.24—26; 60, 1 ff. In 45, 18—25 the nations are addressed.

[25] A comparison of 45, 14d—17 with 45, 24—25 indicates the likelihood that the former is in entirety the speech of the nations. The speech of the nations begins with *'ăk* (v. 14d.24a), followed by a confession in which Yahweh is spoken of in the third person (v. 14d.15.24a). Then Yahweh's behavior toward his opponents is contrasted with his gracious activity toward Israel (v. 16—17.24b—25), with Yahweh's enemies and Israel both spoken of in the third person.

[26] Cf. above, Chapter Four, footnote 65.

[27] 41, 1—7.21—29; 43, 8—13; 44, 6—8; 45, 18—21; 48, 12—15. Cf. Chapter Four, II.

[28] Cf. e. g., 41, 21; 43, 8. Cf. Westermann, Sprache und Struktur, 136, 137.

[29] Its structure resembles rather closely 48, 12—15.

beginning as is typical of several of Deutero-Isaiah's trial speeches.[30]
Instead, it opens with a lengthy introduction:

> For thus says Yahweh, creator of the heavens, he is God,
> Shaper of the earth and its maker, he established it,
> Not chaos did he create it, he shaped it for habitation;
> I am Yahweh, and there is no other,
> Not in secret did I speak, in a place in a land of darkness;
> I did not say to the seed of Jacob, "Seek me in chaos;"
> I am Yahweh, the one who speaks righteousness, who declares truth.

Those who are left from the nations are then summoned, challenged to
match this claim. But they cannot. The revelation had not been given to
them; Yahweh had spoken to the "seed of Israel" but not the nations.
Thus the structural peculiarities of this trial speech emphasize that
Yahweh has spoken only to Israel and that the nations' gods have not
spoken to them.

c. V. 22—25 display the genre of an exhortation, a type of speech
known elsewhere in prophetic literature.[31] The exhortation in v. 22—25
is an imitation of an exhortation; the nations are not really the persons
addressed. It is instead a literary device which functions as a promise to
Israel (v. 24b—25). To be sure, the deliverance of the "ends of the
earth" is expected (v. 22),[32] yet the emphasis lies on the submission of
the nations before Yahweh and the release of Israel from bondage.[33]

Begrich and von Waldow consider v. 18—21 and v. 22—25 to be
one unit of speech.[34] We shall presently have to consider the relationship
of these verses to one another, but for the moment we may content
ourselves with the observation that *form critically* they can be separated
into two units. V. 18—21 is a typical Deutero-Isaianic trial speech,
structured very much like 48, 12—15. V. 22—25 are an exhortation.
Each unit can stand alone by form, and neither requires the other in
order to be understood.

2. *Arrangement of Genre Units.* a. We must ask at the outset
whether the arrangement is the work of an author or a collector.
V. 18—21 and v. 22—25 are quite closely related. In both, the nations
are addressed (v. 20.22). Both deal with the power of Yahweh's word
(v. 18—19.21.23). Both are concerned with the object of the nations'
worship (v. 20.22—24). Moreover, the two formal units are connected
by verbal repetition: $yš'$ (v. 20.21.22), $ṣdq$ (v. 19.21.24.25), and $zæră'$

---

[30] Isa 41, 1.21; 43, 8. But see 48, 12—15.

[31] See Gunkel's introduction to H. Schmidt's Die großen Propheten, 1915, lxvi—lxvii.

[32] Cf. e. g., Isa 42, 1—4; 49, 1—6; 51, 4—5.

[33] Cf. 45, 14—17; 49, 22—23; 60, 1 ff., particularly v. 10—14.

[34] Begrich, Studien, 13; von Waldow, Anlaß und Hintergrund der Verkündigung des
Deuterojesaja, 1953, 36.

*yăᶜᵃqob/yiśra'el* (v. 19.25). In addition, we find thematic continuity between v. 18—21 and v. 22—25. The disputation is not about Cyrus, as is usually the case in Deutero-Isaiah's trial speeches,[35] but its purpose is rather to show that only Yahweh can "save." The nations' gods cannot (v. 20c). The exhortation in v. 22—25 also shares the theme of salvation; the nations must turn to Yahweh to be "saved" (v. 22).

Whether these connections signify an original association of the two genre units is not clear. If v. 22—25 had been a real exhortation directed to the nations, we might assume that v. 18—21 and v. 22—25 were originally independent utterances; but since the exhortation is a literary device for announcing salvation to Israel, we cannot be sure. The connections between the units are indeed quite strong.

V. 14—17 is also related to v. 18 ff. by theme and verbal repetition. The roots *str* (v. 15.19)[36] and *bôš* (v. 17.24) are held in common. The theme of the nations' worship of Yahweh is found in both v. 14—17 and v. 18—25. Both mention idol worshippers (v. 16.20), as well as the fact that the idols are made by men (v. 16.20). In both, the idol worshippers or those "incensed at Yahweh" will be "put to shame" in contrast with Israel, who is saved by her God (v. 16—17.24—25). Both v. 14—17 and v. 18—25 represent the nations in confession that Yahweh alone is God (v. 14—15.24). Finally, it must not be overlooked that v. 14—17 and v. 18 ff. are connected by *kî*.

Nevertheless, there are discontinuities between v. 14—17 and v. 18—25. In v. 14—17 Zion is the addressee while the nations are addressed in v. 18—25 (explicitly in v. 22—25). The messenger formula beginning each passage (v. 14.18) suggests that v. 14—17 and v. 18 ff. might not have originally been joined. V. 14—17 differ also from v. 18—21.22—25 in that there is no concern for the reliability of Yahweh's word. V. 14—17 emphasize instead the wealth of the nations coming to Zion and those nations making a "pilgrimage" to Zion in chains, bowing down before her. This tradition of the pilgrimage of the nations to Zion,[37] which in Deutero- and Trito-Isaiah depicts the nations as servants of Zion and her children,[38] is present in both v. 14—17 and v. 22—25, but in v. 22—25 the tradition appears in a significantly modified form. The normal usage of the tradition in Deutero- and Trito-Isaiah, and reflected in v. 14—17, emphasizes that the pilgrimage of the nations is for Zion's good fortune. Their wealth is to belong to Zion (Isa 45, 14; 60, 5—7.11); they are to bow down before Zion (45, 14; 49, 23; 60, 14). In general, the nations will be servants, coming

---

[35] 41, 1—7.21—29; 48, 12—15.
[36] Mowinckel, Komposition, 101.
[37] Cf. von Rad, Old Testament Theology, II 294 ff.
[38] 45, 14—17; 49, 22—23; 60, 1 ff.

in chains (45, 14), carrying Zion's children home (49, 22), and perform-
ing services for Zion (49, 23; 60, 10). V. 22—25 retain the idea of the
pilgrimage and the nations' confession before Yahweh, but in other
ways v. 22—25 seem to have departed from the typical features of the
tradition. The second feminine singular reference to Zion disappears.
Moreover, most of the typical features of the tradition mentioned above
drop out in favor of an emphasis on the irrevocability of Yahweh's
efficacious word (v. 23—24). These differences suggest the likelihood
that v. 14—17 and v. 18—21.22—25 were originally unconnected, having later been joined by *kî* because of similar theme and vocabulary.

b. Although the genre units appear to have been arranged by a
collector, they were not ordered without purpose. As we have seen,
they share the theme of the nations' homage before Yahweh who alone
is able to save. The nations who pray to a god who "cannot save"
(v. 20) are exhorted to turn to Yahweh and be saved (v. 22). Moreover,
the repetition of *str* connects v. 14—17 with v. 18 ff.[39] In the juxtaposition of v. 14—17 and v. 18—21, Yahweh's "hiddenness" takes on
dimensions larger than we find in each unit taken separately. Yahweh
has been hidden to the nations until his eschatological victory; up until
that time the nations had no possibility of knowing him (v. 14—17). The
collection contrasts this with the assertion that Yahweh has never spoken
in secret to the "seed of Jacob" (v. 19).

The arrangement of the genre units in v. 14—17.18—21, and
22—25 expresses again the tension which we found in the juxtaposition
of units in 41, 1—42, 13. The defeat of the nations (v. 14—17) and the
deliverance of the nations (v. 22—25) are — by association of genre
units — said almost in the same breath. In the juxtaposition of
v. 14—17.18—21, and 22—25 the relationship between the nations'
defeat and their deliverance is made somewhat clearer than it was in
41, 1—42, 13. In 45, 14 ff. we can see, first of all, that only a "remnant"
(v. 20) who survive the eschatological battle will be delivered. Moreover,
they are delivered to worship Yahweh, but as prisoners. Thus, in the
context of the collection, the servant's bringing forth light, *tôrā*, and
justice to the nations does not remove the slave status of the nations
after the final battle. Even Israel's slaves will know Yahweh and his
*tôrā*!

c. V. 14—17.18—21, and 22—25 relate to the foregoing context in
several ways. First of all, v. 14—17.18—21, and 22—25 all contain the
theme of the eschatological victory over the nations. As 44, 24—45, 13
presents it, the victory by Cyrus means the plundering of the nations
(45, 1.2.3), as well as the release of exiles and rebuilding of Jerusalem
(44, 26.28; 45, 13). The three utterances concerning Cyrus (44, 24—28;

[39] K. Elliger, Deuterojesaja in seinem Verhältnis zu Tritojesaja, 1933, 252.

45, 1—8.9—13) serve well as an introduction to 45, 14—17.18—21. 22—25. Whether the eschatological battle in the latter group of genre units originally referred to Cyrus' activity cannot be known with certainty; they make no explicit mention of him, either by name, or indirectly.[40] But in the present context, the defeat of the nations in 45, 14—25 must be understood as the victories achieved by Cyrus.

The confession of the defeated nations (45,14d.15.24.25) and the exhortation to them to be saved (45, 22) fit well after the oracle to Cyrus. Yahweh announces that he will send Cyrus "in order that they may know from the rising of the sun . . . that there is no one besides me" (45, 6). In v. 14—17 and in v. 22—25 the nations make confession before Yahweh that Yahweh alone is God. Indeed, just as Cyrus, who once did not know Yahweh, is made to know him (45, 3b—4), so also the nations who "do not know" (45, 20) will confess his name (45, 14—15.23—24).

## C. 46, 1—4.5—11.12—13

1. *Form Critical Analysis.* V. 1—4 was analyzed above.[41] I argued that it is a speech of salvation which combines the language of a song of victory (v. 1—2) with the style typically found in speeches of salvation. The mockery of the gods who must be carried away into exile after the catastrophe of the eschatological battle serves as a contrast by which Yahweh gives encouragement to Israel in the affirmation that he carries and delivers.

V. 1—4 are to be distinguished form critically from the disputation speech which follows in v. 5—11. The typical structure of this kind of disputation speech was discussed in Chapter Three:[42] (1) the question, "To whom will you compare me/God?"; (2) sarcastic description of the manufacture of idols; (3) exhortation to remember what has long been known through the cult. As we saw, the structure of this kind of disputation speech is not rooted in a long history of usage in oral tradition prior to Deutero-Isaiah. Nevertheless, Deutero-Isaiah stereotyped its structure to the extent which we commonly require of an oral genre. In this sense, then, Isaiah 46, 5—11 can be isolated from its context. Still, Isaiah 46, 5—11 manifests peculiarities found in no other text. The sarcastic description of the manufacture of idols which is characteristic of this kind of disputation speech (cf. Isa 40, 19—20; 46, 6—7) here takes on a special coloration — the image of worshippers bowing down before a god who must be lifted on the shoulders, carried, fastened

---

[40] Cf. also Isa 41, 2.25; 46, 11; 48, 14b.15.

[41] Cf. above, Chapter Two, II, 2.

[42] Chapter Three, II, 2.

in place, a god who indeed cannot answer the one who cries out to him. The exhortation to remember the "former things" appears in the form of a polemic against sinners who have not had faith in Yahweh's ability to save (v. 8). The implication: they have had confidence in idols, who "do not answer," rather than in Yahweh, who from the beginning speaks what will happen. Thus the intention of the disputation is not only to persuade but also to accuse.

The form of v. 12—13 is as follows: (1) call to hear, with the imperative *šim'û*[43] and Israel directly addressed as sinners (v. 12), and (2) announcement of Yahweh's intervention in the perfect tense, elaborated upon by the equivalent of the imperfect (v. 13): "I have brought near my righteousness" *(qerăbtî ṣidqatî)* and "I will put salvation in Zion *(weⁿnatắttî beṣiyyôn tešûʿ ā)*. This tense sequence, as we have seen, appears often in salvation speech.[44] But here, "Fear not" is absent. Moreover, the verb in the perfect tense is expanded by verbs which are best translated by relative clauses;[45] the clause with the verb expressing the equivalent of the imperfect is general rather than concrete in expression.[46] It is apparent, then, that the form of v. 12—13 is not that of the salvation-assurance oracle, though the tense sequence seems to indicate that the structure was influenced by that genre. The structure of 46, 12—13 is a free creation of Deutero-Isaiah, shaped to some extent by the form of the salvation-assurance oracle. Still, the speech can be distinguished from its context by form; it begins with the typical introductory imperative and continues with the announcement of salvation.

2. *Arrangement of Genre Units.* Verbal repetition is an important factor in the arrangement of units, both in the relationship of v. 1—4, 5—11, and 12—13 to one another and in the relationship of these three units to the foregoing context: *sbl* (46, 4.7), *'śh* (46, 4.6.11), the imperative *šim'û* (46.3.12), *kr'* (45, 23; 46, 1.2),[47] *nś'* (45, 20; 46, 4.7),[48] *lo' yošî'(ænnû)* (45, 20; 46, 7). Is this repetition the result of a collector's arrangement of originally separate units, or have we an author of a lengthy poem?

a. Westermann believes that chapter 46 is part of a long poetic composition beginning as far back as 45, 20 — a composition made up

---

[43] A similar introduction appears in 44, 1; 46, 3; 51, 1.7.

[44] Cf. above, Chapter Two, I.

[45] The verbs *lo' tirhaq* and *lo' teⁿἄḥer* are in poetic relative clauses. Contrast the perfect-tense verbs in the salvation-assurance oracles, e. g., 41, 10.14; 43, 1.

[46] For a contrast with the salvation-assurance oracles, cf. 41, 11—12.15—16; 43, 2.5b; 44, 3—5. In these texts the imperfect-tense verbs aid in painting a concrete image of the future.

[47] Cf. Mowinckel, Komposition, 101.

[48] Cf. also 46, 1.3.

of imperatives (45, 20.22; 46, 3.9.12).[49] This poem emphasizes the contrast between the remnant of the nations (45, 20) and the remnant of Israel (46, 3).[50] I have argued, however, that both chapters 45 and 46 can be broken down into genre units; thus it is best to begin by analyzing the relationship of genre units rather than starting with the assumption of a lengthy composition.

V. 1—4 have in common with v. 5—11 the theme of carrying idols, but there the thematic similarity ends. In v. 1—4 the central theme is the contrast between the idols which must be carried and Yahweh who carries from womb to old age; the announcement of salvation is made believable by contrasting their ability to carry and to save. In v. 5—11, however, the image of carrying idols is not central; the disputation emphasizes instead the deity's ability to declare the future.[51] Moreover, v. 1—4 and v. 5—11 use the image of carrying idols in somewhat different ways. In v. 1—4 we have a contrast between the gods who must be carried and Yahweh who carries. In v. 5—11, the contrast is between the god who, on the one hand, must be carried, who cannot answer, cannot save, and, on the other, the ability of Yahweh to declare the future. In v. 5—11 the fact that the idol must be carried is only one factor among several. Another difference between v. 1—4 and v. 5—11 is that in the former, the promise to Israel as remnant-in-exile (v. 3) is at the heart of the purpose of the oracle; in contrast with the idols who will be borne into captivity, Yahweh carries the remnant of Israel out of captivity. V. 5—11, by contrast, make no mention of the remnant. Indeed, in the latter, the emphasis is upon *sinful* Israel (v. 8) rather than upon *remnant* Israel.

It is probable that v. 1—4 and v. 5—11 did not originally belong together. Not only are they distinguishable form critically, but the emphases in v. 5—11, as I argued, are rather different from v. 1—4. Moreover, each is capable of being understood without the help of the other.

The relations between v. 5—11 and v. 12—13 are much closer. In v. 8 and 12 alike, Israel is addressed as sinful.[52] In v. 8 Israel's sin is her lack of trust in Yahweh and her proclivity to believe that the gods are superior to Yahweh. Israel is exhorted to abandon that belief through the contrast between the gods and what Israel has long known about

---

[49] Westermann, Sprache und Struktur, 151 ff.
[50] Ibid. 152.
[51] Cf. v. 9—10a.
[52] The emendation of 'ăbbîrê leb (cf. Ps 76, 6) to 'obᵉdê leb by Duhm and Westermann is unnecessary. V. 12 supports the present text. Cf. Duhm, Das Buch Jesaia übersetzt und erklärt, 1922, 354; Westermann, Sprache und Struktur, 153, and Das Buch Jesaja: Kapitel 40—66, 1966, 149.

the reliability of Yahweh's word (v. 9—10). The tense structure is
significant in understanding the relationship between v. 5—11 and
v. 12—13: Yahweh has already spoken (*dibbărtî*) and purposed
(*yaṣărtî*); in the future he will bring it to pass (*'ᵃbî'ænnā*) and will do it
(*'æ'æśænnā*). In v. 12 sinful Israel is addressed in a similar alternation of
tenses; first they hear the announcement of salvation in the perfect
(*qerăbtî ṣidqatî*), then in the equivalent of the imperfect (*wᵉnatăttî
bᵉṣiyyôn tᵉśû'ā*). The disputation in v. 5—11 argues that what has
already been spoken will in the future come to pass; the speech of
salvation (v. 12—13) promises that the righteousness which has already
been brought near will result in Zion's deliverance. Whether v. 5—11
and v. 12—13 were originally uttered together is not certain. Form
critically they are independent, but they are closely related in theme,
structure, and meaning.

b. Although the juxtaposition of genre units in chapter 46 is at
least in part the result of the process of collection, the arrangement is
significant. First of all, the reference to Cyrus in 46, 11 is related to the
theme of chapters 45—48. Moreover, 46, 1—4 continues the emphasis of
chapter 45 upon the capitulation of the nations.[53] 46, 1—4 extends that
theme in that these four verses do not simply promise their defeat, but
give us a *picture* of their humiliated and impotent gods being carried
into exile. In addition, the image of the nations left with only a residue
after the defeat (45, 20) is in the collection related to the epithet,
"remnant of the house of Israel" in 46, 3.[54] The larger context, then,
uses the image of the remnant as a means of association: a remnant of
the nations confessing Yahweh before Israel (45, 14—17; cf. v. 22—25),
and remnant Israel (46, 3), both of which inherit the new age. Ironically,
the circumstances of the past and present will in the future be reversed;
remnant Israel, slave of Babylon, will be served by a remnant of the
nations (45, 14—17).

The repetition of other images is important as well. Isaiah 45, 20
pictures the nations as those who "do not know, who carry the wood of
their idols, who pray to a god who cannot save." In chapter 45 that kind
of mental picture is placed in sharp contrast with images of the nations'
bowing down before Yahweh (v. 22—25). When chapter 46 is added to
chapter 45, the image of gods who must be carried, who neither answer
nor save, is repeated. But chapter 46 adds a new dimension when juxtaposed with chapter 45. An ironic reversal of circumstances is portrayed.
The larger context says: Israel was in exile; now the Babylonian idols
which were prominently carried about (45, 20) will indeed be carried —
into exile!

[53] Cf. 45, 14—17.22—25.
[54] Westermann, Sprache und Struktur, 152.

In spite of the fact that 46, 1—4 and 46, 5—11 were juxtaposed by a collector, the repetition of the image of the gods who must be carried is a significant connecting feature. The answer to the question, "To whom will you compare me?" (v. 5), becomes even more obvious when read in the light of the images in 46, 1—4. How can a deity who carries be compared with a god who must be carried into exile?

Finally, chapter 46 introduces into 44, 24—48, 21 a theme not found before in this segment of the collection — the theme of Israel as sinner (46, 5—11.12—13). Thus chapter 46 anticipates what becomes a major theme of chapter 48.

## D. Chapter 47

1. *Form Critical Analysis.* Westermann's insight that chapter 47 is a freely created poem is basically correct.[55] To call it a "mocking song" is not wrong,[56] but the structure of the poem appears to be unique to Deutero-Isaiah. Westermann recognizes this,[57] but he does not work out in detail the implication of his insight.

Isaiah chapter 47 is a taunt to a large extent influenced by the style of the prophetic oracle. The taunt begins in imperative style, but quickly moves to the prophetic announcement of the future:

| | |
|---|---|
| Imperative: | Come down, sit in the dust, O virgin daughter of Babylon, <br> Sit on the ground without a throne, O daughter of the Chaldeans! |
| Announcement: | For you shall no more be called tender and soft. |
| Imperative: | Take stones, grind meal, off with your veil! <br> Strip off your skirt, bare your leg, cross the rivers, <br> Let your nakedness be exposed, your shame be seen! |
| Announcement: | Vengeance I will take; I will not protect a man,[58] <br> Our redeemer, Yahweh of hosts is his name, <br> the Holy One of Israel. |

The images bring to mind the dethroning of a beautiful princess — forced to descend from her throne, to sit in the dust, to become a slave girl.

V. 5—7 have a similar structure: The passage opens with imperatives (v. 5a), followed by an announcement of the future (v. 5b). The announcement of the future is substantiated by means of a style often

---

[55] Westermann, Das Buch Jesaja, 152—153.
[56] J. Muilenburg, The Interpreter's Bible, V 1956, 543, 544; Begrich, Studien, 56; O. Eissfeldt, The Old Testament: An Introduction, 1965, 93.
[57] Westermann, Das Buch Jesaja, 152—153.
[58] Cf. the use of *pgʿ* in Isa 64, 4.

used in the prophetic invective (v. 6—7). The images in v. 5—7, as in
v. 1—4, interrelate, a cluster of coherent word pictures. "Sit in silence"
contrasts with the boast, "I am forever, mistress forever." "You did not
put upon them mercy"[59] contrasts with, "You did not put these on
your heart."

V. 8—9 employ the style of the invective and announcement of
judgment: a call to hear plus accusation in participial style, followed by
announcement of judgment. Here the language typical of the prophetic
oracle is dominated by the verb *yašāb*, which is ironically related to the
imperatives in v. 1. The godlike statement, "I am and there is none but
me, I will not sit as a widow, will not know bereavement" is ironic in
the context of the taunt, "Sit in the dust."

V. 10—11, too, make use of the style of the oracle. And again we
find in the invective a quotation of the statement, "I am and there is
none but me." The verbs *yādǎʿ* and *bôʾ* are repeated from v. 8—9, but the
theme is different. Babylon's wisdom, understood as something evil,
becomes the major theme of v. 11—12; in v. 8—9 it was subordinate to
widowhood and bereavement.

The taunt returns in v. 12 ff. The rest of the poem proceeds from the
sarcastic imperative *ʿimdî*. The caustic verbs preceded by "perhaps"
(v. 12) add to the mocking tone. Thus the poem ends as it begins in
mockery. The entire poem stands apart from its context as a taunting
song delivered by Yahweh to Babylon. Although the structure of the
poem is basically the creation of Deutero-Isaiah as he shapes traditional
language for his own purposes, we can isolate it from the context both
by form and content. The surrounding genre units (46, 12—13; 48,
1—11) are speeches addressed to Israel.

2. *Arrangement of Genre Units.* The placement of chapter 47 in
the collection is intentional. First of all, the tone of the poem is much
like several of the poems in chapters 45—46. In particular, the taunt
directed against Babylon in chapter 47 is reminiscent of 46, 1—2 and
45, 20. Babylon, like the gods, must fall to the ground (46, 1—2; 47, 1).
Indeed, Babylon claims to be a god,[60] but, unlike Yahweh, she does not
know the *ʾǎḥᵃrît* (46, 10; 47, 7). Babylon does not "remember" the "end"
in contrast to Israel's "remembrance" of Yahweh's creative word
(46, 8.9). Neither Babylon's gods nor her sorcery save her (47, 13); only
Yahweh can save (45, 20; 46, 7). Finally, the sarcastic summons to
Babylon to let her "counsels" save her contrasts with the affirmation in
44, 26 that Yahweh "accomplishes the counsel of his messengers."

---

[59] I have used a literal translation for the purpose of showing the contrast between
these two clauses.
[60] "I am, and there is none but me."

## E. 48, 1—11.12—15.16.17—19.20—21.22

1. *Form Critical Analysis.* a. V. 1—11 have already been examined form critically.[61] The passage is a disputation speech for the purpose of arguing that Yahweh will deliver Israel. The form, as we saw, was created primarily by Deutero-Isaiah himself in order to express precisely what he wanted to say. The style of the prophetic invective was employed because the prophet wanted to assert that Yahweh had announced the "former things" before they came to pass because he knew that, otherwise, sinful Israel would attribute them to an idol (v. 3—5). He incorporated also into the disputation a style sometimes used in aetiological narratives[62] explicitly for the purpose of arguing that Yahweh's activity in the future was motivated by Israel's sinfulness. Despite the fact that the structure of v. 1—11 is basically the creation of Deutero-Isaiah, v. 1—11 stand out from the context. V. 12, as we shall see, marks the beginning of a new genre unit.

b. V. 12—15 are a trial speech. The typical Deutero-Isaianic structure of summons to trial and argument by means of a question introduced by *mî* can plainly be seen. As is often the case, Yahweh makes assertions in self-praise style (v. 12—13). Looking more carefully, we can see that the structure of this particular trial speech is similar to 45, 18—21. After the introductory call to attention Yahweh makes the claim that he is God, the first and the last and the creator.[63] Then Yahweh summons his opponents to trial (v. 14aα).[64] The shift from singular to plural address probably indicates that Yahweh has turned his attention from Israel to the nations.[65] This indicates that the speech is a trial speech rather than a disputation speech, for the nations are never addressed in Yahweh's disputation speeches. Yahweh argues his case by appealing to what is already known: "Who among them declared these?" An Israelite would answer on the basis of what he knows by tradition that none of the gods created the earth, but Yahweh instead. The proper groundwork having been laid, Yahweh moves to resolve the case:

Yahweh loves him; he will perform his will on Babylon, his might
(literally 'his arm')[66] on the Chaldeans.
I, I have spoken, yea I have called him.
I have brought him; his way will prosper.[67]

---

[61] Chapter Three, II, 6.

[62] V. 7b. Cf. Gen 3, 21 ff. Ex 13, 17.

[63] 45, 18—21 also begins with a claim made in self-praise style.

[64] Cf. 45, 20.

[65] Cf. above, Chapter Four, footnote 67.

[66] Or, "the Chaldeans will be dispersed," reading *zoreʿû*. Cf. G. R. Driver, Notes on Isaiah, BZAW 77 (1958), 47—48.

[67] For this use of the hiph. of *ṣlḥ*, cf. e. g., Isa 55, 11  Ps 1, 3.

In a word, Yahweh argues that since his prophetic word has been reliable in the past, his hearers may now believe what he has just spoken about Cyrus.

V. 14b is striking if one compares the structure of 48, 12—15 with the structure of other Deutero-Isaianic disputation speeches between Yahweh and the nations or their gods. Normally, the first person of Yahweh appears throughout the unit, but in 48, 14b a shift occurs with the result that Yahweh is spoken of in third person.[68] How are we to understand this shift in the light of the typical structure of this kind of trial speech in Deutero-Isaiah? Since it is unique, it seems best to begin by asking how v. 14b functions in this passage. The purpose of v. 12—15 is to argue that Yahweh's word has creative power in contrast to the gods. Since Israel has experienced the reliability of his word in the past, the people of Yahweh can now have confidence that the word he has uttered about Cyrus[69] will come to pass in the future.[70] V. 14b might be something like a quotation of a previously-uttered word concerning Cyrus. It has the ring of a royal oracle spoken in the third person: "Yahweh loves him; he will perform his will on Babylon . . ." Certainly the freedom of Deutero-Isaiah to fuse and modify traditional genres would allow for this alteration of the usual structure.

48, 12—15 reflects both the typical features of Deutero-Isaiah's trial speeches and the unique features mentioned above. It is sufficiently typical that it stands out from its context by form.

c. V. 16 opens with an address: "Draw near to me, hear this!" Then follows a speech in the mouth of Yahweh (v. 16a.b) and a word of the prophet (v. 16c). A somewhat similar pattern is found in Zechariah.[71] In Zechariah, the prophetic word is attached to a divine promise; when the promise is fulfilled, the prophet's hearers will know that Yahweh has sent him. Isaiah 48, 16 differs in two respects: First, the prophetic word

---

[68] A glance into the history of the textual transmission of v. 14b shows the difficulty of establishing the correct text. In LXX the first stich would presuppose a Hebrew text like the following: 'ohebka 'ᵃśîtî ḥæpsᵉka bᵉbabæl. But 1QIsaᵃ reads: yhwh 'whby wyśh ḥpṣy bbbl. The problem is too complex to be able to arrive at a complete reconstruction of the original text, but it seems likely that MT is in general the best text. Hepæṣ is normally used in Isa 40—55 in connection with Yahweh's purpose (44, 28; 46, 10; 53, 10). Thus it is likely that the "purpose" referred to is Yahweh's purpose, thus ruling out the second person suffix in the Hebrew text lying behind LXX. If Yahweh belonged in the earliest form of the text (it is absent in LXX), we should expect a third person suffix on hepæṣ (against 1QIsaᵃ). Moreover, the third person suffix is supported by parallelism (both MT and 1QIsaᵃ read zᵉroʿô in the second stich).

[69] "I, I have spoken; yea, I have called him; I have brought him."

[70] "His way will prosper."

[71] Zech 2, 13.15; 4, 9; 6, 15.

does not appear in the context of an *Erkenntnisaussage* as in Zechariah. Moreover, Isaiah 48, 16 expresses the divine word as a disputation:

> Not from the beginning did I speak to you in secret,
> From the time that it was I was there.

Because in the past Yahweh did not speak in secret but through the prophetic word, Deutero-Isaiah's hearers may have confidence that he has been sent by Yahweh. V. 16 appears to stand apart by form (new address) and by content (a disputation authenticating the *prophet's* mission).

d. V. 17—19 are also independent form critically. They are a divine word introduced by the messenger formula:

Introduction:  Expanded messenger formula (v. 17a)
                  Expanded self-predication (v. 17b)
**Body:**         An expression of what might have been (v. 18—19)

It is difficult to describe the genre precisely, but the speech is clearly built upon traditional liturgical language, as Psalm 81, 14—17 shows. In Psalm 81, however, the statement introduced by *lû* is a conditional promise; it refers to the future. Isaiah 48, 18—19 speak instead of the past, about what Yahweh would have done had Israel been obedient. Whether there was a conventional setting for the latter in oral tradition or whether it is a Deutero-Isaianic modification we may only speculate. In any event, v. 17—19 may be isolated from the context as a particular genre or genre element unrelated *form critically* to what precedes and follows.[72]

e. V. 20—21 are a short hymn which at the beginning imitate instructions such as we find in Genesis 19, 15.[73] The structural similarity with Isaiah 52, 11—12 is also quite apparent, although the instructions in 48, 20—21 lead to the summons to praise, which is characteristic of the hymn: "Say, 'Yahweh has redeemed his servant Jacob . . .'" V. 20—21 do not appear to be related form critically to v. 17—19. Furthermore, the unit can stand alone in terms of content.

f. V. 22 appears not to have belonged originally to v. 20—21. It is a judgmental speech by Yahweh rather than a form of speech which is closely related to the hymn. Moreover, it is repeated in Isaiah 57, 21 in a totally different context.

2. *Arrangement of Genre Units.* a. The arrangement of genre units is in all probability the result of the process of collection. V. 1—11 and

---

[72] The usage in Ps 81 and the similar kind of thing in Ps 95, 7b suggest that the conditional statement was not an independent genre, but rather a genre element which could sometimes be used with a hymn.

[73] Begrich, Studien, 57.

v. 12—15 are obviously connected by the repetition of the imperative of *šmˁ* (v. 1.12), *ri'šôn* (v. 3.12), and *qr'* (v. 1.2.8.12).[74] Moreover, thematic similarities may be found, especially the theme of the reliability of Yahweh's prophetic word in past and future. Yet there are significant discontinuities between the two genre units. In v. 12—15 the intention of the disputation is in no way related to the sinfulness of Israel. In v. 1—11, by contrast, Israel's sin is at the very heart of the purpose of Yahweh's activity. Furthermore, *qr'* is used quite differently in v. 1—11 and v. 12—15. In v. 1—11 it is used to contrast Israel who calls herself by the name of Israel and the holy city (v. 1.2) with Yahweh who calls her a rebel from birth (v. 8b). In v. 12—15 nothing of that kind is implied; we have rather a connection between Yahweh's election of Israel *(mᵉqora'î* — v. 12) and Yahweh's calling of Cyrus (v. 15).

V. 12—15 and v. 16, as we saw, are independent form critically, yet there are relationships in language and subject matter. Both genre units use *ro'š/ri'šôn* and *dibbārtî*. Moreover, both employ the imperative of *šmˁ* in the introduction (v. 12.16).[75] Both genre units are concerned with the believability of the present word of Yahweh in the light of the reliability of that word in the past. Nevertheless, we must not overlook significant differences. In v. 12—15 the primary intention is to convince Israel by means of her knowledge of the reliability of Yahweh's word in the past that he is powerful enough to call Cyrus. Indeed, the word play on *qr'* (v. 13.15) is a poetic device for that very purpose. V. 16 concerns itself, not specifically with the believability of the prophecy concerning Cyrus, but more generally with the credibility of the *prophet's* word. Thus the two genre units are somewhat different in intent and certainly capable of existing apart from each other. It is probable, then, that they were juxtaposed by a collector.

V. 17—19, too, exhibit verbal repetition in relation to the foregoing context: *mădrîkᵃka bᵉdæræk* (v. 17) in relation to *wᵉhiṣlîᵃḥ dărkô* (v. 15), *lo' yikkaret* (v. 19) in relation to *lᵉbiltî hăkrîtæka* (v. 9). Yet the phrases are used quite differently in each genre unit. It seems probable that, like the rest of chapter 48, v. 17—19 did not originally belong to their present context.

As we observed above, v. 20—21 stand apart form critically. Although we find a verbal connection with what goes before in the repetition of *g'l*, there is no other verbal relationship. It is probable that v. 20—21 were placed here by a collector primarily for the structure of the collection as a whole.[76] Only secondarily is its relationship to its most immediate context of importance.

---

[74] Cf. Mowinckel's understanding of the catchword connections, Komposition, 103.

[75] Cf. also v. 1.

[76] Cf. my discussion above in Chapter Six.

b. Although the arrangement of genre units in chapter 48 is the result of the process of collection, it is not without significance. The rhetorical features which connect the units are used to create a kerygmatic unity. Thus it is no accident that disputation speeches were juxtaposed (v. 1—11.12—15.16), all with the imperative, "Hear!" Two of the three disputations relate the earlier time ($ri'šonôt$ — v. 3; $ro'š$ — v. 16) to the divine word uttered now ('$attā$ — v. 6.7.16). Thus we may expect to find a theology of the relationship between past and future a significant factor in the arrangement of chapter 48.

Another rhetorical feature in the arrangement of the units in chapter 48 is that v. 1—19 are dominated at the beginning and end by genre units which portray Israel as sinful (v. 1—11.17—19). Moreover, v. 1—11 and v. 17—19 both speak of the "name" by which Israel is called (v. 1.19) and language associated with Israel's being "cut off" (v. 9.19).

The collection uses these rhetorical features to develop a meaning for the chapter which is larger than the meaning of any particular genre unit. By itself, the disputation in v. 1—11 aspires to convince sinful Israel that Yahweh's plan which is presently announced is trustworthy; as in the past Yahweh announced his word beforehand so that sinful Israel would not attribute his deeds to an idol, so he waits until now to announce the "new things" in order that rebellious Israel will not deal deceitfully. When v. 12—15 are placed after v. 1—11, they take on a significance which the unit did not possess when standing alone. The Jacob-Israel called by Yahweh (v. 12) must now be understood as a sinful Israel, "called rebel from birth" (v. 8). Thus the summoning of Cyrus to execute Yahweh's "desire" on Babylon (v. 14) becomes in the context of chapter 48 a plan which Yahweh executes "for his own sake" that his glory may not be given to another god (v. 11).

V. 16 also, in the light of v. 1—11, is directed to a sinful people. In the context of chapter 48 they are a people who have refused to hear the prophet. Nothing like that is implied when v. 16 is interpreted by itself. V. 17—19, too, must be seen in the context of v. 1—11. Indeed, these verses take on a new meaning so that a particular understanding of the relation between past and future can be seen: In the past, Israel's name was deservedly "cut off" (v. 19), though Yahweh had hoped otherwise (v. 17—19). But, ultimately, in the future which Yahweh is announcing through the prophet, they will not be "cut off." Yahweh will act for the sake of his name and will not give his glory to another (v. 9.11).

V. 1—19, then, is a kerygmatic unity. Sinful Israel doubts the word of Yahweh's prophet concerning Israel. They have always been prepared to attribute Yahweh's deeds to an idol. Because they have refused to obey Yahweh who led them in the "way" (v. 17), their name has been cut off (v. 17—19). Yet Yahweh will not cut them off forever; he will not let his deeds be "given to another." He announces "now" that he will prosper the "way" of Cyrus (v. 15), so that the glory may be given to him.

c. Chapter 48 is related to the foregoing context by verbal repetition: qr' (47, 1; 48, 1.2.8.12.15), yhwh ṣᵉba'ôt šᵉmô (47, 4; 48, 2), the phrase, "suddenly it comes/suddenly I did and it came" (47, 11; 48, 3), and the repeated use of the imperative of šmʿ (46, 3.12; 47, 8; 48, 1.12. 14.16).[77] The theme of the sinfulness of Israel is continued from chapter 46 and intensified. But the most important connection with the preceding context is that chapter 48 relates back to the beginning of the section 44, 24—48, 21. 44, 24 ff. begins with speeches about Cyrus (44, 24—28; 45, 1—8.9—13), and it ends with a complex of units in which deliverance through Cyrus is a major component (48, 12—15). As Cyrus fulfills Yahweh's "purpose" in 44, 28, so also in 48, 14b.

d. V. 20—21, as we saw, end the Jacob-Israel section of the collection. Yet these verses also relate in a peculiar way to the section of the collection which begins in 44, 24. 48, 20—21 relates to 45, 6, where Cyrus is commissioned "in order that they may know from the rising of the sun . . . that there is no one besides me." At the exodus from Babylon the "ends of the earth" will indeed know; Israelites can be summoned to praise: "Bring it to the ends of the earth; say, 'Yahweh has redeemed his servant Jacob!'"

e. V. 22 is related to its context by the repetition of šalôm (v. 18. 22). Precisely when the verse entered the collection we do not know. Perhaps it was included when chapters 40—66 as a whole were united as a collection.[78] However that may be,[79] in the context of the emphasis in chapter 48 upon the sinfulness of Israel, v. 22 appears to suggest a distinction between the destiny of the righteous and the fate of the wicked. Without v. 22 we should never have read chapter 48 in this way. But, as I shall presently argue, the collection makes this kind of distinction in chapters 49 ff. Isaiah 48, 22 anticipates it.


## II. ISAIAH 49, 1—6.7.8—12.13


1. *Form Critical Analysis.* I argued in Chapter Five that Isaiah 49, 1—6 is a report of the commissioning of the servant. Like many of

---

[77] Particularly, "Hear this!" (47, 8; 48, 1.16). Cf. Mowinckel, Komposition, 103.

[78] Note the appearance of the judgmental saying in both 48, 22 and 57, 21.

[79] It is not my intention here to speculate on the process of the growth of chapters 40—66. As I indicated in Chapter Six, I intend to interpret the collection in its final form.

Deutero-Isaiah's poems, it cannot be said to be an example of a genre customarily used in Israel. Although the language of commissioning and elements of other genres appear in the poem, its structure is ultimately the creation of Deutero-Isaiah. He wanted to set the high calling of the servant in contrast with the servant's past experience of failure.[80] Thus he used elements from the thanksgiving psalm in connection with the language of commissioning. As we saw in Chapter Five, the poem does not make clear whether it is the commissioning of a prophet or of a king or of some other kind of official. This is because the intention of the speech is to express Yahweh's commissioning of Israel (v. 3). Israel, who is consumed by a sense of utter defeat (v. 4a), should take comfort; "now" Yahweh gives his people a significant new task (v. 5—6). Even though the form of 49, 1—6 is the creation of Deutero-Isaiah, it stands out from its context by form and content. What precedes is in no sense directly related to the speech of the servant, and 49, 7 is a fresh announcement of salvation, complete on its own.

V. 7, an announcement of salvation, begins with an expanded messenger formula:

> Thus says Yahweh, the redeemer of Israel, his Holy One.
> To one despised to himself, abhorred by the foreigner, servant of rulers.

Then follows the announcement of salvation and the goal of Yahweh's intervention:

> Kings will see and arise, princes will bow down
> For the sake of Yahweh who is faithful, the Holy One of Israel
>     who chose you.

Form critically, v. 7 is a complete oracle of salvation. Moreover, its content differs from the oracles in the surrounding context. Its intention is quite specific: Israel, despised and oppressed, will find princes bowing down before her. This reversal of circumstances is grounded in the faithfulness of Yahweh's election of Israel.

V. 8—12 begin a new oracle with messenger formula and fresh content. Begrich understands it as a prophetic imitation of the "priestly salvation oracle," while von Waldow sees it as a genre from cultic prophecy.[81] The truth of the matter is that we lack sufficient evidence to determine precisely the original setting for this form of speech. It appears to make reference to the cultic complaint,[82] and it has perfect-tense verbs with general meaning, so that we are reminded of the salvation-assurance oracle.[83] Yet the structure is different from the salvation-

---

[80] See my more detailed discussion of the intention of the poem in Chapter Five.
[81] Begrich, Studien, 14—26; von Waldow, Anlaß und Hintergrund, 86 ff.
[82] "At an acceptable time I answer you."
[83] Cf. above, Chapter Two, for a discussion of the form.

assurance oracle. "Fear not" is lacking; the *assurance of salvation* is abbreviated;[84] the *announcement of salvation* is quite extended, and, moreover, it is in the plural rather than the singular (v. 9 ff.). Have we a freely-formed prophetic speech which is an imitation of a more rigidly structured prototype? Or is it a highly stereotyped kind of speech, the form of which we happen to possess only in this one example? We cannot know with certainty. Given what we know about Deutero-Isaiah as a whole, we are inclined to suspect that the form is to a considerable degree the creation of Deutero-Isaiah, conforming roughly to the typical pattern of the "announcement of salvation," but influenced by the "assurance of salvation" as well.[85] The content of the oracle is distinctively Deutero-Isaianic: The one whom Yahweh addresses is given as a $b^e$rît 'am;[86] also the image of the shepherd is Deutero-Isaianic.[87] The Exodus imagery of not thirsting in the desert and the making of a highway in the desert is characteristically Deutero-Isaianic. Even the close of the oracle (v. 12) is quite typical of Deutero-Isaiah.[88]

V. 13 is an eschatological hymn.[89] It has the summons to praise in imperative style, followed by the substantiation, expressed by a verb in the perfect tense and continued by a verb in the imperfect.[90]

2. *Arrangement of Genre Units.* Isaiah 49, 1—13 is composed of formal units which can stand alone both by form and content. Yet we find a number of connecting features. Most obvious is the relationship between $un^e$tāttîka $l^{e_2}$ôr gôyim in v. 1—6 and $w^{e_2}$ættænka librît 'am in v. 8—13. Also, in v. 1—6 the purpose of Yahweh's servant is $l^e$haqîm 'æt šibṭê yă$^{c a}$qob; in v. 8—12 the one to whom Yahweh addressed the oracle is given a mission: $l^e$haqîm 'æræṣ. The servant in v. 1—6 and the one addressed in v. 8 ff. are both understood as agents of Yahweh's "salvation" (v. 6.8). In v. 1—6 the servant is a "light to the nations" (v. 6); in v. 7 Yahweh's despised one is "abhorred by the nations." V. 8—12 and v. 13 are joined by the repetition of hăr (v. 11.13) and the pi$^c$el of rḥm (v. 10.13).

a. It is difficult to determine whether these verses were originally uttered together or whether they were associated by means of the process

---

[84] Compare with the fuller forms of the assurance of salvation: 41, 8—10.14. Other examples are shorter.

[85] It would be interesting to know whether there existed a form in the plural corresponding to the oracle in the singular which begins with "fear not."

[86] Cf. 42, 6.

[87] Cf. 40, 11.

[88] Cf. 43, 5b.6.

[89] Cf. H. Gunkel, Einleitung in die Psalmen, 1966, 32 ff.; Westermann, Sprache und Struktur, 157 ff.

[90] Cf. Isa 44, 23.

of collection. Certainty eludes us, but I would argue that 49, 1—13 is a collection. Not only is each genre unit capable of standing alone by form and content, but each has its own particular intention as well. The report of the commissioning in v. 1—6 has as its purpose the furnishing of a new self-understanding in the face of despair. V. 7, though not in the form of a commissioning oracle, has a somewhat similar purpose; its intention is to announce a reversal of circumstances for one who is despised. V. 1—6 and v. 7, nevertheless, have different foci: v. 1—6 emphasize the servant's mission in connection with the *salvation* of the nations, while v. 7 accents the *submission* of the nations. V. 8—12 betray still another emphasis; this oracle promises Israel's return home. The fact that these differences in purpose correspond with the genre unit divisions suggests that each unit originally had its own separate function and only later was placed in its present context.

b. Nevertheless, in the present arrangement of units a kerygmatic unity is apparent. Yahweh's servant Israel will be a light to the nations when the nations see a change in the fate of the despised one, the collection implies in its juxtaposition of v. 1—6 and v. 7. And what kind of change in his status will they see? They will see Israel returned to her land (v. 8—12). The word play on "to restore the tribes of Jacob" (v. 6) and "to restore the land" (v. 8) intensifies the rhetorical unity of the juxtaposition of units and enhances the essential place of Israel's return to her land in the collection's understanding of Yahweh's plan to save the nations. Yahweh's salvation will reach the "ends of the earth" (v. 6), says the collection, only when princes "see" (v. 7) the restoration of Israel (v. 6.8). Just as elsewhere in Isaiah 40—55 Yahweh's saving deed is performed so that all will see that he is God,[91] so also in 49, 1—13 the collection relates the nations' "seeing" with their salvation. The hymn in v. 13 also contributes to the kerygmatic unity of v. 1—13. The land and the mountains which played a major role in v. 8—12 are summoned to rejoice.

c. An important factor in the placement of 49, 1—13 in the collection is that these units respond to what was begun in the collection in chapters 40 ff.[92] As in 42, 22 so also in 49, 2 we find that the servant was hidden; but the understanding of his hiddenness in 49, 2 puts 42, 22 in larger perspective. The servant was indeed hidden as punishment (42, 22 ff.), but 49, 2 makes it clear that he was hidden only for a time. He was hidden (49, 2) until "now" (49, 5) so that Yahweh's purpose may be accomplished. Thus once again the collection's understanding of the relationship between past and present appears.

---

[91] Cf. 41, 20.

[92] See in particular my comments on 40, 27—31 on the relationship between 40, 27—31 and 49, 1—6: Chapter Seven, I, 2.

The relationship between 49, 1—6 and 40, 27—31 is particularly significant. In 49, 4 Israel complains, "For nought I became weary, for nothing and vanity I spent my strength." This language reminds us of 40, 27—31. But unlike 40, 27—31, the servant in 49, 1—6 expresses confidence: "My *mišpaṭ* is with Yahweh, my reward[93] is with my God" (v. 4b). Indeed, 49, 1—6 is intentionally placed at the end of the Jacob-Israel section of the collection to recapitulate the language of 40, 27—31.

We saw in our discussion of the arrangement of units in 41, 1—42, 13 the tension between the servant who defeats the nations in battle (41, 8—13.14—16) and the servant who brings justice and *tôrā* to the nations (42, 1 ff.).[94] 49, 1—6 shares a similar tension. The servant's task is to restore Israel, but that is not enough; he must also be a light to the nations.

Finally, the servant's mission to glorify Yahweh (49, 3) by restoring Israel and giving light to the nations (49, 6) continues the emphasis on Yahweh's glory in the Jacob-Israel section of the collection. The release of prisoners and the return home is for Yahweh's glory (42, 7.8; 43, 6.7);[95] the servant is a "light to the nations" for Yahweh's glory (42, 6.8); all flesh is to "see" Yahweh's glory (40, 5; cf. 49, 7).

d. The text in chapter 49 clearly identifies the servant as Israel.[96] Moreover, the collection as a whole up to this point seems to understand the servant as Israel.[97] This identification is, however, not without problems. For example, the familiar question emerges: how can Israel restore Israel? The various solutions to the problem in the form of theories such as ideal Israel, remnant Israel, corporate personality, or the like are but hypotheses not explicitly stated in the text. When one reads 49, 1—6 without presupposing one or another of these theories, one is struck by the fact that the text itself gives us no clues to solve our problem. We simply have a servant Israel who is nevertheless in some fashion given the task of restoring the tribes of Israel. Precisely what is meant is not explained; it is as if the ambiguity were deliberate.

We must content ourselves with a kind of ambiguity which cannot satisfactorily be resolved by any of the theories. Moreover, it is unlikely that we shall be able to find new theories which overcome the vagueness of the language of the text. Thus we must be satisfied with a few observations: Without backing away from our insistence that the collec-

---

[93] Cf. 40, 10.

[94] Cf. above, Chapter Seven, II, B, 2, b.

[95] The return home from the four directions (43, 5—7) is equivalent to "restoring the tribes of Jacob" (49, 6) and "restoring the land" (49, 8).

[96] The evidence for deletion is not weighty enough to consider it probable. At best it remains a mere possibility.

[97] See my discussion of 42, 1—4.5—9.

tion understands the servant as Israel, we do find signs that in the collection the servant is sometimes closely related to the prophet who has spoken the oracles in Isaiah 40—55. In Chapter Six we discovered that the "I" of 40, 6 seems to be at once prophet and people.[98] Furthermore, the terms "servant" and "messenger" in Deutero-Isaiah are employed somewhat ambiguously. In 44, 26 we find the terms used to refer to prophetic activity; Yahweh "confirms the word of his servant,[99] the counsel of his messengers." Yet in 42, 19 the blind and deaf "messenger" and "servant" seems to be exiled Israel. It is as though the collection has deliberately blurred the line between prophet and Israel.

e. Isaiah 49, 1—13 not only relates itself to the foregoing context but also anticipates what is to follow. The picture which 49, 7 gives us of the exaltation of the despised anticipates both 50, 4—11 and the fourth "servant song." 49, 7 in its announcement that "kings will see and arise, princes will bow down," anticipates what we find in 49, 23, in the Zion-Jerusalem section of the collection:

> Kings will be your foster fathers, queens your nursing mothers,
> Prostrate they will bow down before you;
>> the dust of your feet they will lick.

Finally, the promise of the restoration of the $n^e\dot{h}al\hat{o}t$ $\check{s}omem\hat{o}t$ in 49, 8 anticipates what follows in 49, 14 ff. (cf. v. 19).

---

[98] Chapter Six, II, A.

[99] Or perhaps, "servants."

10*

# Chapter Nine: Isaiah 49, 14—55, 13

This chapter will examine the arrangement of genre units in the Zion-Jerusalem segment of the collection. Although certain portions of 49, 14 ff. do not speak of the people of Yahweh in the feminine as the mother-wife Zion,[1] the feminine of Zion-Jerusalem address predominates. "Jacob" or "Israel" never appears. 49, 14—55, 13 is divided by the hymn in 52, 9—10 and the command to leave the city in v. 11—12.[2] The fourth "servant song" comes between the two halves. The first half of the Zion-Jerusalem section of the collection opens with genre units which are heavily disputational in tone (49, 14—26), as is the case with the beginning of the Jacob-Israel section (40, 12—31).

Westermann has contended that most of chapter 49—55 is composed of lengthy poetic compositions rather than units which can properly be called *Gattungen*.[3] This assumption must be tested form critically, for our conclusions concerning the arrangement of units cannot be separated from our understanding of the nature of the most basic units.

## I. ISAIAH 49, 14—52, 12

### A. 49, 14—21.22—23.24—26

1. *Form Critical Analysis.* Begrich, followed by von Waldow, holds that v. 14—21.22—23, and 24—26 are separate speeches.[4] For Begrich, v. 22—23 illustrate clearly the parts of the salvation oracle.[5] V. 22a, following the messenger formula, states Yahweh's intervention. V. 22b— 23b declare the consequences of Yahweh's intervention, and v. 23c contains the purpose of that intervention. V. 24—26 also display the

---

[1] 51, 1—8; 52, 3—6.11—12; 55, 1 ff. 51, 12—16 is mixed, partly second masculine plural, partly second masculine singular, and partly second feminine singular. The two "servant songs" (50, 4—11; 52, 13—53, 12) do not employ Zion language.

[2] Cf. 48, 20—21 for a similar phenomenon.

[3] Westermann, Sprache und Struktur der Prophetie Deuterojesajas, Forschung am alten Testament, 1964, 164, and Das Buch Jesaja: Kapitel 40—66, 1966, 26.

[4] Begrich, Studien zu Deuterojesaja, 1963, 14—16, 26; von Waldow, Anlaß und Hintergrund der Verkündigung des Deuterojesaja, 1953, 28.

[5] Begrich, Studien, 16.

[6] Ibid. 16, footnote 7.

structure of the salvation oracle.[6] The purpose of Yahweh's intervention
is found in v. 26b.[7] V. 26a expresses the consequences of Yahweh's intervention. The typical form of the first part of the oracle has undergone
considerable transformation. The doubting question of the lament is
quoted (v. 24), to which Yahweh answers that the unbelievable is
possible (v. 25a).[8] V. 25b, according to Begrich's scheme, is the statement
of Yahweh's intervention. V. 14—21 also display the form of the
salvation oracle, in Begrich's judgment. V. 14—15 dispute the people's
complaint that Yahweh has forsaken Zion; v. 16 is the statement of
Yahweh's intervention, and v. 17 expresses the consequences of Yahweh's intervention. The second part of the oracle, v. 18—21,[9] exhibits
member *a* in v. 18a.[10] Member *b* is present in v. 18b, expanded by
v. 19b—21.[11]

Westermann does not dispute the contention of Begrich and von
Waldow that these salvation oracle structures can be seen, even though
he does not agree that they are imitations of the cultic salvation-
assurance oracle. Nevertheless, he believes that v. 14—26 should be seen
as one poetic composition in which three salvation oracles are imitated.[12]
This long poem combines the language of the disputation and the speech
of salvation to argue against Zion's continuing in the state of lamentation. The poem is a three-part disputation and promise to counter three
complaints: "Yahweh has forsaken me" (v. 14), "I was childless and
barren" (v. 21), and, "Can booty be taken from a mighty man?" (v. 24).
These three complaints, in Westermann's judgment, correspond to the
three complaints of the cultic lament psalm — the complaint about the
lack of Yahweh's saving activity, the complaint about the woeful state
of the supplicant, and the complaint about the oppression of the
enemy.[13] Thus the prophet has composed a long poem, using parts of the
lament psalm as a model and fusing the language of disputation and
speech of salvation as the answer to each of the three parts of the
lament psalm.

Westermann is correct that 49, 14 ff. is not simply a modification of
the salvation-assurance oracle.[14] Moreover, the modification of the

---

[7] Ibid. 18.
[8] Ibid. 21.
[9] Ibid. 25.
[10] The part of the form which expresses Yahweh's intervention.
[11] The elaboration of Yahweh's intervention.
[12] Westermann, Das Heilswort bei Deuterojesaja, EvTh 24 (1964), 366—368. Cf. also
Sprache und Struktur, 121, 132—133, and Das Buch Jesaja, 177 ff.
[13] Westermann, Heilswort, 368.
[14] See my form critical discussion above in Chapter Two.

language of salvation speech by incorporation of disputation style is undeniable. In addition, we must not overlook the thematic continuity of the return of Zion's sons as an indication that the arrangement of these verses is not accidental. But Westermann's view that we have a long poem based on the three parts of the lament psalm is unsatisfactory. First of all, v. 14—26 in their entirety do not dispute three real complaints. Only v. 14 and 24 represent real questions to be disputed: V. 14 has the appearance of an actual complaint that Yahweh has forsaken Zion. V. 15—16 dispute that complaint by arguing that Yahweh has continually been concerned about Zion. Then follow the concrete details of his intervention on Zion's behalf.[15] The mother Zion is told to look at the return of her sons; the children of the bereaved mother will be so many that the land can hardly contain them. Indeed, the miracle of the return will so surprise the mother that she will ask, "Who bore me these?" I was bereaved and barren, exiled and put aside. Who has brought up these . . .?" V. 25—26, too, seem to dispute a real question, quoted in v. 24. V. 21, however, is not a genuine question to be answered. It is rather an intensification of the announcement of salvation. The mother Zion is not really asking a question; she is expressing amazement before the wonder of her sons' return. Therefore, v. 21 must be taken as a part of the promise rather than as a new question to be answered, as Westermann would have it.

A second objection to Westermann's view that v. 14—26 are a long disputational poem, based on the three types of complaints from the lament psalm, emerges from an examination of v. 24. Westermann, following Begrich, assumes that v. 24 is a question typical of a lament psalm.[16] But I do not believe this is true. The lament psalm never questions whether Yahweh can deliver his people from the clutches of the powerful. The lament psalm presupposes that he can and does. In v. 24, however, the question seems to be whether there is any reason to expect Yahweh to deliver from the might of the tyrant.[17] Thus v. 24—26 are not derived from the conventional cultic complaint but rather from the doubt occasioned by the exile. Therefore, v. 14—26 as a whole are not based on the structure of the lament psalm as Westermann argues.

---

[15] Read *bônăyik* with lQIsaᵃ. V. 19a is perhaps corrupt. But note 51, 2b—3 for a similar pattern of two clauses introduced by *kî* in which the second clause reflects a time which is to be compared with the earlier time mirrored in the first clause.

[16] Cf. Begrich, Studien, 21; H. Gunkel, Einleitung in die Psalmen, 1966, 127.

[17] In the laments the supplicant often cries, "Why?" or, "How long?" But we have no examples of a question like Isa 49, 24. Even in Gunkel's discussion of Isa 49, 24 (127) one is aware how unique Isa 49, 24 is.

Form critically we have three genre units: v. 14—21.22—23, and 24—26. Each has the structural elements necessary for a complete speech of salvation:

V. 14—21  (1) Quotation of complaint (v. 14)
          (2) Disputational pronouncement of salvation (v. 15—21)

V. 22—23  (1) Messenger formula
          (2) Announcement of salvation
          (3) Purpose of Yahweh's deliverance
              (*Erkenntnisaussage*)

V. 24—26  (1) Quotation of complaint
          (2) Messenger formula
          (3) Disputational announcement of salvation
          (4) Purpose of Yahweh's deliverance
              (*Erkenntnisaussage*)

Not only is each unit complete in terms of form; each is capable of being understood without the other.

2. *Arrangement of Genre Units.* a. Although v. 14—21.22—23, and 24—26 are capable of standing alone both by form and content, Westermann has rightly seen that these three genre units hang tightly together when compared with the surrounding context. The addressee throughout is Zion,[18] and the theme of the return of sons to the bereaved mother is reflected in each unit. Indeed, these three units all reflect the same kind of traditionary complex.[19] Moreover, in the present context the arrangement of units appears to involve movement from one unit to the other. V. 14—21, answering the complaint that Yahweh has forsaken Zion, promises that so many of the mother's sons will be returned home that she will ask in surprise how all this happened. In the present context, v. 22—23 provide the answer: the nations will carry them home. Though the questions in v. 21 were not genuine questions to be answered, in the present arrangement of the text the rhetorical questions in v. 21 are provided with an answer. V. 24—26 answer the doubt provoked by the promise that the nations will carry Zion's sons home. Can the tyrant be expected to do something as incredible as that? The juxtaposition of v. 22—23 and v. 24—26 causes the issue to be put in precisely that sense. The answer, of course, is: Yes, Yahweh will deliver from the power of the oppressor (v. 25—26). Whether the present text is due to an author or collector is uncertain. However that may be, the arrangement of genre units is kerygmatic.

b. Isaiah 49, 14—21.22—23.24—26 also serve the collection as an introduction to chapters 49 ff. Just as the disputational 40, 12—31 began

---

[18] See the masculine singular in v. 8—13 and the second masculine plural in 50, 1—3.
[19] Cf. G. von Rad, Old Testament Theology, II 1965, 239—240, 293 ff.

the Jacob-Israel section, so 49, 14—26 introduces the Zion-Jerusalem
segment of the collection. Indeed, much of the imagery of chapters
49—55 concerns the mother and her children (49, 14—21.22—23.24—
26; 50, 1—3; 51, 17—23; 54, 1—3).

Isaiah 49, 14—26 is related also to the foregoing context, as we
saw in the discussion of 49, 1—13. Yahweh will be "merciful" to his
chosen (49, 10.13.15);[20] the "desolate places" will no longer be abandoned (49, 8.19). The nations will bow down before the one who has been
oppressed (49, 7.23). Finally, the progession in 49, 1—6 from Yahweh's
intention to restore Israel to his plan to give light to the nations (v. 6)
appears also in the way the collection has arranged the units in 49,
14—26. First, Zion receives a promise "in order that *you* may know
that I am Yahweh" (v. 23). But the next unit says the goal of Yahweh's
deliverance is that "all flesh may know that I am Yahweh your savior"
(v. 26).

### B. 50, 1—3.4—11

1. *Form Critical Analysis.* The form of v. 1—3 was discussed in
Chapter Four.[21] It is a disputation speech, the first part of which imitates
the language of the trial. The purpose of the speech is twofold: (1) to
dispute the complaint, "Yahweh has divorced our mother and sold us to
pay his debts," and (2) to argue against the view that Yahweh is powerless to save. The structure of the poem, we argued, is the creation of
Deutero-Isaiah. Nevertheless, it is independent form critically. The preceding context is composed of three announcements of salvation (49,
14—21.22—23.24—26); what follows is a speech by the servant (50,
4 ff.) and is to be distinguished from the disputation speech in the mouth
of Yahweh (50, 1—3).

Isaiah 50, 4—11, as we saw, is an imitation of a psalm of confidence uttered by the servant (v. 4—9), followed by a sarcastic word of
judgment in the mouth of Yahweh (v. 10—11).[22] A real psalm of confidence employed in its usual setting and for its normal purpose probably would not have included at the end a divine speech of the kind
represented by v. 10—11.[23] Thus the particular structure and purpose of
this poem is the result of Deutero-Isaiah's peculiar intentions. Deutero-
Isaiah combined the psalm of confidence and the divine word of judgment because he wanted to distinguish between the faithful servant and
those who were unfaithful. Indeed, he condemns the unfaithful for

---

[20] Read *mrḥm* as a pi'el participle (49, 15).
[21] Chapter Four, I, B, 2.
[22] Cf. above, Chapter Five, III.
[23] K. Elliger, Deuterojesaja in seinem Verhältnis zu Tritojesaja, 1933, 35.

refusing to hear the voice of the servant. The purpose of the psalm of confidence, then, is not primarily to express trust; it is rather to lay the foundation for the condemnation of the unfaithful. Even v. 8 and 9 in the psalm of confidence proper lay the foundation for v. 10—11.

2. *Arrangement of Genre Units.* a. V. 1—3 and v. 4—11 are quite separable form critically. If each were used originally in the respective settings for disputations and psalms of confidence, the juxtaposition could not have been original. But the psalm of confidence appears to be an imitation. Moreover, stylistic similarities unite v. 1—3 with v. 4—11. Both employ questions introduced by *mî* followed by assertions which begin with *hen* (v. 1.8.9.10.11).[24] Both v. 1—3 and v. 4—11 employ legal language (v. 1—2a.8—9).

Have we in v. 1—11 a unified composition in which more than one kind of speech is imitated, or is the structure the product of compilation? A definitive answer seems impossible. The fact that genre units can be isolated suggests the possibility of a collection. That would indeed correspond to what seems to have been the case elsewhere in Isaiah 40—55. On the other hand, one might argue that the stylistic similarities could be the sign of a unified poem. This is even more persuasive when we recognize that the genre units in Isaiah 50, 1—11 are imitations.

b. Whether or not v. 1—3 and v. 4—11 originally belonged together is not clear. But the shared rhetorical pattern of questions introduced by *mî* and statements begun by *hen* connects the otherwise unrelated types of speech. In the disputation (v. 1—3) the purpose of this question-answer rhetorical pattern is to persuade Israelites to believe that Yahweh has neither divorced nor sold them without cause and that he is able to deliver. That same rhetorical pattern in v. 4—9 expresses the servant's confidence. The confidence on Israel's part for which Yahweh argues in v. 1—3 is verbalized by the servant in v. 4—9.

If, as has seemed to be the case elsewhere in the collection, the servant in v. 4—9 is Israel, the juxtaposition of v. 1—3 and v. 4 ff. exhibits a transition from doubt to confidence. Yahweh's disputation (v. 1—3) effectively overcomes the doubt, with the result that the servant Israel utters a psalm of confidence. Yet the ambiguity in the portrayal of the servant complicates the problem of interpretation. That v. 4—9 do not give him an explicit identity is not in itself problematic, nor is the fact that he appears to be assigned a prophetic mission[25]

---

[24] J. Muilenburg, Interpreter's Bible, V 1956, 579.585.586.587.588. V. 2 has a rhetorical question, not introduced by *mî*, but still followed by a statement begun by *hen*.

[25] Cf. above, Chapter Five, III. For a detailed discussion see O. Kaiser, Der königliche Knecht, 1962, 66 ff.

troublesome. Such a personification of Israel would be perfectly in keeping with Deutero-Isaiah's style.[26] Moreover, his identification as a disciple exhibits a term which is applied elsewhere to the sons of Zion (54, 13).[27] But if the weary to whom he is sent are the people Israel, then we would appear to be confronted with Israel the servant sent to Israel the weary.[28] And the situation is just that indeed! In the only other Deutero-Isaianic poem in which Yahweh helps the "weary" (ya'ep — 40, 27—31), the word in question seems to refer to the people Israel. Against the complaint that Yahweh has forsaken Israel (40, 27) it is argued that Yahweh gives strength to the weary; those who hope in him will not be weary. To interpret: Yahweh will give strength to weary Israel. In 50, 4—9, although the weary are not explicitly identified, the term ya'ep would indicate immediately to one who is familiar with the collection that Israel is meant. Such an interpretation is by no means unlikely. It would not be unseemly at all for Israel to have a prophetic mission to her own weary.

Apparently those to whom the servant speaks do not respond; at least some of them do not. V. 4—9 indicate that the servant has experienced opposition (v. 6.7.8). V. 10—11 condemn those who do not "fear Yahweh and obey the voice of his servant." Such language would seem to indicate a distinction between the servant and those to whom he is sent. It is understandable, then, why some have understood the servant as an individual prophet who was rejected by his hearers.

Without doubt Deutero-Isaiah's own experience as a prophet has colored his portrayal of the servant. The trial and disputation speeches indicate how reluctant his hearers were to accept his message. Still, we should not go so far as to conclude that the servant is simply the prophet. The collection understands the servant as Israel. Yet the collection creates an ambiguous relationship between Israel and prophet. We have seen that in Deutero-Isaiah the terms "servant" and "messenger" refer both to Israel and to Israel's prophets.[29] We saw, too, the equivocation in the identity of the "I" who speaks in 40, 6 f.;[30] he seems to be at once prophet and people. A similar ambiguity is apparent in 50, 4—11. In this text the servant seems to have a prophetic mission with an accompanying rejection by those who hear his word; at the same time, in the context of the collection, he is Israel who moves from doubt (50, 1—3) to confidence (50, 4 ff.).

---

[26] Israel is personified as David in 55, 3—5, and elsewhere as a mother and bride.
[27] J. Smart, History and Theology in Second Isaiah, 1965, 165.
[28] This is somewhat like the commission of Israel to restore Israel in 49, 1—6.
[29] Cf. above, Chapter Eight, II, 2, d.
[30] Chapter Six, II, A.

Why the fluidity between the servant as Israel and Deutero-Isaiah's prophetic ministry? At this point the theory of "corporate personality"[31] is useful, although we should be careful not to use it as a panacea to solve the problem of the "servant songs."[32] In Deutero-Isaiah, Israel is seen as a "corporate personality." Abraham is at once Israel (41, 8) and an individual figure for Israel to remember (51, 2). Yet the Abraham who can be distinguished from the present Israel (51, 2) is ultimately not separated from Israel; he and they are one. In the same way Israel and the prophet are at the same time distinguishable and indistinguishable. The prophet is a particular person with a particular message in a particular situation. Yet as the one who utters Yahweh's event-creating words concerning the "new things," he is in a very real sense Israel. His words constitute Israel; his words inaugurate the age of redemption; he (and his followers?) are the Israel of the new age; his task is Israel's task; his word is the word of Israel the servant. He stands in the tradition of the prophetic "messenger" and "servant" (42, 19). The ambiguity is intentional: Deutero-Isaiah is the servant, but only in the sense that he shares in Israel and embodies Israel in a certain sense. His ministry is a kind of archetype for the mission of Israel. Thus Deutero-Isaiah and Israel are inseparable, with the prophet losing his personal identity in the people.

The blurring of the distinction between the servant Israel and Deutero-Isaiah the servant is analogous to the ambiguity we find between servant Israel and apostates who do not obey the servant's word (50, 10—11). They and the servant are in one sense indistinct and in another quite separate. Throughout the collection there are ambiguous hints that there is a distinction between Yahweh's acts toward faithful Israel and those among his people who are unfaithful. In 42, 14—17, when Yahweh promises to lead the blind in the desert, he speaks as if he will deliver Israel as a whole. Nevertheless, v. 17 is an announcement of judgment against those who trust in idols. In 41, 24.29, too, idols and those who make them are condemned. We are not told whether or not the prophet is condemning Israelites. But when we read 50, 10—11 in the light of these texts, we become aware of a pattern in the collection which distinguishes between the faithful and the faithless.[33] Even the question in 42, 23, "Who among you will give ear to this?" reminds us of, "Who among you fears Yahweh?" (50, 10); thus 42, 23 at least hints

---

[31] O. Eissfeldt, The Ebed-Jahwe in Isa xl—lv in the Light of the Israelite Conceptions of the Community and the Individual, the Ideal and the Real, ExpT 44 (1932—33), 261—268; H. W. Robinson, The Hebrew Conception of Corporate Personality, BZAW 66 (1936), 48—62.

[32] See my comments on 49, 1—13 in Chapter Eight.

[33] Smart, Second Isaiah, 165—167.

at a distinction between the righteous and the unrighteous; in the context
of the collection it becomes part of a pattern.

c. Isaiah 50, 1—3.4—11, then, is a kerygmatic unity. Following
Yahweh's attempt to persuade Israel to have confidence that Yahweh
has neither divorced nor sold them and that his arm is not too short to
save (50, 1—3), the servant expresses confidence. His confidence prevails in spite of adversaries; indeed, Yahweh will help him, and those
who refuse his word will suffer at Yahweh's hand.

There are certain relationships between 50, 1—11 and the foregoing
context. We find that 49, 14—26 and 50, 1—3 share the image of a
mother and her children. Moreover, 49, 14—26 and 50, 1—3 both have
a decided disputational flavor. Yet 49, 14—26 differs from 50, 1—3 in
that we find there second feminine singular address to Zion instead of
second masculine plural. Moreover, 49, 14—26 pictures the mother Zion
as located in her original geographical place as a mother whose children
have been taken away and are to be returned. In 50, 1—3, however, the
mother has been sent away. In addition, 49, 14—26 is centered exclusively on the question of the return of the mother's children. There is no
indictment of her children for sin, as in 50, 1—3. These differences
suggest that 50, 1—3 was not originally a continuation of 49, 14—26.
Nevertheless, the collection uses the image of the mother and her
children as the basis for juxtaposition.

## C. 51, 1—3.4—5.6.7—8

1. *Form Critical Analysis.* Form critical research has not been in
agreement concerning 51, 1—8. Mowinckel, Köhler, and Fohrer consider these verses a unity.[34] Gressmann, Begrich, and von Waldow, on
the other hand, regard them as separate units.[35] A glance at the introductory formulae suggests that these verses might be broken down into
the following parts: v. 1—3.4—5.6.7—8. Now we must look carefully
at each of the parts from a form critical perspective.

V. 1—3 are seen by Begrich and von Waldow as disputation
speech.[36] Those who doubt the promise of comfort to Zion are exhorted
to look to the past (v. 1b—2). Since an Israelite presumably would not
doubt Yahweh's saving activity in the past, the prophet can now move

---

[34] Mowinckel, Die Komposition des deuterojesajanischen Buches, ZAW 49 (1931),
108; Köhler, Deuterojesaja stilkritisch untersucht, 1923, 108; Fohrer, Das Buch
Jesaja, III 1964, 141 ff.; cf. also Westermann, Das Buch Jesaja, 188 ff., but with
considerable rearranging of the text.

[35] Gressmann, Die literarische Analyse Deuterojesajas, ZAW 34 (1914), 264; Begrich,
Studien, 13, 20, 50; von Waldow, Anlaß und Hintergrund, 28, 36.

[36] Begrich, Studien, 50; von Waldow, Anlaß und Hintergrund, 36.

confidently to speak of Yahweh's intervention on Zion's behalf in the present and future (v. 3). The disputational character of these verses is clear. Still, we notice that the language of salvation speech (v. 3)[37] has been fused with a style characteristic of disputation. This kind of combination of genres is undoubtedly the result of Deutero-Isaiah's creativity. He structured v. 1—3 in this manner because his intention was to persuade his hearers that Yahweh comforts Zion as surely as he called Abraham and blessed him.

V. 4 might be construed as a new beginning, with v. 4b—5 the announcement of salvation, structured as a substantiation to v. 4 a. V. 4—5 are also independent in terms of content. V. 1—3 constitute a promise of paradise to Zion, with the promise grounded in a disputation. In v. 4—5, by contrast, the promise has to do with Yahweh's *tôrā* in the judgment of the nations. The imagery has changed completely from v. 1—3.

V. 6—8 can be separated form critically into two "units." V. 6 is introduced by an imperative with an announcement of salvation, introduced by *kî*, serving as the substantiation of the imperative. V. 7—8 also open with an imperative, but the next structural element is the exhortation, "Fear not." The announcement of salvation, also introduced by *kî*, follows. Begrich's arguments that we have one formal unit in two parts are questionable on form critical grounds.[38] He contends that the cultic salvation oracle imitated by Deutero-Isaiah, like the corresponding lament psalm, contains two parts. But v. 6 is not an imitation of the salvation-assurance oracle, so that Begrich's particular arguments cannot be sustained. I doubt that we can determine with certainty whether v. 6 and v. 7—8 were originally uttered together. Each is capable of standing alone form critically, however, as a complete salvation speech. Moreover, each can be understood without need of the other.

2. *Arrangement of Genre Units.* a. Although each "unit" is capable of standing alone both by form and content, we cannot ignore the rhetorical features which bind them together.[39] They share a second masculine plural address and Yahweh is the speaker in each "unit." All begin with imperatives: *šimʿû ʾelăy* introduces the first and last units; *hăqšîbû ʾelăy* (v. 4) is stylistically quite similar to the imperatives in v. 1 and 7. All units share vocabulary: One notices the repetition of *hăbbîṭû* (v. 1.2.6), *tôrā* (v. 4.7), *rodᵉpê ṣædæq/yodᵉʿê ṣædæq* (v. 1.7),

---

[37] V. 3a contains the perfect tense, which is often used to express the fact that Yahweh has turned to intervene.

[38] Begrich, Studien, 13, 20.

[39] Muilenburg is particularly sensitive to the rhetorical features of the text; cf. The Interpreter's Bible, V 589.

*wîšû'atî/w<sup>e</sup>ṣidqatî l<sup>e</sup>ôlam tihyæ* (v. 6.8), and the similarity between the phrases, "the earth will wear out like a garment" (v. 6), and "like a garment the moth will eat them" (v. 8).

There is a pattern in the arrangement of material.[40] V. 1—8 begin and end with a call to the "pursuers/knowers of righteousness" (v. 1.7). Moreover, the entire passage is framed by units in which the "genera-tions" is an important part of the material of the unit. In v. 7—8 Yah-weh's deliverance is "from generation to generation." In v. 1—3 Israel can take hope from her memory of the "rock" from which her genera-tions were hewn.

The four genre "units" exhibit indeed a coherent pattern of arrangement. V. 1—3 are distinguishable not only by form, but they are a unity of language and imagery as well. Israel is exhorted to look to Abraham; just as he was called as one but multiplied, so Zion is changed from desert to Garden of Eden. The entire structure reflects this unity. After the command to hear (v. 1a), the exhortation to look to Abraham has two parallel imperatives: "Look to the rock;" "look to Abraham." The suffixes *kæm* and *tæm* dominate (v. 1b.2a). The com-parison between Yahweh's calling Abraham and comforting Zion appears in parallel clauses introduced by *kî*. The general nature of the verbs in v. 2b—3a leads to the concrete promise. The promise at the end has unity of imagery and sound: third feminine singular suffix and third feminine singular noun endings; also a dominant *š* sound.

V. 4—5 do not build directly upon v. 1—3 in theme, form, or style. Indeed, v. 4—5 form a homogeneous unit. The imperative in v. 4a relates to the rest of the unit. "My people" are exhorted to listen to a promise concerning the "peoples." The repeated *'elăy* of v. 4a corres-ponds to the heavy use of the first person suffix in v. 4b—5. The language about Yahweh's "arm" and Yahweh's "judgment" (both verb and noun) expresses the main theme of the unit. V. 4—5, then, are a distinct unit of form, style, and meaning. Still, an important connection between v. 1—3 and v. 4—5 is observable. The "pursuers of righteous-ness" (v. 1) are promised that Yahweh's "righteousness" is near (v. 5).

Verbal repetition in v. 6 connects that verse with v. 1—3 (*hăbbîţû* — v. 1.2.6); and in addition to this, the parallelism between *ṣidqatî* and *y<sup>e</sup>šû'atî* in v. 6 joins that verse with v. 5. The repetition in v. 7—8 ties everything together: *Šim'û 'elăy yod<sup>e</sup>'ê ṣædæq* (v. 7), in its relation to v. 1, makes the entire kerygmatic unity (v. 1—8) concern itself with the establishment of God's righteousness. Those who know or pursue his righteousness can expect his righteousness to rule the peoples (v. 5). Yahweh's people, who live in a time when they bear the "reproach of men," are reminded that his "righteousness" is forever (v. 6.8). *'Ăm*

---

[40] F. Holmgren, Chiastic Structure in Isa li 1—11, VT 19 (1969), 196—201.

*tôratî beʿlibbam* in v. 7, seen in relation to the appearance of *tôrā* in v. 4, connects the indwelling of the *tôrā* in God's people to the hope of its ruling function in the world. Those who have *tôrā* in their hearts need not fear the reproach of men; not only will a moth eat them, but (says the juxtaposition) Yahweh's *tôrā* will rule the world in place of its present oppressors (v. 4—5).

It is quite difficult to determine whether the unity of v. 1—8 is the work of an author or collector. The relative autonomy of each "unit" suggests the latter, but we may not be certain. In any case, the present arrangement creates a kerygma of its own.

b. Isaiah 51, 1—8 is related to the foregoing context by verbal repetition (cf. 50, 9b; 51, 6b.8a). This repeated phrase points to a theme which 50, 4—11 and 51, 1—8 hold in common: those who belong to Yahweh need not fear opposition — neither the servant who accepts humiliation faithfully nor those who pursue righteousness. Indeed, the juxtaposition of 50, 4—11 and 51, 1—8 gives a significance to the latter which it does not have when taken alone. The term "pursuers of righteousness" apart from chapter 50 probably meant simply, "Israelite." But when it follows chapter 50, the term comes to mean the faithful as opposed to those who neither "fear Yahweh nor obey the voice of his servant." "Fear not the reproach of men" (51, 7) also takes on a larger significance in the context of chapter 50. In the context of 51, 1—8, it seems to be an exhortation not to fear the reproach of the "peoples." In the context of chapter 50 it continues to mean that, but it includes disobedient Israelites as well.

## D. 51, 9—11.12—16.17—23; 52, 1—2.3—6.7—10.11—12

1. *Form Critical Analysis.* Among form critics widely divergent opinions concerning the literary character of these verses have arisen. Köhler, Mowinckel, Begrich, von Waldow, and Fohrer view these verses as a collection of originally short speeches, though there are wide differences among them in the delineation of units.[41] Others, however, such as Haller, think of somewhat larger units.[42] Westermann has argued for the original unity of these verses as a long poem made up of an imitation of several genres.[43] As a result of the lack of agreement, the form critical work must be done again.

---

[41] Köhler, Deuterojesaja stilkritisch untersucht, 108; Mowinckel, Komposition, 108, 109; Begrich, Studien, 13; von Waldow, Anlaß und Hintergrund, 21—25; Fohrer, Das Buch Jesaja, III 145 ff.

[42] Haller, Das Judentum, 60 ff.

[43] Westermann, Heilswort, 368—369, Sprache und Struktur, 121—122, and Das Buch Jesaja, 192 ff.

a. Turning first to v. 9—11, we find that it can be isolated form critically as a part of a lament. V. 9a.b is the introductory cry for help.[44] V. 9c—10 constitute the motivation for Yahweh's help by appealing to his deeds in the past.[45] At this point difficulties arise. Begrich and von Waldow consider v. 11 to be the petition *(Bitte)* of the lament psalm, expressed in the form of a wish.[46] Westermann, on the other hand, suggests that v. 11 is a promise, as it is in 35, 10. In his opinion, this is a sign that Deutero-Isaiah has modified the form of the lament psalm.[47]

The position of Begrich and von Waldow cannot be sustained on grammatical grounds. *Ūba'û* and *nasû*[48] cannot be read as jussives. The view held by Westermann is possible gramatically, and a comparison with 35, 10 gives it added weight. Nevertheless, I would offer another alternative. V. 11 can be read as a continuation of the *motivation* begun in v. 9c. The participles in v. 9c—10, apparently to be translated as an action not limited to one point of time in the past, are expanded upon by verbs which denote incompleted action.[49] If this view is correct, the lament psalm fragment contained in v. 9—11 ends with the motivation. Whether or not my suggestion is correct, it is clear that v. 9—11 can be separated from the context by form. V. 12 begins a new, though related, form.

b. V. 12—16 can be isolated form critically as a salvation speech derived from the cultic lament psalm. It begins with Yahweh's introduction of himself as the people's comforter, followed by a long rhetorical question concerning the people's fear (v. 12—13). The question is a disputational question derived from the exhortation, "Fear not." The promise in v. 14 is the conclusion to the disputation, and v. 15 is the substantiation for v. 12—14. The use of disputation style is a typical Deutero-Isaianic way of adapting the form of a cultic speech to meet the kind of doubt prevalent in the exile.

We encounter certain form critical problems. First of all, the constant shifting from second masculine plural to second feminine singular to second masculine singular is perplexing. Von Waldow is probably right that this speech is patterned as a communal lament directed toward a community which conceives of itself as Zion.[50] This

---

[44] Cf. e. g., Ps 80, 3.

[45] Cf. e. g., Ps 74, 12—17.

[46] Begrich, Studien, 167; von Waldow, Anlaß und Hintergrund, 23.

[47] Westermann, Heilswort, 369, and Das Buch Jesaja, 192.

[48] Or *weʿnas*, if 1QIsaᵃ is correct.

[49] The verbs in the imperfect may be regarded as incompleted action in the past. Even if *nasû* is the correct text, the dominance of the other verbs would not allow us to read this verb as denoting action limited to one point of time in the past.

[50] Von Waldow, Anlaß und Hintergrund, 24.

would explain both the second masculine plural and the second feminine singular, and the second masculine singular would be either the tendency in Hebrew to use the second person masculine for the second person feminine or the tendency in Hebrew to alternate plural and singular.

Another form critical problem is apparent in v. 16. V. 12—15 apparently once existed without v. 16.[51] Indeed, v. 15 is the closing substantiation for v. 12—14. The incorporation of v. 16 appears to add to v. 12—15 a theological perspective similar to 49, 2. The inclusion of v. 16 does not take away from the basic independence of v. 12—16 from its context. 51, 12—16 stands apart as an imitation of a cultic salvation oracle.

c. The form of v. 17—23 has already been discussed.[52] The passage is a speech of salvation which employs language characteristically used to comfort mourners. The fusion of these two kinds of language is the creation of Deutero-Isaiah. His purpose in combining the two kinds of language lies in the image of the bereaved mother; she has lost her sons (v. 18.20). Yet her condition extends beyond the loss of sons; she herself has experienced "devastation and destruction, famine and sword" (v. 19) with no one to comfort her. Deutero-Isaiah has Yahweh announce to the mourning woman that the time of mourning is over. In the announcement of salvation (v. 21—23) he promises that the circumstances which produced mourning are past; soon the present state of affairs will be reversed so that the cup of wrath will be given to the woman's oppressors. The structure and imagery of the speech thus gives a meaningful relationship between past and future.

Although the structure of this speech is the creation of Deutero-Isaiah, it can be distinguished from its context as a speech of salvation. The language used to comfort mourners leads into the announcement of salvation, and the announcement of salvation ends with v. 23.

d. Isaiah 52, 1—2 begins a new genre unit with its own form and images. Begrich views it as a *Gattung* whose speeches he calls *kurze Anweisungen*,[53] which are begun by imperatives and often continued by a clause introduced by *ki*.[54] He sees these instructions as given to the inhabitants of a city. But his view does not give an accurate account of 52, 1—2. The imperatives are not directed to persons within the city, as in Genesis 19, 15 ff. and Isaiah 48, 20—21, but rather to Zion itself as a holy city. Moreover, the content of the speech does not contain the kind of instructions so that 52, 1—2 can be considered an imitation of

---

[51] V. 15 is a closing substantiation to v. 12—14. Moreover, v. 16 seems to be directed to the prophet rather than the community.

[52] Chapter Two, II, 3.

[53] Gen 19, 15 ff.  Isa 48, 20—21; 52, 1—2.11—12.

[54] Begrich, Studien, 57—58.

Melugin, Isaiah  11

the kind of speech seen in Genesis 19, 15 ff. Instead, the speech is more
likely an imitation of a word of comfort. Zion is exhorted to arise from
the dust.[55] The reference to the putting on of clean garments may be
viewed as a reference to the end of a period of mourning.[56] So 52, 1—2
sets itself off from the context as a word of comfort, an exhortation to
the mourner to put on new clothes for a new future free from the
defilement which produces the circumstances requiring mourning.

The prose verses 3—6 cannot be a continuation of v. 1—2, either
by form or content. The language of comforting unclean mourners is
left behind. 51, 17—23, though it employs the language of mourning, is
not form critically a part of 51, 1—2. The imperatives in 51, 17 reach
their goal in the announcement of salvation in v. 21—23. 51, 1—2 is a
different exhortation to mourners. It has its own beginning in the
imperatives directed to mourners; it has its own promise to Zion: "For
uncircumcised and unclean shall no more come into you." It has its own
images — the unclean woman, in contrast with the imagery of the
childless and oppressed woman who has drunk the cup of Yahweh's
wrath in 51, 17—23.

e. Isaiah 52, 7—10 is very much like Numbers 24, 3 ff. The latter
is a speech uttered by Balaam when he is grasped by the spirit of God.
It has the following structure:

(1) Introduction: "Oracle of Balaam . . ."
(2) A vision of the future Israel: "How good are your tents . . ."

It has been suggested that Numbers 24, 3 ff. is a typical form of speech
used by seers.[57] Perhaps this is the case, although we do not have enough
examples of this kind of speech to be sure. But it does seem to be associated with a vision.

Isaiah 52, 7 ff. has a vision expressed in similar language — a vision
of messengers of good tidings: "How beautiful upon the mountains are
the feet of the messenger . . ." But Deutero-Isaiah fuses this kind of
language with the style of the hymn. The messengers speak in hymn
style: "Your God reigns!"[58] Moreover, after the vision of the messengers
(v. 7—8) comes a short hymn (v. 9—10). It is clear that v. 9—10 are a
response to v. 7—8. Just as the watchman "sing" for joy (v. 8), so
Jerusalem must break forth into "singing" (v. 9); just as the "eyes" of
the watchmen see Yahweh return to Zion, so Yahweh will reveal his
arm before the "eyes" of the nations (v. 10).

---

[55] Note the appearance of the imperative of *qûm* and compare my discussion above.
[56] Cf. II Sam 12, 20. D. Baltzer argues that the form and content are shaped by
    cultic material. Cf. Ezechiel und Deuterojesaja, 1971, 17—24.
[57] Von Waldow, Anlaß und Hintergrund, 49—50. But cf. Baltzer, Ezechiel und
    Deuterojesaja, 66, 67, where we find an argument for Wisdom influence (cf. e. g.,
    Ps 133, 1  Sir 25, 4 f.).
[58] Cf. Ps 47, 9.

f. V. 11—12, like 48, 20—21,[59] are in the form of a command to
leave the city with a promise attached as substantiation (v. 12). They are
sufficiently like 48, 20—21 to stand apart from their context by form.

g. V. 3—6 are not easy to deal with, either in terms of genre or in
their relationship to their context. Form critically these verses begin with
a messenger formula and announcement of salvation (v. 3). Then comes
the conjunction *kî* and another messenger formula (v. 4aα). The rest of
v. 4 is a statement by Yahweh concerning the oppression of his people
in Egypt and Assyria. Then Yahweh asks why his people have been
taken away "for nothing." Next comes a complaint in Yahweh's mouth
that the rulers of the people "wail" and that his name is continually
despised. Suddenly, however, Yahweh changes to the language of
promise (v. 6).

We cannot give a satisfactory form critical analysis of the text.
Indeed, whether it is a unity is uncertain.[60] The announcement of
salvation in v. 3 emphasizes that they were sold "for nothing" and that
they will be redeemed "without money." The statement in v. 4 concerning Israel's oppression by Egypt and Assyria indicates also that they
were made to serve for nothing; the rhetorical question, too, repeats the
word *ḥinnam* (v. 3.5). But whether v. 4 ff. were originally a continuation
of v. 3 is not at all clear. The structure of the text is not known elsewhere so that we might compare it with another example of the form. It
is perhaps best to confess that we do not know how to deal with it in
terms of form.

2. *Arrangement of Genre Units.* a. Having tried to show that
51, 9—52, 12 is composed of several "units" which can be isolated by
form, I turn now to the significance of the arrangement of those units.
As we have seen, Mowinckel, Begrich, von Waldow, and others understand the text as a collection of originally separate poems while Westermann thinks of a long poem in which several genres are imitated.[61] For
Westermann, the double imperatives (51, 9.17; 52, 1) and the repeated
'*anokî* (51, 12) are indications of a conscious poetic composition. Moreover the composition reflects a deliberate imitation and interweaving of
the communal lament and the salvation-assurance with the announcement of salvation.[62] 51, 9—10 is the communal lament. 51, 12—13
expresses the assurance of salvation, with the nominal substantiating
clause found in v. 15a and the perfect-tense substantiation in v. 23. The

---

[59] Cf. above, Chapter Eight, I, E, 1, e.
[60] One need only consult the commentaries and other critical works to discover how
    problematic this text is.
[61] Cf. above, footnotes 41 and 43.
[62] Westermann, Das Buch Jesaja, 194.

elaboration of the future, i. e., the announcement of salvation, appears in full strength in 52, 1—2.

This kind of imitation of various genres while at the same time distributing the various parts of the lament psalm and its answering oracle over the whole composition is not in accord with what we have discovered about the composition of the text elsewhere in Deutero-Isaiah. The elements accounted for by Westermann's "distribution theory" can be better understood by looking at each element in terms of its own genre unit. For example, 51, 23 is not the substantiation for the exhortation, "Fear not," lying behind v. 12.[63] Indeed, it is not a substantiating clause at all. It is a simple announcement of Yahweh's intervention. Moreover, its content is closely integrated with the image of the "cup of staggering" which dominates v. 17—23; it is at best only indirectly related to the specific language associated with the fear of the "fury of the oppressor" of v. 12—15.

It is more fruitful to view 51, 9—52, 12 as a group of genre units which are capable of standing alone both by form and content. Nevertheless, the arrangement is not without significance. Most noticeable are the double imperatives (51, 9.17; 52, 1)[64] and the corresponding 'anokî 'anokî (51, 12). Moreover, we find verbal repetition: the verb 'ûr (51, 9.17; 52, 1), libšî 'oz (51, 9; 52, 1), tame' (52, 1.11), ḥamā (51, 13.17. 20.22), z$^e$rô$^{a‘}$ (51, 9; 52, 10), qûmî (51, 17; 52, 2), and g'l (51, 10; 52, 9; cf. also 52, 3). In addition, most of the passages have the second feminine singular of Zion.[65]

These rhetorical features occur in a pattern. 51, 9—52, 12 is dominated at the beginning and end by the image of the "arm" of Yahweh: At the beginning Yahweh's arm is urged to deliver (51, 9); at the end the image appears in a hymn which expresses praise in anticipation of what Yahweh's arm shall have done (52, 10).

The arrangement of units in 51, 9—52, 12 reminds us in some ways of 40, 1—11. Like 40, 1—11, 52, 9 ff. begins with language associated with the Exodus (40, 3.4; 51, 10.11);[66] both employ the verb nḥm (40, 1; 51, 12; 52, 9). The end of 51, 9—52, 12 is a vision of messengers who announce Yahweh's victorious return to Zion (52, 7—10); 40, 9—11 employs similar language. In between the beginning lament with its answering oracle (51, 9—11.12—16) and the speech concerning the messengers to Zion (52, 7—10) we find two speeches derived from the

---

[63] Ibid, 194, 199.

[64] Mowinckel, Komposition, 108, 109.

[65] 51, 9—11 and 52, 7—10.11—12 do not. So also with 52, 3—6.

[66] I am using the term "Exodus" in a broad sense, so that the term includes the wilderness traditions associated with it.

language associated with the comforting of mourners (51, 17—23; 52, 1—2); 40, 1—2 uses *nḥm*, often associated with comforting mourners.[67]

b. Let us now examine more closely the juxtaposition of the individual genre units. The lament (51, 9—11) and its answering oracle (v. 12—16) are not closely related in language and imagery. The repeated *'ûrî* and *'ānokî* are the primary rhetorical features which bind them together. Also the imagery associated with Yahweh's domination of the sea connects the two units (v. 9—11.15).

V. 17—23 are related to v. 9 ff. first of all through the doubled imperative (v. 9.17). They are bound, too, by the common theme of the end of the oppressor's activity (v. 13.14.22.23). Moreover, it is not accidental that *mᵉnăḥæmkæm* in the oracle of salvation (v. 12—16) leads to units which imitate the kind of speech used to comfort mourners (51, 17—23; 52, 1—2). Finally, the "wrath" of Yahweh in v. 17—23 (v. 17.20.22) balances the "wrath of the oppressor" in v. 12—16 (v. 13); one need not fear the wrath of the oppressor now that the cup of Yahweh's wrath has been taken away.

52, 1—2 continues the style of the speech to comfort mourners as well as the style of doubled imperatives. The phrase, "Arise, arise, put on your strength, O Zion" (52, 1) reminds us in particular of 51, 9. In the latter the genre is a lament — a plea for Yahweh to arise and put on strength. In 52, 1—2, as the juxtaposition of units provides, the lament has been answered (cf. 51, 12—16); Yahweh has promised to deliver. Thus Zion may now arise from mourning and put on strength. Indeed, 52, 1—2 unifies rhetorically what has preceded it in 51, 9 ff. The forms associated with the comfort of mourners (51, 17—23; 52, 1—2) are through 52, 1—2 tightly integrated into the larger context by means of the exhortation, "Arise, put on strength" (51, 9; 52, 1). 52, 1—2, however, adds something to the language of the preceding context. The language of comforting mourners with its exhortation, "Arise, arise, put on your strength," takes on the imagery of the cult. Zion is to put on garments befitting a holy city; never again will she wear anything unclean.

V. 7—10 repeat the terms *nḥm* (51, 12; 52, 9) and *g'l* (51, 10; 52, 9). The hope for the return of the redeemed in the lament (51, 9—11) is made secure in the vision of the messenger's report (52, 7—10). The use of the perfect tense in connection with the messengers' report of the victory envisioned as already accomplished (52, 7—10) represents a literary intensification of the language of Yahweh's redemption. The same is true when one compares the self-predication, "I, I am he, the one who comforts you" in the oracle of salvation (51, 12) with the messengers' assertion that "Yahweh has comforted his people" (52, 9).

---

[67] Cf. e. g., Gen 37, 35; 50, 21  II Sam 10, 2.

The final unit (52, 11—12), like 48, 20—21, ends a section of the collection (49, 14—52, 12). 52, 11—12 is related to its immediate context in its use of doubled imperatives. Moreover, in the exodus from the city the people of Yahweh are to touch nothing unclean (v. 11; cf. 52, 1). Indeed, the images of 52, 11—12, like those of 52, 1—2, are cultic. 52, 11—12 relate to the beginning of 51, 9 ff. by sharing with 51, 9—11 the imagery of the Exodus. Thus 51, 9—52, 12 begins and ends with Exodus imagery; it moves from a lament which begs Yahweh to perform an exodus as he had in the days of yore (51, 9—11) to a command which inaugurates a new and better Exodus (52, 11—12).[68]

The arrangement of genre units in 51, 9—52, 12, then, forms a coherent pattern. Whether they originally belonged together or were arranged by a collector we cannot determine with certainty. What we know about Deutero-Isaiah in general leads us to suspect the latter. The answer to this question, however, is ultimately relatively unimportant; in the present context we have a kerygmatic unity. Only 52, 3—6 cannot be incorporated into this rhetorical and kerygmatic unity. It seems to be loosely associated through the term g'l (v. 3) and the language of the Exodus (v. 4).

c. Isaiah 51, 9—52, 12 relates to the context which goes before it by verbal repetition: śāśôn wᵉśimḥā (51, 3.11), tᵉḥôlælkæm/mᵉḥôlælæt (51, 2.9), ḥuṣṣābtæm/ḥămmăḥṣæbæt (51, 1.9),[69] lᵉdôr dôrîm/dorôt ʿôlamîm (51, 8.9), phrases concerning the "arm(s)" of Yahweh (51, 5.9; 52, 10), Yahweh's "salvation" (51, 5.6.8; 52, 7.10), and Yahweh's "comfort" of his people (49, 13; 51, 3.12; 52, 9).[70]

In particular, the vocabulary of the eschatological hymn in 52, 9—10 is related to the section beginning in 49, 14 and ending with 52, 12. That section is framed by hymns which praise God for his "comfort" of his people (49, 13; 52, 9—10), and the promise that Yahweh will act as a comforter appears more than once in that section of the collection (51, 3.12). Moreover, the affirmation that "Yahweh has bared his holy arm before the eyes of all the nations, and all the ends of the earth will see the salvation of our God" expresses an important theme of this section of the collection. The role of Yahweh's "arm" in "salvation" is an important rhetorical feature of this part of the collection (51, 5.6.8.9; 52, 7.10): Yahweh will send forth his tôrā; his "salvation" will go forth, and his "arms" will rule the peoples (51, 4—5).

The expression, "all the ends of the earth shall *see* the salvation of our God" (52, 10), also builds upon what has gone before. In 49, 7 Yahweh promises to the one who is despised that "kings will *see* and

---

[68] For bibliography see above, Chapter Seven, footnote 111.
[69] Cf. Holmgren, Chiastic Structure, 196—201.
[70] Cf. Mowinckel, Komposition, 109.

arise, princes will bow down." Moreover, if one thinks of a relationship between light and seeing, 51, 5 adds to the theme of the nations' seeing God's salvation: "*Tôrā* from me will go forth, and my justice as a light to the nations . . ."

The language of singing hymns of joy is particularly prominent in this section of the collection: "Joy and gladness shall be found in her, *tôdā* and the voice of song" (51, 3); "the redeemed of Yahweh shall return, shall come to Zion with singing, eternal joy upon their heads, joy and gladness shall they obtain" (51, 11); "break forth together into singing, you waste places of Jerusalem" (52, 9).

Finally, the repetition of *ḥārbôt* at the beginning and the end of this section of the collection (49, 19; 52, 9) symbolizes a major theme of this section of the collection. Yahweh will return in victory to his desolate land (52, 7—10); he will rebuild the fallen city of Jerusalem (49, 14—21); he will make the desert like Eden (51, 1—3).

## II. ISAIAH 52, 13—55, 13

### A. 52, 13—53, 12

1. *Form Critical Analysis*. A brief summary of our form critical analysis in Chapter Five will suffice here.[71] The poem is composed of two speeches of salvation, between which we find a confession by the nations. The structure of the poem is related to its intention. Its basic purpose is to announce salvation,[72] but in a very particular way. The announcement of the servant's exaltation (52, 13—15) expresses the incongruity of his deliverance in the eyes of the nations. They are atonished at what they "see" and "hear" (v. 15), for indeed they see and hear what they had not beforehand heard and known.

The confession of the nations (53, 1 ff.) reveals their new understanding of the significance of the servant's suffering; he has suffered for their sins. Yet he suffers also for the sin of "my people" (v. 8).[73] The lack of an explicit identity for the servant and for *'ammi* creates difficulties for the interpretation of the text. It seems to be relatively certain that he suffers for the nations,[74] and it is probable that he

---

[71] Cf. above, Chapter Five, IV.
[72] Kaiser, Knecht, 88.
[73] Cf. above, Chapter Five, footnote 51.
[74] The surprised nations who see what they have not before been told and hear what they have not before understood (52, 15) are surely the speakers of the confession in 53, 1 ff.

suffers for Yahweh's people Israel.[75] The lack of clarity concerning the identity of the servant and "my people" is perplexing. In all likelihood it is related to similar ambiguities in Deutero-Isaiah.

Despite these difficulties, the intention of the poem is to announce that the servant's suffering and his future exaltation are bound together in Yahweh's saving plan. The poet recognizes how startling his message is; indeed, a part of his purpose is to reveal what he regards as astonishing. He presents it as something which surprises the nations, so that his primary intention is undoubtedly to focus on *their* coming to know Yahweh's purposes. Yet one suspects that the poet expects his Israelite hearers to be startled as well.

2. *Relationship to Context.* We notice immediately that Isaiah 52, 13—53, 12 is related to the context which precedes it by the repetition of $z^e r \hat{o}^a$ (51, 5.9; 52, 10; 53, 1) and $r$'$h$ (49, 7; 52, 10.15). Both of these terms occur in the eschatological hymn (52, 9.10) which precedes the fourth "servant song." There is a summons to praise because "Yahweh has stripped bare his holy arm before the eyes of all nations; all the ends of the earth will see the salvation of our God" (52, 10). In the "servant song" we are told that the nations have "seen" what had not been told them before (52, 15), so that they are led to confess: "Who has believed what we have heard, and to whom has the arm of Yahweh been revealed?" (53, 1). We saw that the hymn in 52, 9—10 culminates a section which contains the theme of Yahweh's arm ruling the nations. His arm will bring light to the peoples; indeed, they wait for his arm (51, 4—5). The hymn in 52, 9—10 also reiterates the theme of the nations' "seeing" Yahweh's saving deeds (49, 7).

The "servant song" in Isaiah 53 takes what has gone before and gives it new significance. It serves as an extensive elaboration of the oracle in 49, 7. Isaiah 49, 7 announces that kings and princes will "see" and "bow down" before the one who was despised; an exaltation of the despised one is presupposed. Isaiah 52, 13—53, 12, which begins with a repetition of $r$'$h$ in a similar kind of announcement of salvation, gives an elaborate interpretation of the relationship and significance of the suffering and exaltation. Thus 49, 7 and 52, 13—53, 12 serve as a kind of framework for 49, 14—52, 12.

The fourth "servant song" also reminds us of the very beginning of the collection. The "revelation" of Yahweh's arm in 53, 1 is much like the "revelation" of Yahweh's glory in 40, 5. Moreover, the confession of the nations in 53, 1 ff. is an elaboration of the goal of Yahweh's activity expressed throughout the collection — the promise that the nations would know and confess Yahweh.[76]

---

[75] Cf. the statistics on the use of *'ammî* in Chapter Five, footnote 52.

[76] Cf. 45, 6.14—17.22—25; 49, 26.

The precise meaning of this poem and its significance in the collection remains somewhat of a mystery. The servant is not explicitly identified; nevertheless, as before, we must identify him as Israel in the context of the collection. He suffers for the sins of the nations and apparently for Yahweh's own people as well.[77] The distinction between the servant and the unfaithful among God's people which the collection has already established probably applies here as well.[78] This interpretation does not resolve the tension between sinful Israel and the servant who "did no violence" (53, 9). Kaiser's view that Israel is no longer guilty because the judgment is over (cf. 40, 1 f.; 43, 25) is suggestive,[79] but nothing in the "servant poem" itself points clearly in that direction. I would suggest instead the distinction proposed in the discussion of 50, 4—11, in which the prophetic Israel who "did not rebel" (50, 5) is contrasted with those who do not obey the voice of the servant (50, 10). Isaiah 49, 1—6, too, helps us understand the last "servant song." In 49, 5.6 the mission of the servant Israel is to restore Israel and to be a light to the nations; likewise in chapter 53 the servant Israel suffers to heal the nations and their kings (53, 1—6), as well as for the sins of Yahweh's people Israel (v. 8).

Isaiah 52, 13—53, 12, then, elaborates on the themes of the collection, beginning first with the oracles in 49, 1—6.7 and then the language in the section of the collection 49, 14—52, 12. As we shall presently see, 52, 13—53, 12 is an important bridge to the conclusion of the collection in chapters 54 and 55.

### B. Chapters 54 and 55

1. *Form Critical Analysis.* Form critics are generally agreed that these two chapters can be divided into several units, but there is wide divergence in the delineation of the units.[80] Thus a fresh analysis is needed.

a. In 54, 1—3 the structure is as follows: The speech begins with a hymnic introduction (v. 1a), followed by a substantiating clause

---

[77] See above.

[78] See the discussion of 50, 4—11 above.

[79] Kaiser, Knecht, 116.

[80] Gressmann: 54, 1—3.4—8.9—10.11—17; 55, 1—5.6—7.8—13; Mowinckel: 54, 1—10.11—17; 55, 1—5.6—13. Köhler: 54, 1—6.7—10.11—14a.14b—17; 55, 1—5.6—7. 8—11(13). Begrich: 54, 1—3.4—6.7—10.11—17; 55, 1—5.6—7.8—13 (cf. also von Waldow). Fohrer: 54, 1—3.4—6.7—8.9—10.11—17; 55, 1—5.6—7.8—9.10—11.12 —13. Westermann: 54, 1—10.11—17; 55, 1—5.6—11.12—13. Cf. Gressmann, Analyse, 264; Mowinckel, Komposition, 110, 111; Köhler, Deuterojesaja stilkritisch untersucht, 108, 109; Begrich, Studien, 13; Fohrer, Das Buch Jesaja, III 167 ff.; Westermann, Das Buch Jesaja, 217 ff.

introduced by *kî* (v. 1b). The substantiating clause is in modified hymn style in that it is a promise uttered by Yahweh rather than the usual hymnic recital of Yahweh's past deeds or a catalogue of the general acts of mercy which Yahweh always performs.[81] The imperative style is picked up again in v. 2. This time it does not appear in hymn style but as a command to the barren woman to enlarge her dwelling. This is followed by another substantiating clause introduced by *kî*, again in the form of a promise. The combination of hymn style with the style of the prophetic promise is Deutero-Isaianic; there is no setting for such a fusion apart from his preaching.

b. 54, 4—6 shifts to the form of the salvation-assurance oracle, as *'al tîrᵉ'î* shows. Deutero-Isaiah modifies the usual structure of the genre, however. The appearance of the substantiating clause in the imperfect (v. 4a) seems to be an alteration of the usual structure. Moreover, Zion (or at least a female) is the addressee. We have no examples elsewhere in which Zion is the addressee in this genre, although the absence of numerous examples of this genre outside Deutero-Isaiah limits our knowledge of the original form. Other indications of modification are present also. Following the elaboration of Yahweh's intervention (v. 4b), the promise is substantiated by a rather lengthy group of participial clauses. After this comes a set of clauses introduced by *kî* which speak of the wife's past and present plight (v. 6). Clauses like this at the end of a unit are unusual in speeches of salvation and, in particular, are unknown to us in salvation-assurance oracles.[82] This is without doubt a sign that v. 4—6 are an *imitation* of the salvation-assurance oracle. Having already distinguished sharply between the present and the future in v. 4b, the poet heightens the contrast by adding v. 6, and in so doing, modifies the form.

Even though v. 4—6 are but an imitation of a cultic genre, they stand out from their context. To be sure, Westermann argues that v. 1—3 and v. 4—6 belong together in a lengthy poetic composition. The double imperatives in v. 1, in his opinion, correspond to the twin exhortations in v. 4, and the sustantiating clauses in v. 1b.3 correspond to those in v. 6. But the number of imperatives in v. 1 and 2 does not correspond with the number of exhortations in v. 4—6. Moreover, v. 1—3 reflect imagery of the barrenness of the present time over against the many children of the future, while v. 4—6 have to do with the theme of the wife forsaken by her husband. The fact that the shift in the type

---

[81] Cf. Westermann's categories "declarative" and "descriptive" praise: Das Loben Gottes in den Psalmen, 1961, ET, The Praise of God in the Psalms, 1965.

[82] In fact, the phenomenon is so rare that one might be tempted to place v. 6 with v. 7—10. But v. 6 continues the imagery of the forsaken wife, and that imagery is not present in v. 7—10.

of imagery corresponds with the change in genre units suggests that we are dealing with two originally separate units rather than a longer poetic composition.

c. V. 7—10 shift from the language about the wife to the language of covenant, as the term $b^e r \hat{\imath} t$ indicates (v. 10). This text separates itself from its context as a disputation-like announcement of salvation, in which the promise is made more credible by appeal to the memory of the relationship between Yahweh's anger and his grace in the time of Noah. This disputation-like promise has two parts (v. 7.8). Each part opens with the assertion that for a brief time Yahweh has turned away from Zion (v. 7aα.8a). The preposition $b^e$ is at the beginning of each. The clause expressing Yahweh's temporary abandonment of Zion is followed by another in similar style promising a bright future (v. 7aβ.8b). Then the promises are substantiated by an appeal to the past. Just as Yahweh swore to end his anger in the time of Noah, so now his $b^e r \hat{\imath} t$ and $ḥæsæd$ can be counted on as sure.

The structure of v. 7—10 differs from the imitation of the salvation-assurance oracle in v. 4—6. Moreover, it has nothing to do with marriage imagery. The form of v. 7—10, which arises out of the attempt to counter the complaint that Yahweh has forsaken Zion, differs also from the simple announcement of salvation in v. 11. Thus v. 7—10 are a formal unit. Apparently the structure of v. 7—10 is attributable to Deutero-Isaiah himself. We find this particular structure nowhere else, and we know from other examples in which Deutero-Isaiah combines disputation style with the language of the announcement of salvation that this fusion has its setting in Deutero-Isaiah's preaching.

d. V. 11—17 are difficult to analyze. Most scholars view these verses as a unit. They begin with a direct address (v. 11a) and announcement of salvation introduced by $hinn\bar{e}$ according to the typical style (v. 11b).[83] They end with an impersonal summary statement, which is often used at the end of units in the Isaianic tradition.[84]

Köhler, however, separates v. 11—17 into two units; v. 11—14a and v. 14b—17.[85] He does not explain why he views them as two separate units, although one suspects that his division is on the basis of content. Indeed, the fact that these verses promise riches at the beginning as opposed to announcing freedom from oppression and injustice at the end suggests the possibility that two speeches have been juxtaposed. But

---

[83] Cf. 41, 11.15; 43, 19; 49, 22.
[84] Isa 14, 26; 17, 14. Cf. also 42, 17, in which the summary statement has been modified so that Yahweh is the subject of the clause. Cf. B. S. Childs, Isaiah and the Assyrian Crisis, 1967, 128—136; J. W. Whedbee, Isaiah and Wisdom, 1971, 75—79.
[85] Köhler, Deuterojesaja stilkritisch untersucht, 108.

if that is the case, where should the separation between them be made? Between v. 13 and 14? Or between v. 14a and 14b?[86] We cannot be sure where the division lies, but we are able to note certain elements which connect two probably originally-separate speeches. Both parts have *hinnē 'anokî* (v. 11.16). If v. 14a belongs to the first part as poetic parallelism suggests, the repetition of *ṣᵉdaqā* (v. 14.17) is a unifying factor. In both, of course, the addressee is second feminine singular.

In any event, v. 11—17 can be distinguished from the context by the formal markers described above. Furthermore, there are no direct content connections with the surrounding context: We have already seen the discontinuities with v. 7—10. A shift to a promise on the theme of the Davidic covenant in 55, 1—5 separates 54, 11—17 from the following context.

e. 55, 1—5 begins a new unit. The change from feminine singular to masculine plural is one indication of the new unit. But 55, 1—5 also stands apart from its context as an imitation of the speech of a street merchant, modified by the language of Wisdom and the language of promise.[87] The images, too, relate in no way to what precedes or follows.

f. The form of the units in 55, 6—13 was discussed in Chapter Six.[88] V. 6—7 are a prophetic imitation of priestly *tôrā*, with v. 8—9 (in the present context) as a substantiation for v. 6—7. V. 10—11 also substantiate v. 6—7 in the present arrangement of the text. V. 12—13 are an announcement of salvation. As we saw, v. 6—13 are a kerygmatic unity and constitute the epilogue of the collection.

2. *Arrangement of Genre Units.* a. We have concluded that chapters 54 and 55 can be broken down into genre units, distinguishable both by form and content. Nevertheless, the arrangement is not accidental. Chapter 54 employs feminine singular address throughout. Moreover, as Mowinckel has seen, we find verbal repetition, as well as other stylistic associations.[89] 54, 1—3 and v. 4—6 not only repeat the participle of *bᶜl* (v. 1.5), but also imagery associated with the married woman.[90] In addition, there are stylistic similarities. *Lo' yaladā* and *lo' halā* (v. 1) compare with *lo' tebôšî* and *lo' taḥpîrî* (v. 4). The promises in v. 1b and 4b are both introduced by *kî*. The repetition of *ᶜzb* connects v. 7—10 with the preceding context. In v. 11—17 the phrase *lo' tîra'î* (v. 14) connects this verse with the context (cf. v. 4). Mowinckel

---

[86] Rearrangements of the text are arbitrary and unconvincing. Cf. Begrich, Studien, 20, and Westermann, Das Buch Jesaja, 222—223.

[87] For a discussion of the form, see above, Chapter Two, II, 4.

[88] Chapter Six, II, B.

[89] Mowinckel, Komposition, 110—112.

[90] We have seen above the differences between v. 1—3 and 4—6 in their reflections on the married woman.

notes the stylistic similarity of v. 11a with v. 1a, as well as the repetition of *šalôm* (v. 10.13).[91] 55, 1—5 repeats *bᵉrît* (v. 3) from the foregoing context (54, 10), as well as the word *ḥæsæd* (54, 8.10; 55, 3).
55, 6—13 picks up the imperative style of that which precedes, as
Mowinckel points out.[92]

b. Let us examine more carefully the nature of the juxtaposition.
V. 1—3 and 4—6, we argued above, were originally separate units.
Still, they share the imagery of the married woman, as well as the
stylistic similarities between v. 1 and 4 mentioned above. In addition,
the first verse of v. 1—3 ends with *'amăr yhwh*, and a similar phrase
closes v. 4—6 (v. 6).

V. 1—3 begin the kerygma of chapters 54—55 by the promise to
the mother that her offspring will "inherit nations." The woman's sons
appear again in v. 13, and the theme of the predominance of Israel over
the nations reappears in 55, 4—5. In v. 1—3 the desolate woman will
have more sons than the married woman (v. 1). Thus the future will
contrast sharply with the past.

In the juxtaposition of v. 4—6 with v. 1—3 the image of the
married woman is again used to compare the reproach of the past with
the future. Here, though, the imagery focuses on the forsaken and
shamed wife who will be given a husband. Although the difference in
imagery and form makes it unlikely that v. 1—3 and v. 4—6 were
originally uttered together, they complement each other; the wife and
mother has in store a promising future in contrast with the past.

V. 7—10 repeat *'zb* (v. 6.7) and *g'l* (v. 5.8), and the phrase, "says
your redeemer Yahweh" (v. 8), reminds us of the close of v. 6.[93] The
language of the preceding verses, however, is left behind. The imagery
of the barren and forsaken woman is at best only implicitly present in
the feminine singular address of v. 7—10. Without v. 1—3 and 4—6
no one would think of a marriage relationship in v. 7—10. In its present
context, however, the language of covenant — *ḥæsæd* (v. 8.10), *bᵉrît*
(v. 10), and the reference to Noah (v. 9) — is related to the language of
marriage. Says the present juxtaposition: the wife, once forsaken, will be
restored; the marriage (covenant) will be established by "steadfast
love."

The language of v. 11 reminds us of v. 1. The one who is "not
pitied" is like the one who "did not bear" and who "did not suffer
travail." In v. 11 ff. the contrast between past and future is the contrast
of the "poor one" (v. 11) with the riches which she is to receive. The
promise that "all your sons will be taught by Yahweh, and great will

---

[91] Mowinckel, Komposition, 110.

[92] Ibid. 112.

[93] Cf. also the close of v. 10.

be the peace of your sons" reminds us of the bright future for the mother's sons in the age to come. The term *šalôm* (v. 13) relates v. 11—17 to the covenant language of v. 10. These associations are somewhat loose, but it is clear that the collector combines the imagery of the woman and her sons with the language of the covenant in order to express a rich promise of an expected new covenant.

55, 1—5 renews the language of covenant (v. 3), this time with the tradition of the Davidic covenant. The primary reason for employing the traditional language of the covenant with David is for the purpose of expressing the influence of the covenant people over the nations (v. 4—5).[94] 55, 4—5 reaffirms the expectation of 54, 3 that "your seed will inherit nations."

55, 6—13, as we saw, continues the imperative style of the previous context. These verses correspond with 40, 1 ff.,[95] but they also continue he covenant theme of chapters 54—55. The reference in v. 13 to the "*eternal* sign that will not be *cut off*" relates to the "cutting" of an "eternal covenant" in 55, 3.

Thus chapters 54 and 55 are a collection of genre units, in which the collector has employed a variety of means to associate the units with one another. The dominant connector is the covenant theme; indeed, it is so prominent that it serves as a theological principle of organization instead of a purely mechanical means of association. Nevertheless, chapters 54—55 are somewhat *loosely* organized under the covenant theme. Not all of the texts reflect the covenant theme, and the clusters of images in each genre unit often do not have a tight relationship with the language of other genre units. Despite that, we have seen that the collector has made of it a kerygmatic unity.

c. Chapters 54—55 are a continuation of the poetry which precedes them. 53, 10 promises that the stricken servant will "see seed." In 54, 3 the "seed" of the mother will possess nations. The juxtaposition of 52, 13—53, 12 and 54, 1 ff. manifests once again the collection's tension between the conquest of the nations and their salvation.

The hymn style of 54, 1—3 with its imperatives *rannî* and *pişḥî* goes back to the language and style of 52, 9—10. Yahweh's people are summoned to rejoice at Yahweh's victory before the nations (52, 10; 54, 3). Thus the fourth "servant song" serves as a bridge between the hymnic language of what precedes it and follows it.

We saw in Chapter Six how 55, 6—13 relates to the prologue. The collection ends, then, much as it begins. It is fitting that the collection ends with assertions about the reliability of Yahweh's word (55, 10—11) and a promise of exodus (v. 12—13). The former dominates the first

---

[94] Cf. e. g., Ps 2.
[95] Cf. above, Chapter Six, II, B.

half of the collection; the latter reflects the kind of language which ends each major section of the collection (48, 20—21; 52, 11—12; 55, 12—13).

## III. CONCLUSION

Our inquiry into the formation of Isaiah 40—55 was prompted by the debate between those who saw these chapters as a collection of originally separate utterances and those who viewed them as the work of an author. In the analysis of form I have supported the general approach of the former group, although I have often disputed the assumption that the genre in question existed prior to Deutero-Isaiah.

The results of our analysis indicate, then, that we must begin with the genre as the basic unit. Failure to recognize this can be misleading. We have seen, for instance, how the absence of form critical analysis in Muilenburg caused him in his interpretation of 41, 1—42, 4 to misjudge the nature of the literature and read into the text the setting of the trial when some of the genres had nothing to do with the trial.[96] Examples of this sort abound in works which do not employ form critical research.

Our research has resulted also in substantial disagreement with the understanding of form in Deutero-Isaiah exhibited by Westermann's provocative writings. I have attempted to demonstrate the difficulties with his theory that much of Isaiah 40—55 is composed of lengthy poems made up of a complex interweaving of elements of several genres. It is true, to be sure, that the prophet fused and transformed genres, often to the extent that the structure is essentially his own creation. Nevertheless, his short utterances are capable of standing alone by the test of both form and content.

Isaiah 40—55, then, is a collection of originally independent units, but the arrangement is kerygmatic. In the analysis of the juxtaposition of units I have adapted the method of "rhetorical criticism" as practiced by Muilenburg, applying it to the arrangement of genre units rather than strophes. There are admittedly formidable criticisms which can be leveled against my methods of analysis. Some might contend that the various stages in the growth of the collection have been ignored. And the charge is indeed true! But I have not avoided the issue. I have admitted the probability that chapters 40—55 underwent several stages of growth, but I have argued that it is impossible to reconstruct them. Indeed, it seems to me that in its final form the collection has deliberately eradicated any indicators of the process of growth. It is as if we were intended to see only the final pattern of arrangement.

---

[96] See my discussion above in Chapter One.

The major significance of this study in my judgment has been the attempt to set forth a method for interpreting the message of the collection. It is for this reason that constant reference to the kerygma of the collection has been made. Indeed, I am increasingly aware that the study presented above is but the beginning of what needs to be done in this area. The quest for the kerygma of the collection needs to be broadened. Although chapters 40—55 manifest a literary integrity of their own within the Book of Isaiah, the fact remains that these chapters are somehow related to the whole of Isaiah. Thus our understanding of the kerygmatic significance of chapters 40—55 will remain incomplete until their theological relationship with the entire book is explored.

The need for comprehending the relationship of chapters 40—55 with the whole should, I suppose, be almost self-evident. Yet there are certain unique aspects in the structure of Isaiah 40—55 which call particular attention to this need, for it is apparent that these chapters were never meant to stand alone.[97] Perhaps the most elementary observation in this connection is that chapters 40—55 have no superscription or any other kind of formula to distinguish them as a special body of tradition. Indeed, what initially appears to be a prophetic commissioning (40, 1—8) is really not the call of a prophet in the usual sense of the term.[98] The "I" who is commanded to "cry" (v. 6) is not unambiguously the prophet. He appears to be in some sense both prophet and people.

The ambiguity of 40, 1—8 is characteristic of chapters 40—55 as a whole. The text does not specify at any point the situation to which the speeches were directed. Even the commonly accepted sixth century setting is a scholarly reconstruction. Undoubtedly it is correct, but the redactor has given no indication of a sixth century context. To be sure, there are two references by name to Cyrus and language about the fall of Babylon and the escape from the city. Nevertheless, the text never gives us any specific information about the activity of a prophet during the period. This contrasts markedly with the narratives and

---

[97] By a happy circumstance I have discovered that another form critical scholar and I have independently reached similar conclusions. B. S. Childs, in a lecture delivered at Perkins School of Theology, Southern Methodist University, in the fall of 1972, argued that Deutero-Isaiah should be interpreted, not in reference to the original sixth century context of the exilic prophet's utterances, but in the context of the Book of Isaiah, into which it was placed. His arguments are more detailed than my concluding remarks; thus I hope that he will publish his lecture in order to suggest more fully the direction of inquiry which might be pursued. Another interesting insight on the relationship of Isa 40 ff. to the Book of Isaiah may be found in an article by P. R. Ackroyd, Interpretation of the Babylonian Exile: A Study of 2 Kings 20, Isa 38—39, SJTh 27 (1974), 329—352.

[98] Cf. my analysis above in Chapter Six, II, A.

brief historical notices[99] characteristic of other prophets. The closest thing to a setting for chapters 40 ff. is the prophecy of Isaiah to Hezekiah in chapter 39 concerning the exile to Babylon.

The reason we could not reconstruct the history of the redaction of chapters 40—55 is connected to the nature of the relationships between these chapters and the book as a whole. When chapters 40—55 were placed in the context of the Book of Isaiah, virtually all traces of prior usage of the material in the exilic and post exilic community were obliterated. We were able to deal only with the final arrangement of units because the redactor was not at all interested in the original purpose for which Deutero-Isaiah's poems were intended. Why, we must ask, did he remove all traces of the historical setting when he was so careful to keep them for First Isaiah?

This is not the place for a detailed answer to such a question; another study would be required. Thus I shall attempt only a few observations which might suggest the kind of questions which need to be asked. I suspect that the place to begin is with chapter 39. Why is the last concrete historical reference in the Book of Isaiah the prophecy to Hezekiah of the exile to Babylon? Why did the redactor not place the prophetic utterances of chapters 40—55 in the context of the ministry of a sixth century prophet?

He did not, I suspect, because he was interested in the continuity of the prophetic word, i. e., the relationship between the word given to Isaiah "in the days of Uzziah, Jotham, Ahaz, and Hezekiah" (Isa 1, 1) concerning the events of that time and the divine word in connection with the exile to Babylon. Chapter 39 connects the events in the time of Hezekiah to the calamity of the exile: Hezekiah and his house will be spared; the exile, in which nothing will be left (ytr), will not come in his days (v. 6—8). I suggest that the redactor understood the sparing of sinful Judah in Hezekiah's time as a delay of the full punishment announced by Isaiah until the time of the Babylonian exile. The opening words of chapter 40 are curiously related to the beginning of the Book of Isaiah. In 40, 2 we hear that the iniquity ('awon) of Jerusalem is pardoned. At the beginning of Isaiah this term appears in a word of indictment: "Woe sinful nation, people heavy with iniquity" (1, 4). Significantly, Isaiah 1, 4—9[100] expresses a paradox between the iniquitous nation's punishment and its having been left (hôtîr) a few survivors (1, 9). It is probable that the redactor understands 1, 4—9 in connection with the sparing of Jerusalem from Sennacherib's army.[101] Yet another

---

[99] E. G., Isa 1, 1; 6, 1; 7, 1; 20, 1  Am 1, 1  Hos 1, 1.

[100] Childs, Isaiah and the Assyrian Crisis, 20—22.

[101] I am quite in sympathy with Childs that we should be cautious about harmonizing accounts (cf. Isaiah and the Assyrian Crisis, 120). Thus original intent of 1, 4—9 may have been somewhat different from the redactor's understanding of it.

oracle (22, 1—14), which the redactor probably understands in relation
to the same invasion, expresses a terrifying judgment: "Surely this
*iniquity* will not be forgiven you till you die" (22, 14). [102] Isaiah 30,
13—14, too, understands that Israel's iniquity will be like a collapsing
wall, broken so that not a fragment is left.

A tension is clearly apparent: on the one hand the oath that they
will not be forgiven until they die, an expectation that nothing will be
left; on the other the sparing of a few. It looks as if the redactor who
juxtaposed chapters 39 and 40 ff. understood 1, 4—9 in relationship to
the time of Hezekiah and saw the total punishment of 22, 14 and
30, 13—14 as delayed until the time of the Babylonian exile. The word
about the iniquity which would not be forgiven "until you die" is fulfilled in the exile; only now that the devastation is complete can their
iniquity be pardoned (40, 2).

Another clue to the redactor's purposes might be found in his
understanding of "signs." At crucial points the sign plays an important
role in his understanding of the prophetic word (7, 11.14; 8, 18; 19, 20;
20, 3; 37, 30; 38, 7.22; 44, 25; 55, 13; 66, 19). The sign is crucial in the
Syro-Ephraimite war (7, 11.14; 8, 18); it appears thrice in the narratives about the latter part of Hezekiah's reign, a group of narratives
which are pivotal in the collection (37, 30; 38, 7.22); the carefully
arranged kerygmatic unity composed of chapters 40—55 ends with a
reference to a sign (55, 13); at the end of Isaiah (66, 19) the redactor
has chosen to speak of a sign. The place of Deutero-Isaiah in the collection may well be related to the redactor's theology of the place of signs
in the prophetic word.

These comments are not meant to be definitive but rather provocative. I make them out of a conviction that underlies this work — that
the historical-critical preoccupation with original usage and with reconstructing the process of growth is somewhat one sided. Although its
contribution to our understanding of Israelite religion and culture is of
the profoundest importance, there has been a tendency to miss the
significance of the *literary* relationships of the parts to the whole
because of an almost exclusive concern with reconstructing the history of
the development of the text. Even redaction history, with all of its
concern for the whole of a text, sometimes emphasizes more the process
of growth than the literary or kerygmatic intention of the text in its
final form. A corrective influence is needed to steer us, slightly at least,
away from historical toward literary or kerygmatic exegesis. We should
not abandon historical scholarship, but we should recognize that the
authority of the scriptures is rooted primarily in the completed Biblical
texts.

---

[102] Childs, Isaiah and the Assyrian Crisis, 22—27.

# Author Index

# Biblical Index

# Walter de Gruyter
# Berlin · New York

Beihefte zur Zeitschrift für die
alttestamentliche Wissenschaft

*Zuletzt erschienen:*

R. Braun
## Kohelet und die frühhellenistische Popularphilosophie
Groß-Oktav. XII, 187 Seiten. 1973. Ganzleinen DM 68,—
ISBN 3 11 004050 6 (Beiheft 130)

E. Kutsch
## Verheißung und Gesetz
Untersuchungen zum sogenannten „Bund" im
Alten Testament
Groß-Oktav. XII, 230 Seiten. 1973. Ganzleinen DM 98,—
ISBN 3 11 004142 1 (Beiheft 131)

H. Weippert
## Die Prosareden des Jeremiabuches
Groß-Oxtav. VIII, 256 Seiten. 1973. Ganzleinen DM 88,—
ISBN 3 11 003867 6 (Beiheft 132)

Th. L. Thompson
## The History of the Patriarchal Narratives
The Quest for the Historical Abraham
1974. Large-octavo. X, 392 pages. Cloth DM 108,—
ISBN 3 11 004096 4 (Beiheft 133)

J. W. Rogerson
## Myth in Old Testament Interpretation
1974. Large-octavo. VIII, 207 pages. Cloth DM 76,—
ISBN 3 11 004220 7 (Beiheft 134)

R. N. Whybray
## The Intellectual Tradition in the Old Testament
1974. Large-octavo. XII, 158 pages. Cloth DM 68,—
ISBN 3 11 004424 2 (Beiheft 135)

Preisänderungen vorbehalten

W DE G

# Walter de Gruyter
# Berlin·New York

Beihefte zur Zeitschrift für die
alttestamentliche Wissenschaft